DISCO DUCK
and Other Adventures in Novelty Music

DISCO DUCK
and Other Adventures in Novelty Music

Ace Collins

BERKLEY BOULEVARD BOOKS, NEW YORK

DISCO DUCK AND OTHER ADVENTURES IN NOVELTY MUSIC

A Berkley Boulevard Book / published by arrangement with
the author

PRINTING HISTORY
Berkley Boulevard trade paperback edition / July 1998

The Penguin Putnam Inc. World Wide Web site address is
http://www.penguinputnam.com

ISBN: 0-425-16358-X

BERKLEY BOULEVARD
Berkley Boulevard Books are published by The Berkley Publishing Group,
a member of Penguin Putnam Inc.,
200 Madison Avenue, New York, New York 10016.
BERKLEY BOULEVARD and its logo are trademarks belonging to
Berkley Publishing Corporation.

PRINTED IN THE UNITED STATES OF AMERICA

10 9 8 7 6 5 4 3 2 1

Book design by Lisa Stokes

To Rance, whose eight-year-old curiosity already drives him to dig into and research everything that provokes his interest. I guess this proves my profession has already warped my youngest son. Soon he might just accumulate as much worthless information as I have in twenty years of writing.

T

Contents

Introduction

*T*he odds against landing a hit record are almost as long as the odds of winning at a Vegas blackjack table. Yet that doesn't keep hundreds of thousands of songwriters and performers from trying to beat those odds each and every year. It is a miracle when someone does succeed in striking gold with a truly great song. Yet it is even a greater miracle when a scribe or singer hits pay dirt with a title that is closer to mediocre than outstanding.

This book is largely about the writers and performers who rode to a bit of fame on inspiration that was at best off-the-wall. It is filled with songs that were not just different, but different in a way that helped define their time as well as their message. Many were just outright jokes. Some were serious attempts to write something solid that simply went awry. A few were thought-provoking songs that told their story in a such a novel way as to blaze new trails. These are their creators' often warped stories, some of which are even stranger than the hits they produced.

Maybe the key to really enjoying this book is to remember that a majority of the songs, which we have highlighted, were written and produced for two reasons. The first was to make us smile. The other was to get us to open up our pocketbooks and lay out some ready cash to pay for that smile. Most still work on both counts.

So, in all honesty, these songs may not be the "leaders of the pack," and some are real "hound dogs," but they are honest enough to admit what they are up front. In other words, not one of them is going to really pull the "wooly bully" over your eyes. And certainly, if you will pause and read these pages once in a "blue moon," you might just discover the secret to what makes them all so very special.

Enjoy these stories; you stop and realize just how much joy they have brought to our world. And to those who try to tell you that songs like these novelty numbers are worthless, ask them how much that smile that crosses their lips when they hear a really "good" one is worth. After all, a good joke is priceless.

DISCO DUCK

and Other Adventures in Novelty Music

Abraham, Martin and John

*N*ot *all novelty songs have to be based on a joke. Not all novelty songs have to capitalize on quirks in so-*ciety or fads in the marketplace. Not all novelty songs are silly and meaningless. There are a few that make deep, gut-wrenching points. There are a few that use a time, a gimmick, and a mood to convey something very serious and to ask questions that go straight through the brain and lodge directly in the soul. One of these precious few songs which asked a troubling question that none of us could really answer and therefore caused our collective hearts to sigh was "Abraham, Martin and John."

Dick Holler was a first-rate record producer at Laurie Records who also dabbled in songwriting. In 1966 he had teamed one of his label's acts, the Royal Guardsmen, with one of his own songs that had been based on a comic book character, Snoopy. What resulted was the monster hit "Snoopy Vs. the Red Baron," and a few moments in the sun for a Florida rock group. If he had stopped composing at that point, Dick would have owned a piece that painted all the vivid imagery that was required of a novelty song. Yet Holler would go well beyond "Snoopy," and would challenge the very definition of the song genre, which had helped build his bank account.

Two years A.S. (after Snoopy) Holler was no longer in a funny-pages mood. Still with Laurie Records, the producer had been profoundly impacted by a nation seemingly gone mad. He had lived through the assassination of a president, a civil rights leader, and a presidential candidate. He had seen American National Guardsmen shoot and kill college students. He had witnessed riots in all of the nation's large cities and watched the color images on the network news of young men dying in rice paddies in Vietnam. As he observed what was going on, as the sounds and images of these troubled times echoed in his mind, he couldn't help but wonder what had gone wrong.

Another young man who was searching for answers was Dion DiMucci. The onetime lead singer of the Belmonts was approaching thirty and in a very real sense looking for himself and his place in the world of entertainment. In spite of having tried his luck at a couple of different labels, he hadn't hit the top forty since 1963. And as the Beatles, followed by the Stones and an even harder version of rock, had evicted doo-wop from the playlists, Dion had drifted into trouble with drugs. It was a battle that seemed to offer one of the only escapes from a world he didn't understand.

Dion had come out of the Bronx as a teen with a string of hits that had topped the charts. Most of these dealt with teenage love or boyhood dreams. Still, even though he had sold 15 million records, he hadn't stopped to make too many statements that seemed to have any lasting impact. But as his career grew softer and the sounds of rock grew harder, Dion had begun to reach out to other influences in hopes of both growing as a performer and finding the magic formula that would put him back on playlists. Bob Dylan's writing had intrigued him. So had the blues of the forties and the alternative folk of the sixties. All of these forms of music seemed to have a message and a meaning. While teaching himself guitar, Dion began to attempt to not only end his drug addiction, but to include his own thoughts and ideas in his music.

During Dion's soul-searching period, he essentially came back home to the record label where he had found his initial taste of success. At Laurie he touched base with Dick Holler, and the two began to work together to reinvent Dion the entertainer. The singer was too old to sing about "A Teenager in Love," and he had been a "Wanderer" long enough. He needed to grow up. The fact that Dion was involved in one of the deepest self-explorations Holler had ever seen also indicated that the former rock and roll idol wanted to make a statement that meant something more than just dollars and cents. This sensitive and troubled man wanted and needed to wake people up to all the pain that he was seeing, and all the pain he was feeling.

Knowing his singer well, Dick pitched one of his own folk songs to Dion. The little number which Holler shared was a simple ode to four fallen heroes. In the lyrics the songwriter had not just poetically revealed the acts of violence which took the lives of Abraham Lincoln, Martin Luther King Jr., John F. Kennedy, and Bobby Kennedy, but he'd also wondered aloud what great things they would have been able to achieve if they had been allowed to live life to its fullest. Entitled "Abraham, Martin and John," Holler's song was troubling and almost spiritual; it also dealt with two topics that hit songs almost always avoided—murder and politics.

Dion was moved by "Abraham, Martin and John." Seeing it as much more than just a song to revive a failing career, the singer sensed that this piece was a chance to make people think. In a gentle manner, the very political lyrics transcended politics and musical genres and begged to know why so many promising and courageous men had to be so senselessly killed. Though the song's tone was not angry, it did ask, "What is going on?"

Dick Holler could have been satisfied to have had Dion record "Abraham, Martin and John" in a straightforward folk manner. The song's lyrics would have been strong enough to have made many of those who heard it think. Yet Holler wanted something more. He wanted this song to paint vivid images that would linger in the minds of people long after the song's words had faded into thin air. To accomplish this he used the "gimmick" of cutting the actual words of the Kennedy brothers, as well as those of Martin Luther King Jr., into the song. The effect did not cheapen Dion's effort; rather, it was a novelty that enhanced it.

Martin Luther King's saying "I have a dream" echoed in the minds of listeners as they came to realize that each of these men's powerful dreams had been snuffed out in needless violence. JFK's "Ask not . . ." stayed in listeners' heads even as they again asked themselves, "What can I do." And as they listened to a man who asked "Why not?" many woke up and finally begged to know *why*.

"Abraham, Martin and John" represented a final jump onto the rock charts for Dion. His twenty-first trip would bring him a certified gold record and cement his image as a man who was deeper than most former teen idols. Spurred on at least in part by his last rock hit, the singer's soul-searching continued over the next few years before he finally found peace through an experience that led him to embrace the message of Christian music.

Like Dion, the nation also survived the troubling years which had inspired Dick Holler to pen "Abraham, Martin and John." Yet even thirty years later those who listen to the words and the message of this song are still asking "Why?" and wondering "What if?" The fact that the song's lyrics have these four heroes walking over a hill together brings little comfort when we stop and realize that the world is still killing so many of its best each day.

Wouldn't it be great if the world's greatest and rarest novelty was murder and we didn't have to ask "Has anybody seen . . ."?

Achy Breaky Heart

*T*he verdict is out on whether Billy Ray Cyrus is a novelty act or not. In all honesty, the verdict is out on whether Billy Ray Cyrus is ever going to be a legitimate country music act. What can be established is that in 1992 Cyrus generated tremendous enthusiasm and huge profits for his new record label with a song that became a national phenomenon. But because Cyrus hasn't followed his first hit with anything that has come close to generating as much excitement or sales, the entertainer has yet to find a venue where he can really be taken seriously.

Billy Ray Cyrus was made by writer Don Van Tess's composition "Achy Breaky Heart," and the song was helped a great deal by Cyrus's enthusiastic performance. Yet it was neither the singer nor the composition which made this gimmick-filled single a monster hit; rather, it was the promotional campaign that surrounded both Cyrus and "Achy." It was a campaign that would also affect every facet of the way Nashville created its stars from 1992 on.

When judged on its own merits, "Achy Breaky Heart" works only because of an easy-to-remember chorus and a simplistic melody line. The fact that the song's message is delivered in an almost childlike manner adds a bit of uniqueness to the product, but not enough to vault it past scores of other country songs which have used plays on words to make their point. As a matter of fact, the Bellamy Brothers' "If I Said You Had a Beautiful Body Would You Hold It Against Me" was much more clever than Von Tess's composition, yet in spite of this "Achy Breaky Heart" scored better numbers than a dozen Bellamy Brothers hits.

Most country music stars have been created only after paying long dues and slowly working their way to the top. Unlike in rock, there are few overnight sensations in Nashville, and rarely if ever has a country performer been catapulted to stardom by a unique advertising and promotional campaign. Yet by ignoring every accepted Music City practice, Harold Shedd of Mercury Records not only broke all the rules, he created a very profitable monster as well.

Cyrus had labored for years to get noticed before he earned his first big break. Spotted by Opry star Del Reeves, Billy Ray was put under the wing of one of country music's best managers, Jack McFadden. Somehow Jack got his new client a gig opening for country music superstar Reba McEntire. While he was working in front of Reba, the singer was noted by Mercury Records Artist and Repertory (A&R) man Buddy Cannon. It snowballed from there, and suddenly the thirty-year-old singer had a label and a team interested in finding a way to cash in on a man who looked like a Chippendale dancer and moved like a young Elvis.

When Mercury had Cyrus cut "Achy Breaky Heart," execs sensed that the song alone wouldn't carry their new singer to the top of the charts. What they needed was a gimmick that was an even better gimmick than the number's silly but catchy words. To accomplish the ultimate marriage of promotion and song, they turned to Lee Greenwood's ex-wife Melanie.

Melanie was one of Nashville's top choreographers. While she wasn't being used by a majority of country performers, most of whom simply stood in one spot and sang their hits, she was employed by showmen who used their productions to wow audiences in Branson and other theater settings. It was Melanie Greenwood who had worked out the routines for Louise Mandrell's award-winning Vegas and Branson shows, as well as many of the line dances which were showing up at some of the genre's new dance clubs.

Mercury wanted to use one of Melanie's line dances in its new star's video. To create the illusion that Billy Ray was already a wildly successful draw, the video producers were going to shoot him in front of a huge crowd of screaming fans (mostly beautiful women). In the midst of his song about an "Achy Breaky Heart," Greenwood's dancers (many of whom she'd borrowed from Louise Mandrell's group Spellbound) would break out in a line dance called "the Achy Breaky." The crowd would go wild and would not only "spontaneously" start doing this hot new dance, but would also practically tear the clothes off the man the video seemed to indicate was the biggest thing to hit country music since Hank Williams.

The images caught on the video were great. Greenwood's dance was super, Billy Ray was convincing, and it really did appear as if the crowd was going wild for this hot new hunk. The problem was that no one outside the management team had really heard of Cyrus, the song, or the line dance. So how was Mercury going to use the video to promote a record that hadn't even been shipped? The label answered this question by simply not shipping the record. Instead, it somehow persuaded the only two major country music video outlets, TNN and Country Music Television, to place the "Achy Breaky Heart" video into immediate heavy rotation. So, without a record sold or a single fan request, Billy Ray Cyrus's "dance" song appeared to be a hit of the same stature as those which had worked their way into the top ten by giants such as Vince Gill and Reba McEntire.

For over a month the "Achy Breaky" video ruled TNN and CMT, and audiences, who were caught up by the dance and had been convinced through this promotion that the song was a huge hit, were flooding radio stations and sales outlets with requests for a single which hadn't even been shipped. Mercury was then besieged by orders for a product which it had been holding. Finally, well over a month after the illusion of a nationwide rush for the song had been created, the label shipped "Achy Breaky Heart" to retailers, who gladly hung posters and set up special displays and dumps that trumpeted the arrival of country music's hottest new song-and-dance craze.

With the support of a solid marketing gimmick which had created a hit of a song that hadn't even yet reached audiences (this technique was so successful that the *Wall Street Journal* wrote about it on page 1), Billy Ray Cyrus rode his first song straight to the top. "Achy Breaky Heart" was so hot that it kick-started the country music line dancing craze and a couple of TNN's hottest new shows, and brought millions of people into country dance clubs for the first time. The song was so popular with kids that the Chipmunks cut a version of it.

Five years after he hit #1, Billy Ray Cyrus was still not being taken seriously. As a matter of fact, many within the industry resent the manner in which Cyrus's label manufactured his stardom. Yet by changing the rules to make "Achy Breaky Heart" a hit, Mercury Records changed the industry too. Acts like Shania Twain were made not on the road performing in front of fans, but in the studio and via video. Twain sold more than 10 million records without ever putting her act in front of a live audience via a tour. Sadly, the novelty method used to make "Achy Breaky Heart" a monster also broke with the time-honored tradition that working hard and having talent were the only way to earn a place in Nashville's Walk of Fame.

Alley-Oop

*F*or a while it seemed as though Gary Paxton was doomed to be remembered only as the "Flip" half of the minor fifties Arizona-based rock and roll group Skip and Flip. With one charting single to their credit, "It Was I," and little to follow that up, Skip, whose real name was Clyde Battin, left for the real world. To keep his record deal with Brent Records alive and Skip's professional demise a secret, Gary found a dishwasher to step in as Skip. That duo then cut another record. In early 1960, with yet another Skip, the rotating duet team finally scored another top twenty single, "Cherry Pie."

Tired of working with others who were not as driven as he was, Gary packed up and headed west. He ended up lost and out of gas in Los Angeles. And because of both of those facts he met two other hungry musicians, Buddy Mize and Dallas Frazier, at a gas station. As the trio of young men with big dreams sat around the pumps at three in the morning, Dallas, impressed by the fact that Paxton had actually scored a couple of minor hits, sang one of his own compositions for him. That song, which Frazier had never even cut a demo on, was about a daily comic strip character named Alley-Oop. Paxton liked it a lot, but his contacts in L.A. were even worse than Frazier's, so he could offer the songwriter little more than empty praise.

Renting an apartment in Hollywood for $7.50 a week, Gary ran into another down-and-out music type, Kim Fowley. Gary took Kim to the station where Buddy and Dallas worked nights and had the young man listen to Frazier's novelty song. Fowley also thought it was creative, but as with Paxton, there was not a whole lot he could do. So, with few contacts and no one else to turn to, the four young men formed their own publishing company, using a local pay phone for their business calls, and began to circulate their often strange ideas for songs throughout the music establishment.

In the fast-moving, deal-making, high-finance studio system that was Los Angeles, knocking on doors without an agent or representation shouldn't have worked. But somehow Paxton met Al Kalvin, the owner of Lute Records, and persuaded Kalvin to take a chance not only on him, but on Dallas Frazier's song too. So, within months of arriving in town, the country boy had achieved the Hollywood dream—or so he thought. It was then that a couple of complications began to get in the way of Gary's return to the big time.

First of all, Gary believed that he was still under contract to Phoenix-based Brent Records. Because of possible court action from another label, Kalvin was naturally more than a bit apprehensive about releasing a Paxton cut. To calm Lute Records' legal worries, Gary reinvented himself as a group. He informed the owner that he wasn't Gary Paxton any longer, he was now the Hollywood Argyles (the singer had taken the name from a couple of local streets). Even though this bit of subterfuge didn't really remove the legal barriers, Lute figured that Brent would probably never guess that the Argyles were in reality just Gary. By tossing out a few fake bios and photos, the label could probably escape any problems with the law, just as long as Gary didn't tour or put his face on any of the label's publicity photos. But Gary's name wasn't the only thing bothering Kalvin— the song's subject was also creating legal concerns.

Ally-Oop had been a featured part of the funny pages for years. An unbeatable super caveman, the comic character was syndicated and therefore tied up in a long list of legally protected licenses. What if the creator or the newspaper syndicate sued? Always one to take leaps of faith, Gary wasn't worried, and pushed for Kalvin to let him use the studio to record the song. But even though Gary was completely confident that everything was going to work out for the best, the record company owner was deeply concerned.

Holding his breath, Al Kalvin allowed Gary to cut the song, over several legal experts' objections. Paxton dubbed in the lead and most of the background vocals, using a studio band that included rock and roll's legendary session drummer Sander Nelson to supply what Gary couldn't do on his own. The two-and-a-half-minute single, which sounded so very simple, took an entire day to produce.

Satisfied with the final product, Kalvin printed the records, only to discover that no one would pick up his East Coast distribution for "Alley-Oop." Without outlets in New York, the song would quickly be as extinct as its subject. By the time Lute did work out a deal and got the single shipped out to national markets, two other labels had covered it, and one of those was already moving up the New York playlists. But, probably because it was the best of the trio, the Hollywood Argyles' version came from behind, quickly emerged as the dominant "Oop" on radio playlists, and on June 13, hit the top forty. A month later it was #1.

There was little doubt that this unusual single had climbed to the top because of the arrangement that Gary had worked up. The song's lyrics were elementary, the melody was prehistoric, the beat was as slow as a lumbering brontosaurus, and the cartoon strip on which the song was based, while well-known, was not universally loved by the masses and was barely read by preteens. Yet even in the face of all of those obstacles, "Alley-Oop" thrived, due to the fact that Gary had used his creativity to get more out of the song than anyone else could have. He made it zany, fun, and even singable. And that had been no small task. But by and large, no one knew the man behind this crazy bit of hit making. For Gary, this had to be frustrating.

As the single rose up the charts, Al Kalvin realized that he needed to put the Hollywood Argyles on the road to promote it. The problem was that there was only one Hollywood Argyle, and the label was afraid that if it sent Gary out, Brent Records would discover him, sue

Lute Records, and cost the company all of its unexpected but much-needed profits. Once again Gary had the answers that Al needed. Rounding up a bunch of local musicians, the singer taught them how to lip-sync the song, then sent them out for shows. By some estimates there were as many as five or six different Hollywood Argyle groups touring the country that summer, each claiming to be the real McCoy. Of course, none of them were. It was only after Gary had cleared matters concerning his other contract that he was able to join some of these groups on the road. By then the song was already an oldie.

The singer never again struck gold in the Lute studios, and when Kalvin failed to pay the singer what he felt he should have earned on "Alley-Oop," Gary left to form his own label. At Garpax he would find success in a familiar musical mode as he produced another classic novelty number, "Monster Mash." A couple of years later he discovered Paul Revere and the Raiders, and after helping to kick-start their career, he moved on again, this time to rejoin Dallas Frazier in Nashville. By the early seventies the singer/producer had become a born-again Christian and was spending most of his time working with troubled youth, which he still does today. It is doubtful that many of these young people realize that their mentor once topped the rock charts, and even if they do, it is likely that none of them know who Alley-Oop was. After all, in the minds of today's generation, 1960 *was* the Stone Age.

The Auctioneer

Leroy Van Dyke was one Music City artist who didn't have to depend on each new song and personal ap- pearance to earn a living. Unlike most who worked the long road out of Nashville, Van Dyke had something to fall back on. Leroy was a journalist with a degree in agriculture from the University of Missouri. As a young man Van Dyke had also been assigned to the U.S. Intelligence Department during the Korean War. Good-looking, bright, and well-schooled in a wide variety of fields, Van Dyke knew he could choose from among a host of jobs if he ever decided to ditch his dream of a musical career. But thanks in large part to his first and only novelty hit, once he got into country music, he never had to get out.

A guitar player, Van Dyke had spent a part of his military stint in Korea entertaining his buddies. It was during this time that he and Buddy Black wrote a song which played on one of Leroy's special skills. The first time Van Dyke tried the song out in front of an audience, he was sharing a USO bill with Marilyn Monroe. Somehow the new song not only wasn't completely ignored by a G.I. crowd which was drooling over the braless Monroe, but Leroy even got a nice bit of applause after he finished singing it. Encouragement from a number of the military top brass was then heaped upon Leroy and his song following the performance. And after he sang the song a few more times, there were several well-placed officers who thought their man should try to sell his composition and bring his unit a bit of fame. Van Dyke ignored the encouragement and after being discharged forgot about music and worked as a newspaper writer.

It was in 1956 that Van Dyke finally took seriously the advice he had first gotten while in the service and entered a talent contest. Bob Smith of Dot Records caught the performance and signed Leroy Van Dyke to the label. A few weeks later the singer found himself in a Chicago studio, where he cut "The Auctioneer."

The fact that Leroy Van Dyke was a graduate of an auctioneering school gave him the insight, knowledge, and cadence to not only put together the appropriate lyrics for the song, but to establish a rhythm line that fit an auctioneer's phrasing and style. So with very little effort, and using the world's best-known auctioneer, Ray Sims of Sedalia, Missouri, as his inspiration, Van Dyke had composed the ultimate country gimmick song. And when he sang it, Leroy sounded just like what he really was—a first-class auctioneer.

Released the first month of 1957, "The Auctioneer" hit the country charts right away and became a radio playlist favorite. In the rural regions of the nation, everyone had been to an auction. Most rural adults had gotten their first exposure to this unique art form as youths at livestock sales, and had tried ever since to imitate the auctioneer's method of saying, "Who'll give me five to make it five?" or "I got thirty, who'll make it forty? Do I hear a forty?" Van Dyke's single gave them a chance not only to listen to the story of a young man trying his best to sound like an auctioneer, but also to sing along and work out the nuances that make this unique style of sales banter an art form. Because of all the good memories that surrounded it, how could it help but work?

Leroy Van Dyke's ode to rural sales would not only hit the country top ten, but cross over to the hot new rock and roll charts as well. In a day when Elvis and the Platters ruled, the old country boy managed to place "The Auctioneer" at #19 on the pop charts.

Much like Hank Snow's later hit, "I've Been Everywhere," Leroy

Van Dyke took a bit of Americana and plugged it into a musical format that gave listeners a chance to remember old times and again be fascinated by something that had to be heard to be understood. And while most country music songs from this era have been largely forgotten by the masses—including Leroy's own monster 1961 hit, "Walk On By"—it seems that the novelty associated with "The Auctioneer" will forever keep alive the words, "Going once, going twice, going three times, gone." As long as there are people who have been to a sale, there will always be a place for "The Auctioneer."

Barbara Ann

*T*he birth of one of rock and roll's most unusual and beloved doo-wop ditties was an accident—an accident that was largely ignored for more than two years. And even when "Barbara Ann" did finally strike gold, the only place the record would hit #1 was in the Philippines. Yet the song, which encouraged stuttering and lionized the given names of literally thousands of women (including the likes of country music superstar Barbara Ann Mandrell), is probably one of the best-known nonsensical recordings ever released.

"Barbara Ann" was born on the concrete of the Bronx in the days after the Korean War. In the late fifties four young Italian Americans began to sing songs on New York street corners. This quartet—Guy Villari, Sal Cuomo, Ernie Maresca, and Chuck Fassert—eventually fine-tuned their harmonies well enough to earn time at a local recording label, Seville Records. The young men anticipated that this stroke of luck would lead them to rock and roll fame and fortune. They even spent time practicing their bows for Ed Sullivan. Instead, after "Story of Love" remained unread, and "I Ask You" wasn't answered, the "Montereys" were shown the back door.

Maresca sensed that Seville Records had a good handle

on the Montereys' future, or lack of it, and became involved with the business side of music. Yet even as they watched their friend leave them, the remaining trio refused to give up. They persuaded another friend, Donnie Jacobucci, to join the group. A few months later the four landed a gig as demo singers for Regent Records. As luck would have it, during this period the guys often warmed up before recording sessions with a silly little song which had been written by Chuck's brother about an old girlfriend. Little did the Montereys know that Fred Fassert's infatuation with a high school beauty was going to give them a second, and later a third, chance at the big time.

In the last year of the decade the boys had a few minutes remaining in a demo session and nothing left on their recording agenda. Not wanting to waste a chance to cut something for themselves, the guys asked another Regent studio talent, Ronnie Lapinsky, to sit in with his saxophone and help them with their well-worn warm-up tune. In less than ten minutes the guys had completed "Barbara Ann."

Everyone in the studio who watched and listened as the guys cut loose with the silly little song was caught up in the spirit of the moment. "Barbara Ann," with its "Ba-Ba-Ba-Ba-Barbara Ann," was fun. It was the ultimate doo-wop sing-along. You didn't have to have much talent to sing a harmony part and you could learn the words after hearing it only a couple of times. Besides, in the very simple lyrics could be found the ultimate story of a teenage crush. Here was a guy who had met his dream girl and who, now that he had seen her, wouldn't settle for anyone else. To the storyteller a second with Barbara Ann was better than a lifetime with Buddy Holly's girl Peggy Sue. Yet the lyrics also made it evident that this was going to be an unfulfilled crush, and that bit of unrealized passion made this "happy-sounding" number anything but a fairy tale. With America embracing doo-wop music and songs about teen heartache ruling the charts, how could the story of "Barbara Ann" miss?

To separate themselves from past failures, and probably to "suck up" to their employer and pull down a contract, the quartet changed its name to the Regents. The name had a sophisticated, royal ring, but Regent Records wasn't interested in the boys as a feature act. Determined as ever, Guy, Sal, Donnie, and Chuck shopped "Barbara

Ann" to more than fifty labels—but none wanted to touch it. Just as the singer of the song could never get Barbara Ann to say yes, though they knocked on every door and pursued every lead, the Regents couldn't get a record label to answer in the affirmative either. By 1960, the boys had gone their separate ways and the Regents were history.

"Barbara Ann" would have probably been completely forgotten if it hadn't been for Donnie's younger brother, Eddie Jacobucci. In 1961 Eddie had become a member of a group called the Consorts. As he looked for recording material, he came across an old demo of "Barbara Ann." The Consorts cut "Barbara Ann" in a recording session, but the new version was not up to the standards of the earlier one (the one which had been turned down by every record label that had heard it)! Still, this new recording inspired Fred Fassert to drag out the Regents' cut and to play it for Lou Cicchetti, a record shop owner. Lou was so impressed that he formed his own label, Cousins, and went out looking for the members of the Regents. Cicchetti got everyone but Guy Villari into the studio, cut a new B side, and shipped the few copies of the record he could press to New York radio stations.

From the second the stations played "Barbara Ann," request lines lit up. Everyone loved it. Within days of the single's release kids on street corners all around New York were singing "Ba-Ba-Ba-Ba-Barbara Ann." Soon even parents were helping out with harmonies. Sensing that there was money to be made, Roulette Records stepped in and gained licensing rights to the Regents' local hit, then released it nationwide on the Gee label. Now the group that had been turned down by everyone on the East Coast was singing the song no one had wanted—on *American Bandstand*. "Barbara Ann Fever" spread faster than the Hong Kong Flu. The number was so hot that groups all around the world were recording it, in a dozen different languages. For a month or two it seemed that this song was going to make the Regents even bigger than another local Italian-American doo-wop group, Dion and the Belmonts. But that didn't happen, because the Regents simply lacked the total package to score on their other recordings. By 1962 the group was again without a label.

Yet while the Regents died, "Barbara Ann" lived on. In 1965 the Beach Boys were goofing off in the studio with good friend Dean Torrence of Jan and Dean. In between cuts the guys began to play around with the Regents' old song. Someone at the board began to roll tape, and one of the loosest and most disorganized impromptu recordings in the history of rock music was the result. Sensing that the laid-back style had some commercial merit, and realizing that "Barbara Ann" was still one of the best loved of the old rock and roll classics, Capitol released it as a single. The original version had only hit #13; the Beach Boys and friends rode the ditty up to #2. The Beatles' "We Can Work It Out" was all that kept the band out of the top spot.

Many rock and roll epics have embraced a message that is much less meaty than the one which inspired and drove "Barbara Ann." Yet, while the words or message did not make this number a novelty hit, the song has become one because of the "inspired" way in which the Regents interpreted "Barbara Ann's" rather simple lyrics and harmonies. After all, any song which begins with a "Ba-Ba-Ba" and doesn't include a sheep has to be considered one of the greatest comedic efforts of all time.

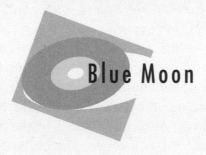

Blue Moon

*M*ost *songs which come off as being unusual or goofy usually begin their existence on an unusual* or goofy whim. But about all that was unusual or goofy about the origins of "Blue Moon" was that it was the only song written by the fabulous songwriting team of Richard Rodgers and Lorenz Hart that was not intended for one of their musicals.

Rodgers and Hart were in the business of writing songs for huge musicals. In the early thirties they were the best-known living composing team in the world. The grand musical motion pictures that were ushered in just after the advent of "talkies" were brought to glorious black-and-white life with the music of Rodgers and Hart. A number of the screen's biggest stars, including many who had problems carrying a tune, like Jean Harlow, lent their talents to the duo's compositions. It was one of these songs, dropped from a Harlow movie, that would eventually become a #1 rock and roll novelty classic.

"Blue Moon" started life as "Make Me a Star" in 1933. When the song was dropped from Harlow's picture, Hart and Rodgers rewrote the lyrics and pitched the number as "The Bad in Every Man." In this form the song was earmarked to play in MGM's *Manhattan Melodrama,* but again it was dropped. As it turned out, this was unfortunate timing, as *Melodrama,* starring two of the silver screen's giants, Clark Gable and William Powell, would go on to be a huge hit. This would also be the film that drew Public Enemy #1, John Dillinger, to Chicago's Biograph Theater on the night the "Lady in Red" sold him out to Melvin Purvis and a score of Windy City G-men. With the kind of publicity that surrounded a top-notch motion picture coupled to the killing of the nation's best-known criminal, "The Bad in Every Man" might just have become one of the most remembered songs of all time. As it turned out, it was quickly forgotten.

MGM eventually used the song in a 1935 movie called *The Night Is Young,* but only after Rodgers and Hart had penned more new lyrics, this time centering on a lonely blue moon. Haunting, beautiful, and sad, the song hit the charts a year later as a single by Glen Gray and the Casa Loma Orchestra. Gray's cut of "Blue Moon" would stay #1 for three weeks. The famous Benny Goodman would take the song to #2 the same year.

Over the course of the next two decades "Blue Moon" would show up on the charts several more times and make appearances in a half dozen movies, the most famous of which was *With a Song in My Heart.* After Mel Tormé hit the playlist with the Rodgers and Hart standard in 1949, the classic next made some noise on one of Elvis's first RCA recordings. Once again, even though a young Presley used a half yodel, half moan for the tune's bridge, "Blue Moon" remained a mournful love ballad. And except for a new group's need for a song to fill out a recording session, it probably would have always stayed in that serious mode.

The Marcels began life in 1959 as a Pittsburgh doo-wop ensemble led by Cornelius Harp, who was backed by Fred Johnson, Richard Knauss, Gene Bricker, and "Bingo" Mundy. All students at Oliver Allegheny High School, they caught the attention of a local talent scout and manager, Jules Kruspir. From there the quintet found their way to Coplix Records. On board, but with no timetable for a single or album release, the group only got into the studio when it wasn't being used by the label's other acts—in other words, once in a blue moon. So when they got there they had to record as much as they could as fast as they could and get it right in a couple of takes.

During one of these quickie sessions a producer asked the group to lay down a version of "Heart and Soul." No one knew it. But one of the members of the group did have a working concept of "Blue Moon," which used the same chord pattern. So he spent an hour teaching the song to the other four. They never did get the melody completely right, but as time was short they returned to the studio to lay down the track. That was when a somewhat demented stroke of genius hit. Bassman Fred Johnson suggested using a bass line similar to the one he had been employing on his version of the Cadillacs' "Zoom" to begin the song. When taken out of context, this idea seemed bizarre. "Zoom" was a long way from Rodgers and Hart—but then again, the Marcels were a long way from Mel Tormé. So Johnson showed them how he would begin the tune. For some reason the guys liked it, and as the bass line worked its way in, it turned the song upside down.

Beginning with "Bomp baba bomp, ba bomp ba bomp bomp," then a few beats later throwing in the essential "Da dang, da dang da dang dang, da ding a dong ding," the group transformed one of the greatest musical embodiments of lost love into a wonderful sing-along doo-wop classic. Within weeks the legendary rock disc jockey Murry the K had played the demo of the record on New York radio station WINS twenty-six times in four hours. His listeners couldn't get enough of this slice of moon pie either, and wanted to hear it more. And because of that the Marcels were on their way and Rodgers and Hart were about to shake up rock and roll in a manner which neither of the two legends could ever have imagined.

The wacky "Blue Moon" officially hit the top forty on March 20, 1961. The group's first single knocked Elvis out of the #1 spot on April 3, 1961. It would hold that position for three weeks in America, and before the bloom was off the flowers would become the top song in England, Spain, South America, Japan, and a dozen other places the Marcels hadn't studied in geography. The single was so hot that the group even sang it in the motion picture *Twist Around the Clock*.

MGM may have shut Rodgers and Hart out of *Manhattan Melodrama,* but the Marcels had opened the door for them to appear with Chubby Checker. Who could ask for a greater billing than that?

In spite of the fact that the bass line which immortalized it was all but born from an accident, and despite the fact that its roots were straight out of musical royalty, more than any other doo-wop classic "Blue Moon" is known and loved. More than thirty-five years after it was recorded, it is still one of the first songs from the early rock era that little children learn to sing. The Marcels' unique cut of "Blue Moon" has been used in many television shows and movies. It has also been sung on millions of bus rides and in football locker rooms everywhere, and almost everyone has tried their own version of Fred Johnson's bass line.

The group that turned so much blue into such a huge amount of gold would never know great success again. Only one of its other recordings charted, and today only one of the original quintet is still performing. Still, the Marcels remain one of early rock's best-known groups because they made history by taking a classic, sad tune and reshaping it into something fun. Yet what isn't remembered is that the racially mixed Marcels (Knauss and Bricker were white, while Johnson, Harp, and Mundy were African-American) scored big when black and white weren't supposed to blend. These men of different colors took blue, mixed it with black and white, and lit up the world with a new kind of sound. In their doing so, the lesson they gave us may have had an even more profound effect than did the crazy song that gave them their brief burst of fame.

Blue Suede Shoes

"*Blue Suede Shoes*" *is one of the most revered and remembered songs of the early rock era. It was a* single which not only deeply influenced and inspired the performers and fans of its day, but that shaped a second generation of rockers such as the Beatles, Johnny Rivers, and the Rolling Stones. The song remains so popular and is still so well-known that its words and music have become a part of the fabric of the American persona. It is doubtful that anyone in the United States has not heard it dozens of times, and tens of millions know all the song's lyrics by heart. "Blue Suede Shoes" is therefore one of the most important cornerstones of rock music, and because of this fact, few stop to consider that it is also one of entertainment's most clever novelty numbers.

Carl Lee Perkins was born in 1932 on a farm in Tennessee. He made his first guitar out of an old cigar box while still a grade school student and was soon taught to play that homemade instrument by a black field hand. By the age of fifteen the teaching had taken hold: Perkins had a store-bought instrument and had landed himself a place on a local radio show. Using the on-air exposure as a launching platform, he formed a band and began to play area hillbilly dances. By the age of twenty-one, Carl was a full-time musician, traveling back and forth across his home state.

In 1955 Perkins wandered into Sam Phillips's Sun Studios in Memphis. Phillips, who had already signed Elvis Presley and Johnny Cash and who would soon add Jerry Lee Lewis and Charlie Rich to his label, had been looking for raw talent that would appeal to kids. He felt that Carl's combination of blues and country would mesh well with Sun's other "rockabilly" acts.

Carl Perkins didn't know that he would soon be an important facet of an entertainment revolution. The singer/guitar player simply saw his new record deal as a way to get a chance to record a country music hit and maybe make a little money in the process. But Sam Phillips had much bigger plans than Nashville or the Opry. And the producer was making good on those dreams by lighting a match that would start a fire which would consume much of what had previously been known as pop music. As it turned out, Perkins would supply a great deal of the fuel for this blaze.

Forty years after the fact, few stop and consider what the merging of gospel, black blues, and white country meant to the music industry. It was in Sun Studios where the idea of a solo entertainer backed by his own band really took hold. In New York, Los Angeles, and other cities where rock and roll was being birthed, the group sound drove the music. Vocal ensembles didn't have their own bands and recorded and performed in a manner that was not dissimilar to the way popular music had been made for years. But Presley, Perkins, Cash, and Lewis came out of a country music environment where a singer had to have a band to make ends meet. House bands didn't back up stars like Eddy Arnold or Hank Snow. Every singer had to have his own musicians, and therefore, because playing together led to growth, each singer and band developed their own style and sound. In the cases of these performers it was the band, not the producers, who really shaped their acts. This approach, which began in Memphis, would eventually spread around the world and sharply influence the way rock music was produced from Los Angeles to Liverpool. But to make this a reality, Sun had to produce hits. By 1955 Presley was on his way and Cash had hit the charts. It was now Perkins's turn to find a bit of magic.

Carl was working a dance with his band in December of 1955 when the singer uncovered a bit of inspiration that would define the rest of his life. As he performed, Perkins was intrigued by a young man who kept mainly to himself. Even when the boy danced, he kept his distance from his date. Carl eventually discovered that the youth had just purchased a pair of special blue suede shoes and didn't want to get them stepped on. So rather than letting himself go and really enjoying the evening, the lad spent the night protecting his footwear as if he were a mother protecting her firstborn. The singer found the boy's extreme actions hilarious.

It was early the next morning when Carl got home, but even though he was tired, he couldn't sleep. The image of the boy with the blue shoes was reeling in his mind. In order to exorcise the demon, Perkins got up and wrote out the words to a song about a man who would give up everything he had to keep his shoes in perfect shape. A few days later Sam Phillips put Perkins into the studio to cut his little ditty about a boy and his "Blue Suede Shoes."

In early 1956 "Blue Suede Shoes" topped the country, R&B and rock and roll charts, becoming the first song to own the #1 spot on all three simultaneously. It seemed that the twenty-three-year-old Perkins was on his way to the big time. He had even been signed to make his television debut, on *The Perry Como Show*. Sporting a new pair of blue suedes, Carl was traveling to New York when he broke his back in a car wreck. A few weeks later, his buddy, Elvis Presley, cut his own version of "Blue Suede Shoes" and bumped Perkins out of the spotlight.

"Blue Suede Shoes" was such a huge dance hit, and had such an enormous impact on the music industry, that few stopped to consider that the story Carl Perkins had told through the song's lyrics was as timeless and deep as many of Mark Twain's tales of American life.

People have always saved their money to purchase special things, such as cars, china, clothes, and even blue suede shoes. Then these same people often become so paranoid that something will happen to their purchase that they don't allow those items to be used as they were intended. The special new car with the wonderful leather interior and sported plastic seat covers is not driven during the rain. The fine china is kept in the cabinet and saved for special occasions which never seem to arise. And that expensive suit or dress is wrapped in a hanging bag and lost in the back of the closet, because it is just too pretty for any of the normal events of life. Carl's "Blue Suede Shoes" simply, but eloquently, told the story of all the things which are just too special to use and the people who simply can't enjoy themselves when they finally do take these "treasures" out for a night. Perkins's song presented the foolishness of man's lust for things, a lust which brings mainly worry and very little happiness.

"Blue Suede Shoes" was a novelty song which never was recognized as one. Too successful to be categorized alongside other gimmick tunes, this rock and roll classic might just rank as one of the most clever exposés ever scribed on America's materialism. Yet the fact that most folks miss this message and just see "Shoes" as a great song is just as well. After all, Carl Perkins is still wearing his "Blue Suede Shoes" and still getting a standing ovation every time he says, "It's one for the money." This one sure was!

# A Boy Named Sue

As a boy in Chicago, *Shel Silverstein seemed destined for great things. Probably a certifiable genius, he* was composing lyrics to songs and scripting and illustrating stories before he was in first grade. Later, in the army, his cartoon work highlighted many issues of the service newspaper *Stars and Stripes*. After serving his country Shel drifted back to his hometown and eventually landed at *Playboy* magazine. It was there that he made his name as one of the country's best-known illustrators.

Silverstein had always been interested in music, composing an album of jazz numbers in the early sixties and writing pop songs throughout this period. But by the last few years of the decade the artist had begun to devote more and more time to country music. Shel seemed drawn to the way that the lyrics, rather than the beat, drew country fans into songs. His original work, released on Atlantic Records, was fairly unsuccessful if judged simply by sales, but the fact was that a number of the quirky songs he wrote and sang often found their way to hit status via other artists. One of those who discovered Shel rather early in his country period was Johnny Cash.

Few entertainers' stories are better known than that of the "Man in Black." Along with Elvis Presley, Jerry Lee

Lewis, Carl Perkins, and Charlie Rich, Cash had put Sam Phillips's Sun Studios on the map. With his long list of hits coupled to an equally long list of personal problems, Johnny's hit train had run into several bumps over the course of fifteen years in the business. But in 1968 he was again riding high and ruling the charts.

A week before a scheduled performance at San Quentin Prison, Johnny had gathered a number of the nation's best songwriters at his home in order to hear their latest work. Along with Shel, Bob Dylan, Graham Nash, and Joni Mitchell were pitching their best stuff. While Joni tossed out her very serious-minded "Both Sides Now," Silverstein opted for a song about a man whose father had given him a girl's name and then deserted him.

June Carter Cash, Johnny's wife and a member of the famous Carter family, had been so taken by "A Boy Named Sue" that she begged Johnny to sing it for the prisoners at San Quentin. Cash didn't want to. He hadn't rehearsed the song, didn't know the lyrics, and wasn't all that sure that it was his type of material. Yet as was often the case, June won out and Cash performed the song for the first time reading the words off a sheet live in front of a "captive" audience.

The convicts immediately fell in love with the idea of a father cursing his son with a sissy name. The fact that the boy named Sue had grown up to be the toughest, meanest, most profane man alive appealed to them too. As Johnny told more and more of Shel's story, the prisoners went crazy. As luck would have it, Columbia Records was recording the concert for a live album and captured the first take of "A Boy Named Sue" on tape.

Columbia knew that the live version of "A Boy Named Sue" had "hit" written all over it. This "talk" song was perfect for Johnny's limited range and the lyrics worked with Cash's own gruff appearance and somewhat sordid background. Yet the label had a problem with the fact that Johnny had used the term "son of a bitch" rather than the cleaned-up "son of a gun" when he'd performed the song for the prisoners. While the audience at the prison may have loved the expression, the radio programmers, record execs figured, wouldn't. Yet Columbia sensed that it would never catch Cash any better than he had been on this cut. So, in a stroke of futile genius, the label opted not to bring the singer back into the studio for a recording session and simply bleeped the profanity, thus allowing the audience to fill in the word on their own.

"A Boy Named Sue" would race up the charts in the summer of 1969, hitting #1 in country music on August 23 and holding that position for five weeks. On the rock side only the Rolling Stones' "Honky Tonk Woman" would keep Cash from earning his first #1 pop single. Still, "Sue" was at #2 for three weeks.

Johnny Cash's successful run with Shel's novelty song would lead to the singer's trying the tactic again some seven years later with "One Piece at a Time." This song about an autoworker who steals a piece from the plant every day and builds a bizarre car of his own at home would bring Cash another #1, but the single would not find the universal acceptance of "A Boy Named Sue."

"Sue" was a monster hit probably because of when and how it was recorded. As with so many novelty hits, timing was probably more important than the wonderfully written tale that the imaginative Shel Silverstein had woven into the piece. But it represented more to some people than just another quirky song. "A Boy Named Sue" gave thousands of men who had been teased about having "sissy"-sounding names, such as Carol, Francis, and Robin, a chance to stand up and be proud. Maybe Shel actually brought a boy named Francis or Carol and his father back together again.

Okay, probably not, but it is a nice way to try to imagine "A Boy Named Sue" as having had some kind of social significance!

The Chipmunk Song

The fifties were the golden age of close-harmony rock and roll groups. But most of these groups, even the Platters, Coasters, and Drifters, would a decade later find their days of fame and fortune fleeting. By the mid-sixties the great original rock and roll trios and quartets were largely a part of the past. Yet one group that began life in 1958 is just as strong today as it was when it recorded its first #1 record. And even more amazingly, its members haven't aged a day.

Ross Bagdasarian, a.k.a. David Seville, was on the verge of starving to death in the music business when he discovered that the process of using lyric lines recorded at one speed and then played at a different speed could be a gimmick that would sell to both rock and children's audiences. Ross (under the Seville name) proved this gimmick was marketable and saved his skin with the #1 hit "Witch Doctor." Yet the good physician and his unique chanting music only bought Bagdasarian a brief moment in the spotlight. In order to capitalize on the silly sound of extraordinarily high voices singing normal songs, Ross was going to have to be inventive enough to score again using the process. This was on the songwriter's mind as he took a vacation at Yosemite National Park.

It has long been said that nature's wonders have given great men great thoughts. Whether this axiom ties in with what happened to Bagdasarian is open for debate. Yet it is a fact that it was in Yosemite that Ross's inspiration for a new use for his recording technique sprang forth. The group that would change his whole life was apparently conceived when the songwriter saw a small chipmunk stubbornly refuse to give up its spot on a California highway bridge, thus forcing Ross to wait on the rodent. While this was the spark that gave birth to the Chipmunks singing group, there can be little doubt that the cartoon characters Chip and Dale, who spoke in squeaky, high-pitched tones, also had to play a part in linking Bagdasarian's observations of the cute rodent on the bridge to the production technique he used on "Witch Doctor." As he would soon find out, this was a marriage made in musical heaven.

The writer knew from firsthand experience that selling bizarre ideas to a major label was never easy. It had taken a stroke of luck and the help of some friends to turn his first novelty concept into a hit. So once Ross wrote some songs and recorded some demos with his new trio of blended voices, he came up with his ultimate brainstorm. His contract was with Liberty Records, so the Chipmunks would sport the names of the three most powerful men Ross knew at the label: Simon Waronker, Theodore Keep, and Al Bennett. They were the movers and shakers; surely they would be honored to have his cutest creations christened after them. The ploy worked. But getting a record deal for the Chipmunks was just the beginning in Bagdasarian's mind.

Ross wanted to create a Disney-like product with his new group. He wanted the Chipmunks not to be just voices on a record, like the "Witch Doctor" had been, but "real" characters. Bagdasarian saw himself creating a group that could perform via cartoons, make television shows and sing in motion pictures, have their images on everything from lunch boxes to coloring books, and keep his bank account healthy for years to come.

Liberty Records probably didn't see the big picture the way Ross did, but execs there liked the Christmas song that the writer had cut a demo on, and they understand that quirky songs had long had a positive effect on the charts during the holiday season. They had no problems pushing the product; in fact, they were behind it all the way!

Released around Thanksgiving of 1958, "The Chipmunk Song" raced up the charts, thanks to the combination of the recording's special effects and the humorous attempts of "David Seville" (Ross) to keep Alvin, the stubborn member of the group (remember the chipmunk who wouldn't move off the bridge for Ross's car?), in line. By Christmas week the Chipmunks had their first #1 hit. They were a national phenomenon, and Ross was caught up in the complete merchandising of all things Chipmunk.

Within three months the trio had landed in the top five again with "Alvin's Harmonica," a few weeks after that the group had won three Grammys (Best Recording for Children, Best Comedy Recording, and Best Engineered Record), and within six months the Chipmunks had been signed for their own prime-time network show on CBS. (Many in the entertainment business have long cited *The Monkees* as the first attempt by a network to sell a musical group via a sitcom. In truth, three rodents beat the four simians by several years.)

"The Chipmunk Song," with its seasonal flavor, remains one of the most played Christmas "classics," and probably ranks only behind "Rudolph" in holiday novelty appeal. The guys are also going strong with new recordings, this time produced by Ross Bagdasarian Jr., a new television show, and numerous other product lines. The Chipmunks are hanging as stubbornly on to their fame and status as the original chipmunk held on to its spot on that bridge—a bridge that Ross Bagdasarian crossed to go from one-hit wonder to the creator of perhaps the most beloved novelty act of all times. If a novelty song hall of fame is ever created, there should be a statue of a stubborn rodent holding his position on a California bridge near the entrance.

 Convoy

*Country music performer C. W. McCall was actually
a classically trained art director for an Omaha-based*
advertising company whose real name was Bill Fries.
C. W. McCall, who would become Bill's more famous alter ego in the mid-seventies, began his existence as a fig-
ment of Fries's ever-expanding imagination. It was for an
ad campaign that helped the Metz Baking Company sell
a lot of loaves of its Old Home Bread that the artist
dreamed up a trucker named McCall and put the man on
the road looking for clear traffic, good love, and a great
sandwich. What old C. W. found was a grateful sponsor
and a bit of regional fame, as some of the folks around
Nebraska began to believe that the country boy really existed.

Sensing that Fries had created something special, MGM
Records approached the advertising worker and asked if
he thought he might want to spin C. W. off into the world
of music. Always in a need of a little extra cash, Bill
agreed, signed a contract with the label, and took a turn
in the recording studio. Yet even when his first release,
"Old Home Filler-Up an' Keep On A-Truckin' Cafe," sold
into the six figures, Fries hung on to his day job.

Now almost consumed by the character he had created,

when he wasn't drawing for Bozell & Jacobs Advertising Bill was transforming himself into a latter-day David Dudley (of "Six Days on the Road" fame). He got so caught up in the life of truckers that he even purchased a citizens band radio so that he could listen to the men who had inspired him to create McCall. It was while stuck behind a long line of trucks trading small road talk with other CBers that Bill was consumed by an idea that he thought would make the greatest trucker song of the modern age.

During the mid-seventies CB radios had become the mobile phone network for the nation's truck fleets. Though the radios had been around since the fifties (Lassie had even used one to save Timmy in the TV series), it had taken the Arab oil embargo and the fifty-five-mile-an-hour speed limit to make them popular. By the time Fries began to experiment with his trucker character and to consider using the trucker CB lingo for a story line in a song, it was estimated that almost 4 million units were being employed on the open road. It was hard to find a trucker who didn't have one and who hadn't created a handle—an on-air name—that was even more colorful than the lines these men often gave truck stop waitresses.

Bill's handle was Rubber Duck. Whenever the truckers heard the voice of the old Rubber Duck, they knew that they had latched onto the dude in the jeep who wanted to ride the concrete ribbon like they did. When they found out that this Duck was making their profession a bit more respectable through the identity of C. W. McCall, the men behind the wheel gave the songwriter all the help he needed. He was even made an honorary member of their gang.

Using the evolving CB language that he had learned from the guys in the big rigs, Fries composed a song in the tradition of talking-story numbers such as "Big Bad John." Except this time the hero was not a large man of steel, but rather a trucker named Rubber Duck. Bill put his song's subject in the midst of a convoy that was rolling across the United States led by a group of militant truckers who were going to make their own rules, drive at the speed limits they set, and run over any Smokey (cop) who got in their way. It was the first time a hardworking trucker had ever been considered in the same class as a Hell's Angel. And for some it was an image that just didn't fly.

Probably because of this antihero status, MGM Records was not too impressed with what Fries had created. Besides, the label had argued, how many people really understood the lingo that Bill had used to tell his story? MGM refused to release the song as a single.

Not discouraged, Fries cut the song as McCall and put it on his newest album in 1975. It was then that the radio disc jockeys put the metal down. Rather than promoting C. W.'s latest release as a whole, the jocks went to the LP and pulled "Convoy." And while this move may have been initiated in order to inject a little laughter onto the airwaves, what MGM found out was that it lit up the phone lines too. Within weeks the label had pressed hundreds of thousands of copies of "Convoy" and had shipped them to country stations and retail outlets nationwide. MGM execs then discovered to their amazement that that first shipment wasn't large enough—rock stations and rock outlets were demanding copies too. And so were suppliers in Great Britain—and that nation didn't even fully understand what a CB was. Within weeks the song went absolutely crazy, hitting #1 in country and pop markets and adding dozens of special trucker phrases to everyday conversation. It literally changed the way people talked, but that was only the beginning.

"Convoy" had been inspired by a fad, the truckers' use of the citizens band radio, but the song took this fad further than had ever been imagined. Suddenly, thanks in no small part to the publicity that the hit song had given to the units, CB antennas were appearing on everything from VWs to Lincolns. Everyone from lawyers to housewives had a handle, could use the lingo, and was on the lookout for Smokeys. Hollywood, sensing that there were scripts to be written around the fad, created movies which starred folks like Burt Reynolds and Kris Kristofferson. Television followed with scripts embracing the CB language, and men who had never been to a truck stop were dropping the pedal to the metal and riding past the double nickel.

The CB fad did two very important things. First, it paved the way for the mobile phone business, which grew by leaps and bounds in the nineties. Second, it lasted longer than disco. Yet it had to die, and when CB units began showing up at garage sales for ten bucks, Bill Fries realized that his career as C. W. McCall was over too. With his profits in his fist, he waved to his fans, said, "We gone, bye-bye," and signed off.

But the old writer didn't leave until he had truly spotlighted and taken advantage of an American craze that was bigger than Super Balls, hula hoops, and skateboarding. And just think—without the CB most of us would have never had the chance to be called "Good Buddy." Maybe that was what Timmy would have called Lassie if Fries had written the script that first spotlighted the CB. *Scary thought!*

# Dang Me

*O*ver its seven decades, recorded music has been blessed with a number of geniuses. The industry has also had its share of eccentrics. But there has been only one man who took his eccentricity and his genius and put them together in a way that somehow made sense to millions while also leaving everyone wondering, "Where is this guy coming from?"

Roger Miller was one of the most unique talents to ever find the entertainment spotlight. A product of Fort Worth, Texas, orphaned before his third birthday, he was raised by relatives in Erick, Oklahoma. Like so many who would gain stardom, he was a victim of the Depression. Poor, undereducated, forced to go to work before he had entered his teens, Miller grew up in a world that was both hard and unfair. World War II broke out when the boy was five, but even as the economic state of many farm families improved, Miller's life changed little. When the fighting ended and the nation embraced real prosperity and growth, Roger still lived in a world that was filled with blighted hopes and unreachable dreams. Yet somehow, through the bleakest times, the boy joked, laughed, and smiled. He survived even the toughest days with a warped grin on his face.

After years of ranch work and some time on the rodeo circuit, Miller found a steady paycheck, plenty of food, and brand-new clothes in the army. For the young man who had grown up eating turnips and dehorning cows, the military was a walk in the park. Overjoyed to be in a place where he had everything he needed, Roger often picked up a guitar and sang off-the-wall songs to make some of his homesick buddies laugh a little. This performing talent was soon noticed and earned the young man a transfer to special services, where he was assigned to play with an army hillbilly band. Writing much of the outfit's material, picking up drums and fiddle as well as his guitar, Miller was not only the group's star, he was their happiest member. He had never dreamed that life could be this good.

Discharged in the mid-fifties, Miller found that the real world was not nearly as accepting of his humor or his whimsical view of life. With an elfish grin, he talked himself into and then out of a number of jobs before thumbing to Nashville. Working as a bellhop, he began to write a few songs and to meet other struggling writers. He received a lot of tips, but no offers, and for a while it looked like he would spend his life carrying other people's bags.

Country music star Ray Price finally picked up on Miller's talent and placed the songwriter's "Invitation to the Blues" on the flip side of one of his huge hits, "City Lights." Now Nashville had to notice him. Roger took that as a good sign, of course; with his natural optimism, he took rejections, and even disasters, as good signs too!

Thanks to scoring a Ray Price record, Miller would write for the publishing company of another country star, Faron Young, for a while. His work on a host of future hits, including "In the Summertime," convinced RCA to give him a shot at recording. He produced one minor hit for the label, "When Two Worlds Collide," before being cut loose.

There was little doubt that Roger was talented, but to many it appeared that he was also crazy and prone to wasting time on compositions that were written just for laughs. While "normal" scribes spent days perfecting serious songs, Miller was often content to while away his time writing things that made no sense at all. More and more his songs seemed to have no commercial value. Many of these

Miller products were so strange that they made most novelty songs seem downright serious. More often than not, even those who called him a genius also labeled him a flake.

Somehow Smash Records saw a method in the madness and caught on to what country music had missed. When Roger toured, those who bought tickets to his show liked him best when he made them laugh. In many ways he was a stand-up comedian who delivered his jokes in lyrics and music. His skewed point of view always seemed to hit home, particularly with the younger crowd. Without even knowing it, Miller had invented a type of funny folk music. Sensing that there was some value here, the label thought it would be worth the risk to release one of Roger's most unique songs.

"Dang Me," complete with a bizarre nonsensical chorus line and a mostly dialogue-driven verse, somehow became a major hit. Where did Miller come up with such a strange idea? Who knows—this was the same guy who would come up to his blind friends, put his hands over their ears, and say, "Guess Who?"

"Dang Me" was the story of a man who had been a loser at just about everything he had tried. How much of it was autobiographical is anyone's guess. Heaven knows that Roger had seen his share of losing. But even if the song did represent Roger's assessment of his own lot in life, it showed his humor as well. By and large he just didn't take himself, or any given situation, very seriously. As the song's secondary message revealed, life didn't make a lot of sense to Roger, but it was kind of fun anyway.

"Dang Me" stayed at #1 on country playlists for five weeks in 1964, and also made rock's top ten. The equally strange "Chug-a-Lug" and "Do-Wacka-Do" climbed the charts that year as well. Partly singing, partly talking, mostly laughing, the poor boy had suddenly become a star whose royalty checks could now buy him anything he wanted. And with this quick, crazy success, Roger suddenly found the world taking him ever so seriously. Those who had recently called him a flake were now discussing the artistic value of songs like "You Can't Roller Skate in a Buffalo Herd." The stranger Roger's lyrics, the more he seemed to be embraced.

With "Dang Me" leading the way, Miller won five Grammys and

countless other awards just months after emerging from nowhere. In spite of the fact that most writers and singers of novelty songs fade away as quickly as they appear, the ever-quirky Miller stuck around. Just a year after recording his first hit record, Miller had become country music's most visible national star.

Over the course of the next three decades, Roger Miller's songs would be learned and sung by adults and children everywhere. Millions who cannot remember their anniversaries and who have never bought a single Roger Miller record can sing every word of "Dang Me," "England Swings," "Kansas City Star," "You Can't Roller Skate in a Buffalo Herd," and "King of the Road." Miller would use his songwriting and performing skills to gain notice as an actor, a humorist, and a Broadway composer and star. Before his death in 1992 at the age of fifty-six, he would be recognized around the world as one of the brightest talents of modern music—a modern-day Will Rogers.

Hank Williams left the world with songs of heartache that made fans want to cry. Merle Haggard gave the world songs that celebrated the sacrifices of the workingman and the downtrodden. John Lennon defined love in countless ways. Roger Miller left us with something not nearly as dramatic, but maybe far more meaningful. He gave the world a smile because he knew that a smile, accompanied by a whimsical outlook, made everyone feel a lot better while not giving too much of a dang about their problems. Now that is a novel idea we could all use!

Dead Skunk

There can be little doubt as to where the inspiration for Loudon Wainwright's only chart-making single came from. As Wainwright had always been a bit off-the-wall, the subject matter for this hit song was not surprising to his friends; what was most surprising to those who knew him best was that the songwriter never made a bigger splash on the music scene than he did. Those who made up his small core of fans thought that he was one of the most talented and original solo acts of the rock/folk era. They still wonder why he didn't make it big.

Wainwright had come to San Francisco in 1967 at the age of twenty. He had spent his first two decades in North Carolina, and his thoughts and the pattern of his speech often revealed his rural slant on life. Not long after arriving on the West Coast, Loudon, a bit of a loner, got caught up in the folk movement of the period and began to play solo coffeehouse-type gigs in front of the flower children of the time. His performances were static and stark, and he took each show along at a pace that allowed for a lot of conversation and humor. A poet as much as a songwriter, seemingly more interested in making statements than gaining fame, Wainwright nonetheless caught the attention of Atlantic Records, and he signed a contract less than a year after arriving on the West Coast. The label saw Wainwright as the next Bob Dylan.

In many ways Loudon did remind those who knew him of Dylan. His vocal style showed limited range and was highly unstructured. His almost spoken manner of sliding into notes left many wondering if he really could sing, or even carry a tune. His compositions, which were often stark and plaintive, nevertheless seemed to contain many layers of meaning. His writing also possessed a bit of sly humor. As per the thinking of the time, this appeared to make Wainwright a genius.

While many critics of the era raved about the young man and his unique talents, others wondered if he was anything more than a pretender. After a couple of dismal album failures, Atlantic joined those who questioned his potential. After pouring tens of thousands of dollars into his career, the label determined that Wainwright was not even close to being the next Dylan, and cut him loose. This seemingly huge setback didn't destroy the young man's dreams of becoming a recognized artist. Continuing to write and plug his own thoughts and style in small venues around the country, Loudon had another record deal by 1972, this time with CBS.

With the exception of a solitary song, Wainwright's time with CBS was not much more successful than his initial days in the Atlantic recording studios had been. What the label soon found out was that Loudon was more a comedian than a songwriter or recording artist. Those who caught him in the small clubs he played found him to be insightful, bright, and incredibly funny. But Wainwright's humor and talent seemingly couldn't be turned into pay dirt in the studio. From a commercial standpoint, he seemed like a lost cause.

One of Wainwright's self-penned numbers that had generated a great deal of audience response concerned an animal that had been violently stopped in mid-trip during a jaunt across a highway. When writing the simple ode to this fallen creature of the woodlands, Loudon had been inspired by all the times he'd driven along rural highways and smelled a dead skunk that had been given his ticket to mammal heaven by a truck or car.

CBS decided to record and release Wainwright's "Dead Skunk (in

the Middle of the Road)" in the winter of 1972. Hoping just to generate a bit of air play for an artist who was not headed much of
anywhere, the label soon discovered that this Bob Dylanesque
"Skunk" had much of the rock world laughing. Maybe it was only
because everyone could identify with the single's story line, but within
just a few weeks Loudon Wainwright found himself in *Billboard*'s
top twenty. More amazingly, his song would spend more than three
months on most major playlists (surprisingly, "Skunk" never cracked
the charts on the country side).

The timing of CBS's release of "Dead Skunk" had been perfect.
Bob Dylan and his music were being lionized by music critics, John
Denver had taken the folk/country sound and made it hot, and it
seemed that in the wake of Watergate the country needed a laugh.
Yet if the label was hoping that the silly number about a smelly and
deceased pest was going to pave the way for Loudon Wainwright's
career to explode, they were wrong.

Loudon would never again manage to find a spot on the pop
charts. Maybe partly because of his early comparisons to the man,
Wainwright would never escape Dylan's shadow long enough to be
recognized on his own merits. But just as Loudon Wainwright may
never be inducted into the Rock and Roll Hall of Fame or labeled as
one of the greatest influences in modern music, Bob Dylan will probably never write or record a song that touches people's *senses* as
profoundly as "Dead Skunk" did.

It has been said that the smell of success varies greatly from man
to man. In the case of Bob Dylan and Loudon Wainwright, this proverb has never been more true.

Disco Duck

*M*any view the disco craze that tore up the charts and influenced dance clubs in the mid-seventies as one of the most insipid periods in modern music. There were #1 hits that made songs like "The Twist" sound almost symbolic and intellectual. It is therefore not surprising that in 1976 a Memphis disc jockey, Rick Dees, sensed that the craziness which had taken over playlists was ripe for exploiting. Seizing upon a dance hit from the sixties, "The Duck," as his inspiration, Dees put together two senseless verses about a dancing fool who couldn't stop his fowl movements. In retrospect it seems appropriate that "Disco Duck" would find a place on playlists during the same era as Johnnie Taylor's "Disco Lady"—that is just how little taste the buying public was exhibiting during this time (which may have accounted for the millions of listeners who moved from rock to country in the late seventies)—but the mere fact that a label would actually cut and release a song whose best line was "Flapping my arms I began to cluck" shows the mentality of the entire music business during the golden age of disco.

Resting his hopes for finding a sucker at a studio who would like his composition on lines like "Don't be a cluck," Rick took his new song to a friend who owed him a favor. That fact didn't prevent Estelle Axton of Fretone Records from informing the DJ that he had been spinning too many records and suggesting that he forget the whole idea of a novelty number about disco. After all, as anyone with any sense could reason, disco was a novelty and a parody already! Yet Dees, who had been a party to some of Memphis's zaniest promotions (world's largest fruitcake, largest jelly donut, etc.), wouldn't give up. From time to time he would circle by the studio and beg Estelle to cut his "Disco Duck."

Finally, after three months of witnessing his pleading, in what had to have been a moment of great weakness, Axton gave in and let Rick use several of her session players to put his record together. Once he had a copy of the "Duck" in hand, the hard part should have been over. It should have been easy for Dees to get his single on the air and promote it; after all, he was the #1 record spinner in Elvis's hometown. Yet his station, WMPS, refused to allow Dees or anyone else at the station to air "Disco Duck." WMPS informed the jockey that it had a rule against both "self-promotion" and "cross-promotion" (the station probably had certain standards of taste, too). So, just as any other performer would have had to do, Rick had to ship the "Duck" to programmers at other stations. On the basis of his lack of a track record and the fact that there wasn't a large market for popular music about ducks, Dees would seem to have stood a slim chance of getting his song played.

For some unknown reason a station in Birmingham jumped on "Disco Duck" in the summer, generating play on other southern stations and in the dance clubs that tuned in to these outlets. Just off these "Dixie plays," Dees had quickly exhausted his supply of product and had been forced to seek a larger label to handle distribution and pressing of his novelty release. By October of 1976, RSO Records was shipping "Disco Duck" by the hundreds of thousands, and from coast to coast millions were listening to Rick Dees and His Cast of Idiots and liking what they were hearing. Yet as the leaves changed colors in Memphis, Dees's single was nowhere to be heard in the Delta area. WMPS still wouldn't play it, and neither would the city's other disco and rock outlets. Then Rick was fired from the station in October (it seemed that management was embarrassed that one of their own was party to something like "Disco Duck"). By that time "Disco Duck" was the #1 song in the nation and Dees could have cared less about losing his job.

Dees would move his radio show to Los Angeles and go on to become one of the nation's best-known on-air forces. Syndicated shows and television gigs would make him a household name and celebrity image—but his "Duck" would not fare as well, nor last as long.

Disco was a craze that was short-lived. It might have been the computer-generated synthesized sound, the polyester suits, the constant moaning of lead singers, or just a sudden awakening of the public's taste that brought disco down. It died suddenly, and odds are that the songs which sold millions during disco's peak years will not be revived by oldie stations anytime soon. With that in mind, Dees will probably see very few royalty checks generated in the future by "Disco Duck."

But in 1976 the song proved its point. By and large the disco sound was being fueled by buyers who didn't take their music too seriously. In this case, maybe they should have. After all, one of the key lines in Rick Dees's classic is "Don't be a cluck." This bit of advice was followed by the word "disco" seven times, and then the word "duck." Nonetheless, this single—which didn't even realize that it is chickens, not ducks, that cluck—made more sense than Donna Summer's "Love to Love You Baby" (though Donna's single did probably have more hidden symbolism than "Disco Duck"). If this point doesn't make all of the hits of disco music candidates for this book, then what does?

# Do Wah Diddy Diddy

*W*hen millions of American kids first heard Manfred Mann's "Do Wah Diddy Diddy," they assumed that the Fab Four had just released another hit. Certainly the song's arrangement, lead vocal, and harmonies sounded like the Beatles, and even the single's somewhat unusual and offbeat lead line about a girl warbling a non-sensical bit of jive wasn't all that far removed from the wisdom shown by the boys from Liverpool when they had uttered, "It's been a hard day's night," or "She loves you, yeah, yeah, yeah." Yet not only was Manfred Mann not a mop-headed, English-bred member of the leading force of the British invasion, the central "Mann" of the group was not even born in England.

Michael Lubowitz, the man who essentially was Man-fred Mann, was born and raised in Johannesburg, South Africa, in the forties and fifties. In 1961, at the age of twenty, he had left his homeland and journeyed to London to study classical music. From there Michael moved on to the Juilliard School in New York. By 1963 Lubowitz had traveled back to England and formed a band, the Mann-Hugg Blues Brothers. This time it was jazz, not classical music, that was motivating Michael. A few months later the group had moved to a rock sound, had a record deal,

and was known as Manfred Mann and the Manfreds. By the time
MM walked into the studio to record for the first time, the eight-
member group had been reduced to five and the band had become
known as simply Manfred Mann.

Solid musicians, Manfred Mann quickly became one of England's
leading groups, scoring several hit records and selling out club and
concert dates. Steeped in jazz and classical music, the boys were
poised and ready to become international stars when the Beatles made
the trek across the Atlantic and reshaped American music. Still, in
order to make a Beatles-like move, Manfred Mann needed a solid
single that would translate well to a U.S. audience, an audience which
seemed hungry for anything British. Ironically, EMI Music, MM's
recording label, didn't capitalize on the group's ability to perform
some of the world's most challenging music. Instead EMI searched
for a simple ditty and found the boys a hit by listening to the work
of two American songwriters who had carved out a career based
largely on the unique and shallow whims of American teenagers.

Though they didn't brag about it, Jeff Barry and Ellie Greenwich
had made a host of car and house payments by writing songs which
had embraced young people's unique social perspectives while retain-
ing few redeeming social qualities. "Da Doo Ron Ron," "Leader of
the Pack," "Tell Laura I Love Her," and the song which would eventually bring Tommy James out of retirement, "Hanky Panky," were
all theirs. To be fair, so were a host of really good tunes, including
"Chapel of Love," "The Look of Love," "River Deep—Mountain
High," and "Then He Kissed Me." The problem was that when EMI
directed demos toward Manfred Mann it fished out one of Jeff and
Ellie's lesser songs, one which the songwriting duo (known professionally as the Raindrops) was about to record as one of its own
singles. As it turned out, the Raindrops' loss was Manfred Mann's
gain.

Much like the writers' "Jingle Jangle" and "Da Doo Ron Ron,"
"Do Wah Diddy Diddy" made little or no sense. But as Barry and
Greenwich would prove on countless occasions, words didn't have to
have a meaning to score big in a teenage record buyer's mind. The
song scribes seemed to know that teens who couldn't recite even half

of their multiplication tables could remember lines like "Do wah diddy diddy dum diddy do" from the first time they heard them. Then, as if given some kind of special gift, these same teens would also be able to actually use these words in a conversation and have all their peers understand just what they meant. This fact confounded adults, but made cash registers chime and Jeff and Ellie smile.

In September of 1964 Manfred Mann landed on the American charts with "Do Wah Diddy Diddy." Within a month MM had knocked "Pretty Woman" out of the #1 spot and would spend several weeks ruling American music with its "British but made in America and South Africa" sound. The boys would also field a hundred questions from the press and fans as to just what "Do wah diddy diddy" meant. If they knew, they didn't let on, which probably somehow helped the song continue to sell.

The last two months of 1964 were the best of days for this eclectic band. Yet in spite of possessing more talent and musical knowledge than probably any other group of the era, MM simply couldn't follow up its wildly successful debut American hit with anything meaningful. Perhaps that was due in part to the fact that "Do Wah Diddy Diddy" didn't have any meaning either. Still, it came as some surprise that when Manfred Mann released the deeply spiritual "Sha La La" as its next record, American audiences pretty much decided that the Rolling Stones and Herman's Hermits had a bit more to say than Manfred did. How did teens come to this conclusion?

Manfred Mann didn't die just because it couldn't hit it big a second time on *Billboard* charts. Even though American audiences had written the band off, back in England it continued to record and tour. And the hard work paid off. Four years after "Do Wah Diddy Diddy," Mann again resurfaced in America's top ten. Learning from its first hit, MM this time rode up the charts on one of the most meaningful songs of the rock era, Bob Dylan's "Mighty Quinn (Quinn the Eskimo)." It took an almost spiritual reawakening eight years later, in 1976, for Mann to finally hit #1 again, with a song which finally got the musical world to take this talented group seriously, "Blinded by the Light."

# Duke of Earl

*B*y *the early sixties rock and roll was struggling to redefine itself. The business had been overrun by teen* idols, and though many of these, such as Bobby Darin, were extremely talented, most of these primarily white acts who had stolen the spotlight from more deserving performers were cardboard cutouts. Because of this influx of new "talent," many of the great doo-wop groups had been washed out, and the once driving and revolutionary sound of rock had given way to a softer, less hostile product. In other words, by pushing the likes of Jerry Lee Lewis, Little Richard, and Chuck Berry to the side, and by taming the wild facets of Elvis Presley, the charts were "safe" again for America's youth. Unfortunately, "safe" wasn't very stimulating, and even worse, it wasn't much fun.

Eugene Dixon had cut his teeth on music during rock and roll's more creative and less professional time. He had sung the music of the great R&B groups and learned lead by listening to folks like the Platters. He understood the need for youth music to be rebellious, but he also knew that at the same time it had to be spontaneous and happy. His neighbors in Chicago, who fought day and night just to make it through life, didn't want to be spoon-fed or lulled to sleep, and most didn't want to wallow in self-pity by singing the blues; they wanted to laugh, smile, and strut. So did Eugene. He also wanted to carve out his niche in the world of entertainment.

Dixon had performed with a couple of Chicago high school groups before landing with the doo-wopping Dukays in the mid-fifties. Though still in his teens, the youngster had style. He not only sang with passion, but he wrote a great deal of what he sang. He also understood that through music he could get out of Chicago, see the world, and maybe even mingle with royalty. But before he got the chance to take his show on the road, he was inducted into the service.

The world of rock and roll was much different in 1957, when Eugene first put on his nation's uniform, from what it was in 1960, when he returned to civilian life. In 1960, a lot of the musical punch was gone and groups were suffering, while solo acts were grabbing up more and more of the limited airtime. Nevertheless, Dixon jumped back into his lead singing spot with the Dukays, who were now managed by Bernice Williams, and dreamed of making it big. Sitting down with Williams to plot the future, Eugene scribbled out some words and shared some of his song ideas. The two then put together several new songs from Dixon's creative bursts.

Williams interested Nat Records in the group, and the small label put out two of the Williams-Dixon efforts, "The Girl's a Devil" and "Night Owl." Neither made much more than small vibrations on the underside of the top 100 charts. Williams then tried to sell the label on following up the first releases with a song that Dixon had written around the theme of a man who took the notion that he was the ruler over his own small corner of the world. The song made no real statement, was not like any of the more traditional love songs which were scoring on playlists, and claimed only a unique musical pattern climbing up and down a scale using a repetition of the word "duke" as a sales point. It was no wonder that Nat's executives suggested that the Dukays go back and seek out new material. But Williams simply wouldn't give up. She took the demo of "Duke of Earl" to another Illinois recording company, Vee-Jay.

For some reason A&R man Calvin Carter flipped over the sparse arrangement and Dixon's treatment of "Duke." When he discovered that Nat cared nothing about the song, he purchased all rights to the demo. But he soon had to confront the cold hard fact that he couldn't release it because while he owned the song and the recording, Nat owned the Dukays. It looked for all the world as if Carter had bought a lemon.

Dixon solved a major part of Vee-Jay's problem when he quit the Dukays and signed with the new label as a solo artist. He suggested that the company now simply rerecord "Duke of Earl" and beef up the song's bare feel with strings and full orchestration. But while Eugene wanted to do "Duke" up in a royal fashion, Carter didn't; he liked the original record. With Dixon already in his camp, he decided to simply release the demo, but to label it as a solo effort.

Though Dixon was now no longer legally a member of the Dukays, the new label thought it would be in its best interest to make sure that it distanced itself even more from Eugene's association with Nat Records. He was told to come up with a new name. Choosing Chandler as a way to honor his favorite actor, and pulling the last part of his first name, Dixon created Gene Chandler while Vee-Jay made sure the world got the chance to hear its newest act under his new name.

"Duke of Earl" was shipped in late 1961, and the song, which the singer/writer himself had not particularly liked, jumped from #93 to #49 on January 20. By February 3 it was in the top ten. Two weeks later it was #1, a spot it would hold for three weeks. By simply making it to #1 it would continue a strange musical trend. "Duke of Earl" became the fourth straight "unique" song to rule the charts—"The Twist," "The Lion Sleeps Tonight," and "Peppermint Twist" had been #1 in the months before "Duke of Earl." These four songs, while some of the era's best remembered, point out just how quickly rock and roll had lost its punch and drive. It had gone from being rebellious and creative to being safe and formulaic.

When Gene Chandler's "Duke of Earl" took off, Dixon—now Chandler—decided that this taste of rock and roll royalty was to be enjoyed to its fullest. Buying a cane, a dress suit with tails, and a top hat, and sporting a monocle, the singer became an even bigger joke than the song. By the time he released an album a few months later, Dixon had dropped the "Chandler" handle in favor of simply referring to himself as the "Duke of Earl." Yet his subjects were fickle and the Duke's reign didn't last long. By 1964 Dixon had been cut loose by Vee-Jay, had landed with Constellation, and was again recording under the name Gene Chandler. He had changed his wardrobe, too. It did little good. In the face of the Beatles and other English rock groups, Dixon couldn't compete. Though he kept plugging and even scored a modest hit in 1970 with Mercury, "Groovy Situation," the Duke would have no stage kingdom from which to rule. But behind the scenes Dixon did manage to secure a title, one that gave him more real power and influence than his unique creation ever would. Eugene became CEO of Bamboo Records, producing many hits for them before forming his own label and creating an even larger kingdom to rule.

Meanwhile the "Duke of Earl" has continued to reign as one of the most remembered and beloved rock and roll numbers of all time. Though it is now often mistakenly labeled a fifties song, Gene Chandler's hit belongs to the ages, and its kingdom includes millions all over the world who have never wondered just how a song with so little substance and meaning could rule the rock charts for three weeks. What those fans may intuitively realize is a piece of wisdom that Eugene Dixon learned on the streets of Chicago: Music doesn't have to make sense; it just has to be fun. Certainly the "Duke" was fun, for Dixon and for us!

Eat It

In 1984 Michael Jackson was not a strange tabloid personality, he was the King of Pop. The former cute kid from the Jackson Five, who had successfully groomed his image to that of an "all-American" pop icon loved by kids and tolerated by parents, was largely thought of as a talented and gentle soul by much of the media. He had just begun to alter his look via cosmetic surgery and bizarre makeup. In other words, he was cool and becoming very wealthy, and the weirdness that would soon eclipse his tremendous talent was just beginning to surface. As a matter of fact, about the strangest thing to come into Jackson's never-never land at that time, at least publicly, was an accordion-playing polka freak who liked nothing better than making fun of Jackson and any other musician whose products were commercially successful.

Al Yankovic had to have been born with a unique viewpoint. He simply didn't see things the way normal people did. Where others saw anger, pain, or nothing, Al saw a laugh. It would be his special sense of humor that would soon pave the way for some very special rewards.

By the time he was in high school Al was playing his accordion at weddings, bar mitzvahs, and other ethnic parties which demanded the presence of a squeeze box and someone who could properly squeeze it. While other kids were picking up the guitar and learning to rock, Al seemed content to simply add his own riffs to the "Beer Barrel Polka" while making a few dollars on the side. Then lightning struck! Using his inimitable sense of humor and music which he arranged for the "instrument from hell," Yankovic began to spend some of his spare time writing parodies of the era's best-known standards. These bizarre tunes got the New Yorker so many laughs from his school chums that he began to tape them on a cheap home recorder and to send them to one of the city's strangest and most popular radio programs, *The Dr. Demento Show*. Surprisingly, the good Doctor played a few of Al's originals, and this bit of local fame inspired the young man to churn out some more. It soon seemed that nothing was held sacred by Yankovic, who, as "Weird Al," was making fun of everything from polka standards to Queen's "Another One Bites the Dust" (in Al's world it was "Another One Rides the Bus"). Sensing that it was time to lift his act to a higher level, Yankovic put his accordion in its case and took his show on the road. That was when reality set in, big time.

Though Yankovic would have seemed perfect for a guest shot, Chuck Barris, a man who had the lowest of performance standards, turned him down for *The Gong Show*. One would think that anyone who failed to exhibit enough talent to qualify for the strictly-for-laughs *Gong Show* would have seen the writing on the wall and given up. Yet for a reason known only to him, Al didn't. He continued to write and continued to knock on doors.

The songwriter's parody of "My Sharona" landed him a spot with Capitol Records, which released Al's homemade version, "My Bologna." Yankovic thought this might signal an improvement in his fortunes, but when the tune didn't take off, he quickly found himself back in the real world. In his mid-twenties, working in a radio station mailroom, Yankovic should have been contemplating a change of careers. Instead he was continuing to pick up his accordion and record more new original parodies.

Thanks in large part to his mentor, Dr. Demento, Al landed a few gigs. During these shows in small clubs, his most requested number was a bit lampooning the nation's hottest songs. But in his version

"Maneater," "Whole Lotta Love," and other hits were turned into food epics. One of the songs which he had rewritten for this strange package was Michael Jackson's monster "Beat It." Al simply dropped the first letter in the title and sang number as "Eat It."

Sensing he might just have something special, Yankovic sent his one-verse parody to Michael Jackson. How the song worked its way through the recording giant's maze of mail handlers and found its way into the King of Pop's hands is unknown. What is known is that Jackson, who was just beginning to emerge as a parody of himself, loved Yankovic's parody. With Michael's approval and blessing, the accordion player rewrote the song, landed on the Rock 'n' Roll label, and put together an incredibly funny video featuring special fat makeup and two gangs fighting over a chicken.

It was the video spoof of Jackson's creative videos which really displayed Al's genius for the first time. As Dr. Demento already knew and the world was soon to find out, this was classic "Weird Al." The "Eat It" video was a combination of *Laugh-In, The Milton Berle Show*, and *The Twilight Zone*. The concept, a takeoff on Jackson's "Beat It" video, made Mel Brooks's stuff look pretty normal. Deemed perfect for the MTV audience, Yankovic suddenly went from unknown to heavy rotation. Thanks to the impact of video, "Eat It" also made it to #12 on the rock charts in the late spring of 1984. And suddenly, "Weird Al" had what he really craved: a spotlight just for him.

Yankovic, whose look was closer to Tiny Tim's than to that of most of the day's top pop artists, could sell his unique work on the strength of his appearance. One has to even question if he would have ever made it without video. (Then again, what kind of impact would Jackson himself have had without MTV?) Yet to credit the success of "Eat It," as well as the scores of successful Yankovic parodies which followed, to the visual strangeness of his curly locks, his huge glasses, his long face, and his special wardrobe, would be to underestimate the man's talent. Much like the early creative geniuses of television, especially a Sid Caesar or Ernie Kovacs (who couldn't have made it without television), Yankovic knew how to poke fun at the seemingly serious bits of life and to reveal that they were anything but serious.

In short, he made us laugh at ourselves. As it turned out, "Weird Al" might not have married Elvis's daughter or signed hundred-million-dollar record deals, but in 1996, when many countries were banning the "King of Pop," few were telling Yankovic to "Beat It."

# Flying Saucer

In 1956 Dickie Goodman, a comedy writer for Jackie Mason, took a concept that had been used not only during the golden age of radio, but also in several comic film shorts created during the first years of talkies, and put it to work in the recording medium. Joining him in the initial attempt to merge technology, studio cutting and mixing, sound bites from the day's hottest rock and roll hits, and a simple plot premise was writing partner Bill Buchanan. Buchanan and Goodman had begun to work together during their days with the Twentieth Century-Fox music department. Using a zany approach to writing, they had teamed for a few off-the-wall concepts that didn't fly before they made their ideas mesh in a record which they initially called "Back to Earth."

Even though their number would become a best-selling single, it was never really a song; neither Buchanan nor Goodman sang a note on the recording. Rather, they became the reporters who were on the scene to interview people who had witnessed a flying saucer land on earth. Instead of simply giving the two men straight answers to what they had seen, these witnesses spoke, or rather sang, in the youth language of the day—rock and roll music.

The main creative force behind "Back to Earth" was

Dickie Goodman. Goodman had picked out key phrases in songs like "Heartbreak Hotel" and "The Great Pretender," then linked them to questions which he had written into his unusual news script. Hence, when he needed an answer to "What would you do if the flying saucer landed?" he played Little Richard singing, "Duck back in the alley," or Elvis wailing, "I'd take a walk down lonely street."

Working through the hit parade of the day, Goodman used more than two dozen musical clips to fill out his unique vision of a flying saucer landing on earth. Then, after cutting a final product in their studio, Buchanan and Goodman rushed out copies to radio stations under the Luniverse label (thus making the company name almost as campy as the single). There can be little doubt that every disc jockey who received the Buchanan-Goodman single knew that the song was being self-marketed and that this was usually the kiss of death, but the idea was so strong and the production so "spacey" that those who programmed the hits didn't turn their backs on it.

One of the shrewd moves the duo had made before printing the record's labels was changing the song's name from "Back to Earth," to "Flying Saucer." This took advantage of some of the more sensational news stories of the day. Thanks at least in part to that fact, Buchanan and Goodman's single hit the charts with some force in the late summer of 1956. With a host of UFO movies playing at drive-ins, the air force studying the existence of flying saucers via Operation Bluebook, and radio jumping on the youth-oriented rock and roll music explosion at an accelerating rate, the "Flying Saucer" single flew up near the top of the charts by early fall. The single would hover at #3 for a week and remain in the top forty for almost three months.

Buchanan and Goodman probably broke a host of copyright laws when they produced their gimmick single. They were using cuts from scores of songs without permission. But just as the timing of the song had assured it a great deal of exposure, the performers were probably saved from the legal system by timing too. Because few in the entertainment industry had really figured out just how much money could be made by exploiting the law through the court system, America was not yet being flooded by copyright-violation lawsuits. If this legal stance had become popular in the mid-fifties, "Flying Saucer," as well as a host of imitators, would have never been heard over the airwaves.

Dickie Goodman would rework his cutting-and-splicing concept a few more times, and even though his "Mr. Jaws" was certified gold in 1975, the writer would never gain much fame via novelty songs. In 1989, evidently dissatisfied with his lot in life, Goodman scripted his own ending, using a more abrupt punctuation method than he had ever employed in his comedy writing. Dickie stopped the laughter forever when he shot himself.

Get a Job

*W*here's Shorty?
      A better question might be, Who is Shorty?

Shorty was the name of one of the four original members of a small-town North Carolina gospel group known as the Gospel Tornados. Bill Horton, Raymond Edwards, and Earl Beal filled out the quartet, who specialized in spiritual renderings of religious classics. Seeing the wind of inspiration dropping off and the money not blowing in, Shorty (it seemed no one knew his last name) dropped out of the group less than a year after the Tornados' inception. He was replaced by another man in his twenties, John Jenkins.

The Gospel Tornados all felt that they had been called by the Lord to specialize in bringing people to a belief in Christ through the use of music. Yet even though a number of local folks were caught up in the religious fever of their songs, this fever failed to generate much in the way of love offerings. By and large, if they were to eat, the Tornados were going to have to get another job. With the doors of the church only open on Sunday and Wednesday, they went in search of jobs at venues which stayed open more than two days a week.

Even though they didn't want to become a part of the

club scene, the quartet began in 1956 to sing R&B standards at black honky-tonks. Sensing that he didn't belong in this smoke-filled environment, John Jenkins went out to look for Shorty and was replaced by Richard Lewis. Throughout the next year the gospel/R&B group's membership was stable, and as they groomed their sound, they found themselves in more demand on the secular than on the sacred side of the musical shore.

Lewis, who had served a hitch in the air force, played a large part in not only the maturation of the group, but in the direction it would head. Sensing that black entertainers were being given access to white America's pocketbooks via rock and roll, Lewis steered the Tornados into doo-wop. As he positioned the group to compete with other doo-wop acts, Richard pulled out a song that he had never intended to drop into this often silly version of musical expression.

While in the military Lewis had spent his spare time writing songs. One of these compositions concerned a man who was looking for but could not find a job. Richard had seen many who'd found themselves in this position end up in the service. But all the time they were being paid by Uncle Sam they were still concerned that there would be nothing for them when they got out. Worse yet, many had a fear that their wives wouldn't give them any peace until they did find employment. They were looking forward to getting out of the military, but dreading the double dose of hell that might greet them when they jumped back into the real world.

Lewis's "Get a Job" was written as a straight song. It was simple, too. He had included nothing but an elementary lead line surrounded by a somewhat humorous story told verse by verse of a hounded and luckless man. In a way it represented a new version of the blues. And like "Blue Moon," "Get a Job" was intended to be a song which addressed a serious subject in an entertaining fashion.

But no one had much interest in the song or the group, and the Tornados were turned down by almost all the major labels. Some even suggested that the group's members might just want to follow the song's advice and get a job in the real world. For a while it seemed that if they didn't look for work they might just starve to death.

In 1957 the Tornados were finally noticed by a talent scout while playing in a small Philadelphia club. Through this contact they were given a shot in the Uptown Theater. Spotted by the owner of Junior Records during the show, the Tornados were signed to a contract and rechristened the Silhouettes. As it would turn out, the name change was not the only transformation that took place in the Junior studios.

The group began to play with "Get a Job." In the course of the Silhouettes' going through it scores of times, the Lewis ode about looking for work had been turned upside down and had become a doo-wop dream. This had come about because the label's arranger-producer, Howard Biggs, suggested that the backup vocalists have some real fun. Hence came the most famous of all nonsensical rock and roll lyrics: "Sha-na-na-na, na-na-na-na." With that line, others, including such wonderfully emotional statements as "Yip," Boom," and "Ba-doo," sprang forth. In the course of an hour, what had been a straight quartet song had become a composition whose lead line was completely buried by the strange stuff that was backing it. For perhaps the first time in the history of rock and roll, the doo-wop lyrics had supplanted the song's lead lyrics.

When "Get a Job" was released in Philadelphia (at that time the center of rock and roll) as a B side to "I Am Lonely," disc jockeys immediately flipped the record and it became a hit. Meanwhile "I Am Lonely" joined Shorty as a forgotten part of the group's history. The Silhouettes' initial single sold more than nine thousand copies in its first week. Ember Records in New York then purchased distribution rights for "Get a Job" and put it out nationally. By New Year's the song was well on its way to not only the #1 spot, but to selling more than a million copies. The Silhouettes, who could never generate much power when they were the Tornados, now had more jobs than they knew what to do with. One of them was an appearance on Dick Clark's *American Bandstand*. For a moment, this made them national celebrities!

"Get a Job" would become one of the greatest group sing-along numbers of all time. The lead lyrics were often viewed as not being important enough to learn, but everyone, it seemed, could do all the "sha-na-nas." Many kids would stand on city street corners or in rural schoolyards and just sing the background music.

But, after roaring up the playlists in the winter of 1957–58 with "Get a Job," the Silhouettes soon found themselves without a job or a label, unable to put together a follow-up hit. By the early sixties most of the group had departed, to look for real employment or to search for Shorty. It seemed that the Silhouettes had proven just how fleeting fame could be and how very few long-lasting jobs there were in the world of entertainment.

But though the Silhouettes would die a largely forgotten death, their song would not. A group of college kids got together one night in the late sixties to stage a few fifties numbers for a fraternity dance. The song which seemed to turn the crowd on the most was "Get a Job." Sensing a hunger for old rock and roll, these students worked out some more crazy routines, learned fifty rock classics, and christened themselves after the first line of "Get a Job." College studies would soon be forgotten as Sha Na Na stormed the nation, gaining far more fame and making far more money than the Silhouettes had ever dreamed of. And even though Sha Na Na never charted on their own, they had a great deal to do with the renewed interest in rock and roll. This led to the Silhouettes' re-forming in 1980, and finally getting some good-paying jobs, too.

Wonder if Shorty was as lucky.

Hanky Panky

In 1963 Jeff Barry and Ellie Greenwich had formed a group called the Raindrops. As writers the duo had scored with songs like "Da Doo Ron Ron," so they had long ago realized that meaningful lyrics were not a necessary ingredient to a hit song. Coming to the conclusion that there was more money to be made if they combined writing and performing, the pair went to work on another masterpiece, this time intended to launch their own recording careers. Grabbing the slag expression for playing around—hanky panky—the duo cut a single by the same name. In the midst of the era of teen idols and beach songs, the song was thankfully lost, and Jeff and Ellie eventually went back to composing.

While most rock and roll fans quickly forgot the Raindrops, the "Hanky Panky" number somehow hung around—in, of all places, Indiana. As a matter of fact, just off the hallowed campus of Notre Dame, the old tune was still being played in a dance club, even after the Beatles had turned the music world upside down. One teenager who wandered in and heard it was Thomas Jackson.

Jackson had been born in the years right after World War II, and like most baby boomers was just getting interested in music when Elvis hit the big time. Inspired, the youngster bought a guitar and learned to play. By the time he was a Michigan junior high student he had formed a group. Jackson had given the group a very rock and roll moniker—the Shondells.

Jackson was ambitious, and had a mother who encouraged him to go all out in everything he did. By twelve Thomas had recorded a song. By the mid-sixties he had a job with a small record label. One of the songs which Thomas pitched to his producer was "Hanky Panky."

The "Hanky Panky" which the Shondells cut in 1964 was a bit different from the one which had been released two years before by the Raindrops. James had ad-libbed many of the lyrics, simply because he couldn't remember them all. Yet the story of a young woman who did the "Hanky Panky" as she walked down the street made no less sense in Thomas's hands than it had in the writers'. A listener might imagine what the singer meant, but no one could really know for sure. Initially, few would care, either.

While still not a meaningful view of teenage love or life in general, the Shondells' version of "Hanky Panky" was superior to the first release because of the solid and entertaining musical accompaniment James had provided. It had a party feel to it. And for a high school band, the group was pretty good. Yet up against the sounds of the British invasion, the record, released on the small Snap label, was quickly lost in the shuffle, as were the Shondells.

Twenty months later, an almost twenty-year-old Jackson, now professionally known as Tommy James, had let his band go and all but given up on the music business. He had tried the road, and it had ridden him harder than he had ridden it. He had pitched his songs to numerous record labels, only to be shot down again and again. And a trunkful of old copies of "Hanky Panky" were simply not getting him any work. Depressed and considering his career options, he returned to his family home in Niles, Michigan. There, fate stepped in.

A Pittsburgh radio station had found a copy of the Shondells' version of "Hanky Panky" and had played it on the air. For some reason, the teens in the steel town couldn't get enough of it. Within weeks it had climbed to the top of the request charts—but even as the song was spun over and over again, no one could find it. And outside of Pittsburgh, no one had even heard of it.

A radio station tracked James down and asked him to bring the members of his group to town and perform the song for their teen fans. There were no longer any Shondells, but the lead singer went to Pittsburgh anyway. Searching the local clubs, James discovered a solid-sounding area band, sold its members on a chance to appear as the group with the hotly requested "Hanky Panky," and then billed this "newly formed old band" as Tommy James and the Shondells.

After playing before screaming fans in Pennsylvania, James took his clippings and his record to New York. There he finally found a label that was interested in giving him another chance. A few weeks later, using the recording that had been cut two years before in Michigan with the original band, Roulette Records took a gamble and released the single for a second time.

When writer Jeff Barry found out that his "Hanky Panky" had been reissued, he wanted to deny that he had any part in writing the song. He thought that this version was so bad it might hurt his professional standing. Now if Barry, who had composed such classics as "Leader of the Pack," "Bang Shang-a-Lang," and "Chip Chip," was embarrassed by the song, the sanity of sending it out to the marketplace had to be questioned. Yet for some reason, America suddenly fell in love with the girl who was involved in all that "Hanky Panky."

The song only spent ten weeks on the charts, but that was enough time for it to pass such musical giants as "Strangers in the Night" by Frank Sinatra, "Paperback Writer" by the Beatles, and "Paint It Black" by the Rolling Stones. And then, instead of disappearing as quickly as it had surfaced, "Hanky Panky" kept showing up at dances and on radio flashbacks for years. And as the royalty checks kept rolling in, even Jeff Barry fell in love with his old composition.

Over the course of the next fourteen years, Tommy James would chart sixteen more times. His biggest hit, "Crimson and Clover," seemed to make about as much sense as his initial plunge on the charts. Yet even in the face of that fact, there was no denying that James was talented enough to stand out in an age when the playlists were dominated by the British invasion and acid rock. And while

Tommy has now spent as long a time off the charts as he did on them, his classic "Hanky Panky," along with the Shondells' great testament to the meaning of life, "Mony Mony," are still requested at dances around the world. And who can now doubt the importance of a higher education? After all, "Hanky Panky" would never have become a hit if it hadn't been for the dedicated students of Notre Dame.

"Let's play one for the Gipper!"

Harper Valley P.T.A.

*I*f country music has a Mark Twain, it is probably Tom T. Hall. In Nashville he is known as "The Storyteller," and it does seem that his songs stand apart from most because they speak lyrically of normal life and normal people in a manner that reminds one more of e. e. cummings than Ernest Tubb. Even though Hall has always remained almost G.I. style and clean cut, his soul must contain a bit of a flower child. There is a childlike quality about his songs, evident in both their innocence and their direct, simple story line. But while Tom's compositions may appear simplistic, there are really built-in layers, with each piece of fabric revealing a little bit of Hall's own life experiences. And as it turned out, it would be an experience from his own life that would put him on his way to stardom.

Born in Kentucky, Tom began to play guitar toward the end of World War II when he was just eight. His was not an idyllic life. His mother died when the boy was just eleven and his father was injured and forced to quit work a few years later. By sixteen Tom had left school, gone to work in a factory, and formed a band which played backwoods schoolhouses and small fairs. At that time his main goal was to have a group in which everyone got to dress alike. Hall's band ended up on radio, and it was there that Tom's show business career was born in earnest. A few years later he was the area's top disc jockey and making fairly good money, but at twenty-one he grew restless. He wanted to see the world. About the only way for a poor boy to manage that was to join the army. In 1957 he did just that. Three years later Tom had been a lot of places, seen a lot of things, and thought he knew what he wanted to do with the rest of his life.

For a while he went home and spun records as a disc jockey. Then he bought a store. Finally he went to college, where he worked toward a degree in journalism. Still dabbling in music, Tom sent a few of his compositions to Nashville. That was the beginning of something that would become very big.

By 1965 Hall had left college, worked several different clubs, and won a songwriting contract. He seemed on his way to penning major hits. Then reality kicked in. The songs which Hall wrote were much different from those the established writers were turning out. Like Roger Miller's songs, Tom's stuff was considered a bit too off-the-wall for the big artists. While a few of his tunes found homes, most gathered dust. Finally, against Hall's own desires, Mercury decided to have the songwriter sing his own stuff. Beginning in 1967 Hall charted consistently. His "A Week in the County Jail" even topped the playlists in 1969. Yet by and large Tom still considered himself a songwriter. That's what he really wanted to do. Touring and working the road just didn't have much luster for him.

In the middle sixties Tom T. journeyed home to visit with family. He was not there to bask in his burst of newfound fame; rather, he was looking for ideas for new songs. While visiting with his father he heard the story of a young woman whose child had been spanked in a local school. She had taken on the school board and administration, and before it was over had made them all look pretty stupid. Others might have dismissed this little bit of small-town life as a funny but unimportant taste of local color. Hall sensed that this was a tale that could easily become a song.

Tom T. took that real-life educational confrontation and fleshed it out. Consciously or not, he molded together two old small-town themes. The first was the fact that so many folks said they didn't go to church because there were so many hypocrites there. The second was that each of those hypocrites' favorite Bible verse almost always ran along the theme of "judge not lest you be judged." The song that spewed out of the scribe's somewhat skewed mind was a short story built around a beautiful young single mother who dressed in miniskirts and knew the dirt on everyone in town.

At about the same time that Tom was shopping the "Harper Valley P.T.A." demo, Jeannie C. Riley and her husband had moved to Nashville. Within a few months of landing in town, Jeannie, a former high school majorette from Anson, Texas, had secured a contract at a local recording house and had even released a single. Her first effort failed, and her career went nowhere for two years. She might have remained an unknown if Shelby Singleton, a Plantation Records producer, hadn't heard her voice on a demo and recalled a song that Tom T. Hall had pitched to him about six months before.

Pulling Jeannie into the studio, Shelby offered her a chance to record "Harper Valley P.T.A." She listened to the demo and expressed her reservations about the song. She thought it wasn't country enough for that market, and feared that if it scored well on the rock charts it might just ruin any chance she'd ever have at making it big in Music City. Singleton wouldn't give up on Riley or the song and urged her to cut it anyway. When she did, the producer rushed a copy to Nashville's top disc jockey, Ralph Emery. Emery immediately put "Harper Valley" into heavy rotation. Ralph knew something that Jeannie hadn't—that this was going to be a huge country record.

Plantation Records worked as quickly as possible to turn out "Harper Valley." As the company shipped the single, it also sent out thousands of photos of the beautiful Riley outfitted in a very short miniskirt. It was a marketing ploy that worked so well even the label was overwhelmed. The song was picked up so quickly by both country and rock radio outlets that Plantation had to print copies of "Harper Valley" twenty-four hours a day, seven days a week, just to keep up. Almost 2 million copies were sold during the single's first month of release. It was a monster hit, one that had struck a chord with a nation that had seen its share of stone-throwing by folks whose lives had been stuck in the mud for so long that their hands would never be clean.

"Harper Valley P.T.A." owned the charts for most of the fall, and Jeannie C. Riley was spotlighted as the young lady who would soon own country music. Yet, as is often the case, the singer was simply unable to follow up with another huge hit. Even though her signature song was made into a movie and a television series, Jeannie quickly discovered that she had suffered a fate that she herself had predicted upon first hearing "Harper Valley P.T.A." The song had ruined her chances at ever being taken seriously in the world of country music.

While Jeannie C. Riley disappeared and was replaced by a new crop of women performers, Tom T. Hall would continue to write, record, and tell his stories. Spurred on by the success of "Harper Valley P.T.A.," Tom T. would go on to compose scores of unique hits for himself and others. Happily for his listeners, even when his songs concerned the most serious of subjects, his voice and wit were a most refreshing novelty at a time when nearly everything and everyone in Nashville sounded the same.

Hello Muddah,
Hello Fadduh

"*Hello Muddah, Hello Fadduh*" *combined both classical music and a child's ever-changing view of* life in a way that made it a timeless novelty hit in 1963. The fact that this inspired bit of nonsense became a golden record which had all of America singing is not just a tribute to the creativity of the song's writer and performer, but a testament to millions of American children's summer camp experiences.

Allan Sherman was one of the most inventive minds in early television. Born in Chicago during the early years of radio, Allan came into television when the networks and most live shows still made their homes in New York. Sherman's knack for writing gags and scripts caught the eye of folks like Jackie Gleason, who put him to work creating some of the most colorful comedy dialogue on the then black-and-white tube. Others stole Allan away from "The Great One," and Sherman quickly evolved into one of the industry's most sought-after minds.

In 1952 Allan came up with a concept for a television game show which would help put the CBS network atop the ratings for years to come. Using four panelists and a moderator, Sherman created a show where a guest would come on with a special secret and the panelists would have to question the guest and find out what that secret was. Produced by the famed duo of Mark Goodson and Bill Todman, and using Garry Moore as the host and such personalities as Orson Bean, Bill Cullen, Kitty Carlisle and Henry Morgan as the panelists, *To Tell the Truth* would run for over two decades and become one of the most beloved fixtures on television. The show would also become one of Allan Sherman's greatest and most lasting gifts to entertainment.

While Sherman relished having a hit show, and was involved behind the scenes with dozens of other successful projects, he was still largely unknown by the American public. This began to change in the early sixties when the writer put together a comedy routine that would take him from backstage to center stage and make his name known to millions.

When Allan happened upon the inspiration for his "Hello Muddah, Hello Fadduh," he knew that he was walking on ground that had been covered countless times before. In both movies and television, the stories of homesick boys and girls who were having a miserable time at camp had formed the basis for some great comedy bits. Almost every family sitcom had used, in at least one script, the premise of a kid begging to come home from a mosquito-infested camp ruled by a former marine drill sergeant. Yet while the camp concept had been almost overworked on television and in motion pictures, the world of music had simply ignored it. In most writers' minds it was easier to create a song about a purple space invader or a singing chipmunk than it was to tell about something that happened to tens of thousands of kids each summer. Then along came Allan Sherman.

Using every camp horror story he had ever heard, the television writer wrote and afterward recorded in the Warner Bros. studio a child's letter home. Allan sang and narrated "Hello Muddah, Hello Fadduh" in the voice of a sad little boy who had been forced to leave his comfortable home for a foreign wasteland where the bugs were huge, the other "inmates" were mean, and the food was lousy. Setting the lyrics to the familiar Ponchielli's *Dance of the Hours* seemed to add to the song's wailing, pleading, childlike voice and emotions. The composer's quick surprise turnaround during the final verse and the song's abrupt ending were strokes of real genius that ultimately and fully captured a child's ever-changing point of view. As both a song and a comedy sketch, "Hello Muddah" was perfect.

In order to push his first single and become something of a known personality, Allan hit the television variety show circuit. With his rather rotund form, his rubbery face, and his wide range of expressions, Sherman sold his ode to camp life as no one else possibly could have. Though he was approaching his forties and looked even older, there was a little boy's glint in Allan's eye that made him seem almost childlike. There is little doubt that this quality helped promote "Hello Muddah, Hello Fadduh" on the shows of Garry Moore, Johnny Carson, Tennessee Ernie Ford, and other top television personalities.

Released in the summer of 1963, "Hello Muddah, Hello Fadduh" hit #1 in many markets and managed to peak at the second slot on the *Billboard* chart. It held that #2 position for three weeks, being denied a chance at #1 by the Angels' "My Boyfriend's Back." A child's favorite for summers to come (and if they were to tell the truth, there are still hundreds of thousands of baby boomers who three decades after they last attended a summer camp can still sing every one of the words to Allan Sherman's song), its message and millions of listeners' personal camp memories make this song a novelty classic!

# Hokey Pokey

*S*ome of the best-known lines in the history of song begin, *"You put your right foot in; you put your right foot out."* Then after you do some shaking and turning around, you know what it's all about—at least that's what the "Hokey Pokey" claims. And this number might just also claim to be the most famous recording flop in history!

Larry LaPrise, a little-remembered native of Detroit, was known for most of his life as "Mr. Hokey Pokey," or "The Hokey Pokey Man." After spending some time in military service in Europe during World War II, LaPrise returned to civilian life and formed a musical group known as the Ram Trio. While working the nightclub circuit in Sun Valley, Idaho, the group members tried out a dance number which Larry had taught them. The ski crowd fell in love with it and demanded to hear it again, and soon everyone in Sun Valley was dancing to a little ditty called "Hokey Pokey."

After watching the college kids gyrate night after night in front of the bandstand, Larry thought that this funny dance number which got feet, legs, elbows, and head moving all at once might have some commercial possibilities. About a year later, in 1949, the Ram Trio cut a studio version of what might now be called a calorie-burning workout song. As its version of "Hokey Pokey" was shipped, the Ram Trio waited for things to take off. When the song flopped and their fortunes went flat, the boys found day jobs.

In 1952 bandleader Ray Anthony caught a bit of Larry's special little song, played it for one of his dance crowds, watched the kids eat it up, and decided to find out who held the rights to it. Tracking down LaPrise, Anthony secured all future rights to "Hokey Pokey," paying the song's scribe just $500 for sole ownership. The bandleader then rushed into a recording session and cut his own version of "Hokey Pokey." Unfortunately, Anthony's label, Capitol, decided to use "Hokey Pokey" as a flip side for "The Bunny Hop." It was the rabbit song which hopped into the top twenty early in 1953. "Hokey" was lost in the shuffle.

Over the course of the next decade "Hokey Pokey" was cut countless times, by everyone from the Tommy Dorsey Orchestra to Annette Funicello. Yet in the dozens of times the dance song was reintroduced, it never made the charts. Even though Larry LaPrise no longer owned the rights to "Hokey Pokey," he followed the trail that the song took from studio to studio, artist to artist, and label to label. He also began to note that even though his song had never appeared on a single *Billboard* list, it was getting to be pretty well-known. Even a lot of dances in the backwoods of Idaho and Montana were using it.

In the mid-sixties LaPrise had worked his way to Ketchum, Idaho, and had signed on for duty with the post office. At about the same time, Ray Anthony Music sold the rights to "Hokey Pokey" to Acuff-Rose Music in Nashville. Country music legend Roy Acuff noted that LaPrise was listed as the song's author, but was not getting any royalties from use or sales of "Hokey Pokey." Roy didn't like to see writers being treated unfairly, so he tracked Larry down, listened to his story, and gave the scribe back the royalty rights which LaPrise had once sold so cheaply. Even though the semiannual checks weren't very big, Larry was now reaping at least a little bit of fortune for his ever-expanding contribution to American culture.

By this time the "Hokey Pokey" had become known as one of the easiest dances to teach children. Schools across the nation were using it as a part of physical education classes and school programs. By

1970 it was estimated that every school-age child in America had tried to dance the "Hokey Pokey" at least once. And at dances and P.T.A. programs, adults were joining in.

In 1996 the Macarena crisscrossed the globe as one of the hottest, and dumbest, dance numbers of all time. The mere fact that it was so inane and insipid seemed to get everyone involved in wanting to try it. Like the "Hokey Pokey," the Macarena was easy to learn and impossible to get out of your mind. But unlike Larry's song, the Macarena had a marketing arm behind it, which made sure that it was a hit not only on the playlists, but at the cash register too.

"Hokey Pokey" is probably the best-known modern-era dance song to never become a hit single. The mere fact that this bit of silliness survived and prospered with no radio airplay, videos, or marketing ploys says a lot about Larry LaPrise's songwriting efforts. Would the Twist or Macarena have become dance crazes without radio play? Would they have survived simply on their own merits?

In 1996 Larry LaPrise died in Boise, Idaho. He left his own modest legacy as a small-time song-and-dance man and a darn good postman. As the news of his death broke, a host of stories cropped up that the one thing in life which LaPrise could proudly say was his contribution to the America of his time, "Hokey Pokey," had actually been played in the thirties and forties in Europe and that Larry might have simply been the first to bring it back home and play it in America. Did Larry LaPrise write "Hokey Pokey," or simply import the dance song? Who knows and who cares? After all, Larry never got rich off this song which couldn't find a place on the charts, but he sure did make a lot of people happy. And "that's what it's all about!"

 Hot Rod Lincoln

*I*n the late forties and early fifties, beginning in California, hundreds of thousands of teenagers became obsessed with taking old used-up cars, dropping newer-model hopped-up Ford flathead V-8 engines into them, restyling the old car's appearance inside and out, and then finding a long straight highway. On those lonely stretches of road these kids, in their now meticulously revived autos, would challenge other "hot-rodders" in drag races. The prize at stake was simply the knowledge that their car was the boss of the valley. It was machine against machine in a one-on-one battle for supremacy.

Over the rest of the fifties the hot-rodding craze engulfed much of the country, as kids from coast to coast and border to border where chopping, channeling, and rodding everything from '49 Mercury sedans to rusted-out deuce coupes. Magazines were started that showed the ins and outs of hot-rodding, and an entire car parts industry catered to boys who wanted more and more speed.

By the mid-fifties Hollywood had discovered these teens with the souped-up wheels. James Dean watched a man die in a daredevil drag race in *Rebel Without a Cause*. Elvis's prize possession was a hot-rodded roadster in *Loving You*. In almost every cheapie teen drive-in feature, the bad guy always drove some kind of open speedster with flames painted down the side. The hot rod was so universally accepted that even the character of Bud Anderson on television's *Father Knows Best* bought an old "A" model to fix up as a runner.

Except for a few songs which dealt with someone dying tragically in a car crash ("Tell Laura I Love Her") or humorous numbers about nice cars and bad dates ("Maybellene"), in the fifties the record business mostly ignored the hot-rod craze and stuck with standard doo-wop or teen idol themes. But beginning in 1960 the automobile surfaced as a major player in the music industry. The novelty song which seems to have gotten this automania started concerned a car with a souped-up Lincoln motor and enough speed for the Indy 500. Strangely, this epic's driver was not a speed-crazed teen, but a middle-aged man.

Johnny Bond had been a part of the entertainment world since 1934. Born in Oklahoma, the singer/songwriter/actor had drifted to Hollywood during the Great Depression, earning his keep singing western songs and doing extra work in B movies. Under the guidance of Gene Autry, Bond sang on radio and expanded his acting career. By his thirty-second birthday in 1947, he was cutting country music hits like "Divorce Me C.O.D." for Columbia Records. Johnny would continue a strong presence in hillbilly music for the next decade through both his single releases and his appearances on numerous national and regional television shows.

To really appreciate the man's talents and contributions during this period, one has to go beyond his profound bass voice and smooth singing style. This accomplished songwriter and arranger's compositions, like "Cimarron," were vital to country music's gaining widespread acceptance and expanding out of the southern hills and across the nation. One of the first artists to successfully blend southern and cowboy styles of music, he was very much an innovator and a pioneer, as he played a major role in taking what had been known as hillbilly music and turning it into the genre known as country and western.

By the late fifties Bond's career had pretty much run out of gas. Columbia dropped him, and he might not have been able to find another record deal if his old buddy Gene Autry hadn't called. Gene had just started a new label, Republic, and he wanted Bond to help kick it off. Johnny gladly accepted the opportunity.

While looking for material to plug in the rapidly growing country music market, Bond came across a novelty number that had been cowritten by Charles Ryan and W. S. Stevenson. Stevenson, who composed such classics as "Lonely Street" and "Am I That Easy to Forget," was well-known in country music circles, so his name on a credit impressed most performers. Yet what surprised Bond was that the song he had uncovered was not only a decade old, but centered on something far removed from Stevenson's usual subject matter.

There was little doubt that even if he hadn't known that W. S. Stevenson had had a hand in writing "Lincoln," Johnny would have been familiar with the number. Three-hundred-and-fifty-pound orchestra leader Tiny Hill had recorded "Hot Rod Lincoln" in 1951. Though the single had only stayed on the pop charts for two weeks, it had been one of the high points of Tiny's career; he would soon depart from the national hit parade forever.

Bond, who as a songwriter understood what elements needed to be in place to make a hit, sensed that Hill's "Hot Rod Lincoln" had been a solid musical choice and that Tiny's arrangement had been good too, but that the song's timing had been all wrong. The hot-rod craze was so localized during this period that only a small audience in California could identify with the subject. But now, a decade later, with *Hot Rod* magazine being read by millions of teens each year and drag racing becoming a legitimate sport in many areas, Johnny reasoned that "Hot Rod Lincoln" might just work.

Bond had last seen his own teen years in 1934, so in a way he seemed a bit long in the tooth to be trying to revive his career in the rock and roll market. Yet by using a driving bass guitar, his deep voice, and the phrasing style that he had learned from making dozens of movies, Johnny cut a rousing story-song version of Tiny Hill's old single. One of the keys to Bond's arrangement was the song's pacing, which continued to pick up as the car raced faster and faster. By the end of the recording session the song seemed to be moving at an almost frantic speed.

Like a fine engine tuned perfectly for a race, Johnny Bond's "Hot Rod Lincoln" roared onto the charts in 1960. For seven weeks his song about the fastest car on the road charmed millions who listened to rock music. "Lincoln" probably also inspired scores of young songwriters to stop and scribble down musical versions of their stories of a fast deuce coupe, a killer curve, or a hot-rodding senior citizen. Two years after "Hot Rod Lincoln" raced up the charts, *Billboard*'s playlists were so filled with hot-rod numbers that the subject matter was no longer considered to be a novelty. As a matter of fact, by 1963, car songs were almost a separate musical genre.

Johnny Bond's "Hot Rod Lincoln" didn't really cover any new ground; it succeeded because the singer recognized the opportunity to exploit a fad. Yet even Johnny himself probably didn't realize just how big this fad would become. If he had, he might just have tried to beat the Beach Boys and Jan and Dean to the punch with his own follow-up. Instead, the singer drifted off into the sunset, crashing the country charts a few more times, but never again scoring on the rock side.

But "Hot Rod Lincoln" didn't go away. In 1972, Commander Cody and His Lost Planet Airmen restored the old vehicle and took "Hot Rod Lincoln" for a final ride up the rock charts. The old single didn't run out of gas until it had broken into the top ten.

Hound Dog

*M**ike Stoller and Jerry Leiber were two of rock and roll's most influential songwriters, and they are in* the Hall of Fame today because they probably understood more about the varied roots of rock and roll music than any other songwriting team. These two East Coast natives met on the West Coast while in high school. Though they were from New York Jewish families, in Los Angeles the boys became heavily involved in the local African-American social scene. Not only were most of their friends black, but Mike and Jerry also primarily dated black girls. Therefore the "Negro" culture of the forties, and especially the music of this people and era, became an important facet in developing the duo's mannerisms, style, and social outlook.

In high school Mike and Jerry not only began to write songs together, but they also began to have contests to see who could write the most songs in a single day. Admittedly this practice led to a huge volume of throwaway ditties, but it also unlocked and developed a talent that made the teens wunderkinder. It was through their original music that the two primarily expressed their East Coast/West Coast/Jewish/Negro cultural mesh. And because of that their sound wasn't big band, it wasn't rural, it wasn't blues, and it wasn't bop, but rather contained elements of all four. In other words, it was rock and roll before the term had been invented. The two teens were so original and so talented that they attracted attention, especially in the black music circles where their friends traveled. And by 1950 Mike and Jerry had established themselves as the best and most original up-and-coming R&B tune-smiths in Los Angeles.

"Hound Dog" was inspired when Leiber and Stoller caught Big Mama Thornton's blues act during a studio rehearsal. The boys were impressed not just with her down-and-dirty sound, but with the way Thornton wrapped her whole body around notes and made them say something that seemed to imply more than the lyrics stated. In other words, Big Mama caused folks to wonder if she was hinting at something illicit even when she was telling the story of Mary and her little lamb.

Inspired to come up with something that Thornton could throw her gutsy soul into, the songwriting team composed the two simple verses of "Hound Dog" in one short session. Though Mike and Jerry were in reality big-city boys who wrote for an R&B company, their original take on "Hound Dog" was more along the lines of southern rural blues. It was slow, deliberate, and kind of funky. It is not surprising then, that Big Mama and her producer, Johnny Otis, loved it. Thornton cut the song and took it to the top of the R&B charts, but because this genre played to such a small portion of the American population, most white Americans never heard her "Hound Dog." The dog would have probably been humanely put to sleep forever if not for another R&B group, Freddie Bell and the Bellboys.

If you haven't heard of the Bellboys, don't fault yourself—even very few music experts remember them. In 1956 they were a lounge act that catered to the gamblers who visited Las Vegas. One of those who caught their show was a twenty-one-year-old Elvis Presley. Presley, who was in the midst of a disastrous weeklong series of shows at the Frontier Hotel and Casino, was probably thinking his days as a media and recording phenomenon were numbered. The reviews for his show were terrible and his ego had suffered a huge blow. Many critics were predicting that the Pelvis was simply a flash in the pan who would soon be kicked out of the entertainment business. And Elvis himself was wondering if that wasn't true.

Why Elvis went to see Freddie Bell is unknown. Always restless, Elvis was probably doing nothing more than killing some time and looking over the local competition. (It is known that Presley also caught Derek and the Dominos this same week.) When Elvis heard Bell's somewhat cavalier version of the old Mama Thornton standard, he took note. It certainly didn't take "the King" long to learn the lyrics, and within a week he had added a straight slow blues version of the song to his show. Audiences ate it up like kibble. The number went over so well that Presley used "Hound Dog" for his appearance on *The Milton Berle Show*. Steve Allen, who was fighting for his life against Ed Sullivan on Sunday nights, caught Elvis on Uncle Miltie's show and decided to go Berle one better. He signed Elvis, dressed the singer in tails, and had him sing the comedic number to a basset hound. Presley hated playing the song as a comedy bit, but the audience died laughing and Allen beat Sullivan in the ratings game for the first time ever.

Elvis was now beginning to loathe "Hound Dog." But because of the exposure that the song had gotten on national television, it seemed that the singer and the Leiber-Stoller title were tied together at the hip. Elvis couldn't escape it. When Ed Sullivan booked him in the fall of 1956, the old showman demanded that Presley warble about the flea-ridden canine.

Steve Sholes was calling the recording shots at RCA. Even though Elvis didn't want to record "Hound Dog," Sholes demanded that he do so. But this time the song was played not slow and bluesy; through Sholes's guidance, the number was now frantically paced and basted with a rockabilly flavoring. The recording was a snarling Elvis at his best, and coupled to Otis Blackwell's "Don't Be Cruel," "Hound Dog" would become what is still the #1 rock and roll effort of all time.

The fact that "Hound Dog" was his biggest hit must have confounded Presley as much as the fact that people actually believed that there was some kind of demonic message hidden between the song's notes. Millions of American parents were suddenly demanding to know just what kind of nasty things Elvis was promoting through the song's meaningless lyrics. Preachers and social workers seemed to know that there had to be something dirty hidden between the lines—otherwise why were so many teens rushing out to buy it?

Strangely, *Billboard* did not classify Elvis's version of "Hound Dog" as a novelty song (as a matter of fact, none of Presley's releases, including "Little Egypt" and "U.S. Male," were classified as anything but straight releases). And certainly Leiber and Stoller, who would write numerous comedy hits for groups like the Coasters, weren't going to demand that the music magazine reconsider the song's categorical status, but anyone who had caught Elvis on Steve Allen crooning the song to a disinterested, top-hatted basset hound had to believe that this was one number which was never meant to be taken seriously—this one was a joke all the way!

Consider the song's message—if you don't catch a rabbit you aren't worthy of friendship. Anyone who had ever hunted, including Elmer Fudd, knew that a hound dog was supposed to flush the bunny out of the thicket, not catch it. So why did not doing something he wasn't supposed to do in the first place cost man's best friend his friendship with his man? No wonder parents were looking for some kind of hidden agenda in the lyrics—the song's real message certainly didn't make any sense.

There is an old southern saying that defines a bad idea in these words: "That dog won't hunt." As it turned out, this hound dog didn't have to. The song which Elvis came to hate because it placed him at the butt of so many jokes wouldn't fall out of the #1 spot in 1956 until it was replaced with Presley's ode to a stuffed animal, "Teddy Bear." Of course, by that time the singer had been with this dog long enough that the old hound would follow him the rest of his life. Thus the man who arguably was the greatest entertainment influence of the modern era and who sold more than a billion records would always be coupled to a "worthless" mutt. Of course, in the canine's defense, the hound dog that somehow wandered away from Big Mama Thornton's house and made himself at home in Graceland did make the singer and the songwriters millions of dollars. Lassie was probably the only dog that made more, and the collie had to work a lot harder!

I Saw Mommy Kissing Santa Claus

Christmas is one of the most magical times of the year. For centuries a host of great anthems, hymns, and classical pieces have been inspired by the religious themes which are at the heart of this holiday. But in this century, as Christmas has become more and more commercial, a number of songwriters have seen the lighter side of this season of giving. In a few cases these scribes' work has led to some of the most successful and beloved recordings of all time.

Who could imagine a Christmas without "White Christmas," "The Christmas Song," "Jingle Bell Rock," "Pretty Paper," or even "Rudolph"? When considered on their messages alone, all of these songs could easily fit into the novelty category. Imagining snow in Hollywood is a leap of faith, as is a deer with a glowing nose. Yet in the midst of these numbers is a sentimentality which drives them beyond a gimmick and moves their messages straight to the heart. They have therefore become timeless classics which bring back the warm, fuzzy feelings of Christmases past and present for almost everyone who hears them.

The true Christmas classics escape being labeled as novelty efforts because they were initially written to bring both a smile and a tear. They were songs which didn't apologize for their emotions; rather, they strove to reach the emotional base of everyone who heard them. Yet while many of the true Christmas classic novelty songs may have evolved into numbers which touch a listener's heartstrings, originally their main goal was to hit the listener full force in the funny bone. These songs didn't go for the deep sigh—they begged for a cheap laugh. One of the best of these was penned by a writer who had mainly been known for writing the 1944 Perry Como hit "Lili Marlene."

It is not hard to figure out just where Tommie Connor came up with the inspiration for "I Saw Mommy Kissing Santa Claus." After all, what child hasn't sneaked out of bed to watch for Santa coming to deliver the goods? And how many of these children have actually seen their own parents performing the deed instead? But in a few cases, where parents really went all the way with the trappings of the season, a few children probably did actually see their mother and a man in a red suit alone in a living room sharing a bit of the romance of the season with each other. After all, in the thirties and forties, women were drawn to men in uniform, so some children must have gone to bed a bit troubled by the thought that Mommy had a crush on the jolly old elf from the north.

For Tommie Connor, putting his concept into song was fairly easy, but finding a singer to sell this concept to the adult population, party as it was to the conspiracy to keep the legend of a pure St. Nick intact, was a bit harder. Folks like Bing Crosby and Gene Autry just weren't interested. Columbia Records finally decided to bypass the usual adult recording artists and use thirteen-year-old Jimmy Boyd to launch Connor's novelty song.

The song, released in November 1952 and delivered in a child's voice, hit the top of the charts the first week in December and held on to the top spot for two weeks. It would be Jimmy Boyd's only #1 hit.

The next year Molly Bee, an Oklahoma-born country singer who had made a solid name for herself as a child act on the West Coast and who would soon join Tennessee Ernie Ford as one of the stars of early network television, cut a version of "I Saw Mommy Kissing Santa Claus" from a fourteen-year-old girl's perspective. This time

Santa's illicit peck managed to hit the top twenty before the holiday spirit disappeared. Molly's version of this soon-to-be-classic might have earn broader exposure except for the fact that Mr. Novelty Song himself, Spike Jones, cut it as well. Jones, who had earlier pegged a chart buster with "All I Want for Christmas Is My Two Front Teeth," and his City Slickers orchestra were perfectly suited for anything that was a bit off-the-wall. Their unique look at the Romeo with the white beard hit the top ten.

Though "I Saw Mommy Kissing Santa Claus" never again topped any of the major charts, hundreds of entertainers have put their spin on it in the past forty-five years. From the Osmonds to the Ronettes, group after group has reenacted this bit of holiday tomfoolery. The song has also inspired countless television skits, ad campaigns, Christmas cards, and even men's magazine pictorials. In a very real sense, Tommie Connor's gimmick to sell a new seasonal tune "drew" an impression which is as timeless as a Norman Rockwell painting. And because of the tune's lasting impact, "I Saw Mommy Kissing Santa Claus" has joined "White Christmas" as a Christmas classic. Yet unlike Bing's story of wanting snow in Beverly Hills, Connor's novel fantasy sometimes comes true.

I'm Henry VIII, I Am

*M*ost novelty songs are hits only in their native countries. While there are exceptions, such as the reworking of the Zulu tribal song "The Lion Sleeps Tonight," each culture's humor is usually so sharply defined that even well-developed funny stories rarely make a completely successful transition when transported from one setting to another. So, when Peter Noone suggested that his Herman's Hermits cut a new version of an old English pub song, *one might have thought the old lad a bit daffy!* As it turned out, it was the American consumer who appeared to be short a few marbles.

Noone had grown up acting on television and in plays in his native England. At the age of sixteen, when most child actors have been pushed aside and are retired, Peter became involved in music. He worked with a couple of Manchester bands before being spotted by a record producer who was much more impressed with his "Kennedy-like" appearance than with his voice. It seemed that in the early sixties Britain was as gaga over John F. Kennedy and his family as Americans would be over Princess Di a generation later. Grabbing Noone, the producer, Mickie Most, put the eighteen-year-old together with four other musicians. As few of the boys actually played their own instruments in the recording sessions which followed, Most had essentially manufactured a group in a fashion that would soon be copied by American television executives when they formed the Monkees.

The group's name came about because many people felt that Peter, besides looking like JFK, was also the human facsimile of Sherman on *The Bullwinkle Show* (we will leave it up to you to now compare pictures of JFK and Sherman to see if you can spot the resemblance). But the boys' label, MGM, got the name a bit confused in the promotion department. They thought that Peter looked like someone named Herman (hopefully not Munster), and because of that nonfact the name Herman's Hermits came into existence.

As they were with a hundred other hastily formed English rock bands of the mid-sixties, record executives were trying to mold Herman's Hermits into the next Beatles. But while the quartet from Liverpool was on the edge and featured an evolutionary sound, Peter Noone's group was softer and much more reflective. The Hermits simply paled when compared with the Beatles or the Rolling Stones. Noone and his crew were the guys that Dad wouldn't have minded going out with his daughter, and if they were to get a haircut they might even be allowed to marry her.

Beginning in early 1965 with "Can't You Hear My Heartbeat," Herman's Hermits scored several top ten hits on the American side of the Atlantic. But while the Hermits were officially a part of the British musical invasion, they were more medics than frontline troops. This became obvious when one witnessed the Stones begging for "Satisfaction" while Noone was sweetly crooning "Mrs. Brown, You've Got a Lovely Daughter."

The fact that "Mrs. Brown," an old English folk number, unexpectedly hit #1 in the U.S. sent Peter searching through ancient sheet music to come up with something else that could be updated into a rock hit. Noone found what he wanted in a 1911 music hall number. An old comic, Harry Champion, had made this popular drinking song "I'm Henry VII, I Am" famous in the days before World War I. Because the words made no sense, the music was easy to learn, and the song's message was meaningless, "Henry" had since become sort of a British version of "Row, Row, Row Your Boat." Those who knew it sang it for laughs and usually sang it best after they had put away a few pints of ale. Noone, to his credit, was totally sober when he recommended that the Hermits cut a new version of "Henry" as a follow-up to "Wonderful World."

When the boys gathered at MGM to cut "Henry," it was discovered that no one knew the words to anything but the chorus. They didn't let this lapse stand in their way. Noone simply declared, "The second verse is the same as the first." Peter's claim went unchallenged, despite the fact that the group hadn't even produced the first verse. In its final form "Henry" became a repetitious, boisterous tavern-warbling record that seemed to get a bit more rowdy on each run through the chorus, and it was quickly deemed simply too awful for the British market. Yet while MGM thought that the sophisticated English, who had first popularized the song three generations before, wouldn't spend a plug sixpence on "I'm Henry VIII, I Am," the label was somewhat confident that the American market would buy practically anything that was being sold by a cute British band. Indicating that sharply defined taste had not crossed the Atlantic with the Pilgrims on the *Mayflower*, the youth of America proved the recording giant, which had once sold 3 million copies of a song about a one-eyed, one-horned purple monster, right.

"Henry VIII," which made less sense than "Wooly Bully," was perfect for the teenage mentality of the time. Hitting the charts in July of 1965, within four weeks it had knocked the Stones' "(I Can't Get No) Satisfaction" out of #1. A week later "Henry" was taken down from the throne by a song that probably sounded best after lifting a few pints, Sonny and Cher's "I Got You Babe." *And there are people who believe that this period wasn't the golden age of music!*

Herman's Hermits would continue to mine the vaults of British musical history for a few more years, but sadly, the group peaked with "I'm Henry VIII, I Am." The mere fact that this song, with its mindless chorus that was sung best by those whose tongues were thick with liquor—had made a bigger impact on the charts than the group's "Listen People" or "Just a Little Bit Better" makes one wonder if their rivals, the Rolling Stones, were the only ones not getting any satisfaction at this time. In retrospect, maybe the best thing about

Herman's Hermits' version of "Henry" was that they couldn't remember the verses and didn't bother looking them up. Consider how quickly this song would have gotten on one's nerves if one actually had to stop and think about a story line that accompanied a chorus whose main purpose was to make sure that folks knew Henry wasn't a Sam.

I'm My Own Grandpa

*F*or *many who know and love country music, the names of Lonzo and Oscar mean nothing. This pre-*mier hillbilly comic duo, who made hundreds of thousands laugh each Saturday night at the Opry for more than forty years, has been all but forgotten by those who can only trace the history of country music back as far as Garth Brooks and Reba McEntire. Yet even before the legendary Hank Williams Sr. made his mark in the world of entertainment, Lonzo and Oscar were performing with the likes of Paul Howard's Arkansas Cotton Pickers and Eddy Arnold, as well as charming millions via a national audience on WSM radio.

The roots of the group date back to the Depression and to two brothers, John Y. and Rollin Sullivan. From a poor Kentucky family of ten, in their preteens the brothers began playing local dances with their families, before forming their own group in the late thirties, the Kentucky Ramblers. By the forties Rollin had sought greener pastures, first at a radio station in Louisville, and then as a mandolin player on the Opry with the Arkansas Cotton Pickers. It was during his initial stint on WSM that Rollin began to use the name Oscar and capitalize on his knack for rural comedy. At that time every band needed a clown, and Oscar was the Cotton Pickers' joker.

This move to comedy was not a dramatic departure for Rollin. He had long dressed in an exaggerated rural style and told jokes. Yet he had no way of guessing that his developing act, coupled to a song written for a radio show gag, would soon make him a country music comedy icon.

In 1942 Rollin joined his brother William as a member of the band of country music's hottest act, Eddy Arnold. While both brothers played in the Plowboy band, Rollin was also featured as the act's comedian. While working for Eddy, Rollin met another funnyman, Lloyd George, and the two formed the team of Oscar and Lloyd. With the likes of Hope and Crosby, Abbott and Costello, and Laurel and Hardy, comedy teams were in vogue, yet Oscar and Lloyd's brand of humor, dispensed via rural stories and country songs, was unique; only Homer and Jethro offered a similar kind of act. Soon, as their and Eddy's popularity grew, and as the duo's routines became even more hokey, Lloyd's rather plain real name was dropped in favor of Lonzo. By 1947 Lonzo and Oscar had not only become members of the Opry, but had earned a recording contract at RCA.

Meanwhile, a long way from the Opry stage, Moe Jaffe was hard at work penning songs for some of America's best-known crooners. Frank Sinatra would record Jaffe's "If You Are but a Dream," and the songwriter's "The Gypsy in My Soul" would also find a place in many people's hearts. Jaffe mainly wrote for Broadway-type musicals and big band radio shows, so it would have seemed that a marriage between Jaffe's skills and inspiration and the cornpone humor of Lonzo and Oscar was out of the question, that providence had determined at birth that the songwriter and the country comedians would never travel in the same circles. And indeed their talents wouldn't have ever been successfully merged if Dwight Latham hadn't entered the picture.

Latham was a member of a singing group called the Jesters who performed on NBC radio. As was suggested by their name, the group's specialty was humor. The Jesters often used novelty songs to poke fun at other hot acts, as well as at news of the day, fashion fads, and national trends. Dwight was therefore always on the look-out for any and every kind of funny or off-the-wall story he could find to work into the group's act. And even though he didn't know who Lonzo and Oscar were, Latham was reading the words of an-other country boy, Mark Twain, when he came up with a concept that would put the comedy duo on the map.

Twain had spelled out a way that a man could become his own grandpa by marrying a widow whose daughter had married the man's father. Latham seized upon the concept, expanded it to include a variety of other bizarre steps, and then took the roughed-out prose to Moe Jaffe. The two came up with a novelty song which was to be used by the Jesters on NBC. The number was essentially a "throw-away," meant only as a onetime gag. But one of those who heard the Jesters sing this "throwaway" was none other than Rollin "Oscar" Sullivan.

The Jesters, whose chart appearances had included such numbers as "MacNamara's Band," "The Band Played On," and "Fuzzy-Wuzzy," didn't show much interest in "Grandpa" beyond getting a few laughs on their radio show. But this song seemed perfect for a group like Lonzo and Oscar. The country duo already had a long line of jokes about double cousins. Besides, as the two would often point out, it was the South, where marrying your cousin wasn't as much of a joke as it was a fact of life. And it was in the South where Lonzo and Oscar claimed hundreds of thousands of fans.

Taking the Latham-Jaffe composition to RCA, Lonzo and Oscar brought in the Winston County Pea Pickers as their backup group and set down the tracks on what was to become not only their sig-nature song, but later one of Grandpa Jones's most requested num-bers. Released in January of 1948, the Jesters' "throwaway," "I'm My Own Grandpa," hit the top ten within a month and became Lonzo and Oscar's biggest all-time seller.

During this period, big country hits were often covered by suc-cessful pop artists. Bing Crosby had scored big with both "You Are My Sunshine" and "San Antonio Rose." Tony Bennett and others had also jumped in to cut tunes that had originally been recorded by

Eddy Arnold, George Morgan, and, later, Hank Williams. Still, few in Nashville were figuring that anyone in pop music would opt to cover Lonzo and Oscar. It was thought that their sound was simply too hillbilly for mainstream taste. But despite the number's somewhat monotonous tune, bizarre message, and strange lyrics, as well as the song's tie to real hillbilly music, two acts showed the bad taste to try to churn a pop hit out of the hot country tune.

First to jump on board was Capitol recording star Jo Stafford. Jo had begun her career as the vocalist for the Tommy Dorsey Orchestra and had charted twenty-eight times in her first four years of recording. For some reason the singer, who would sell more than 2 million copies of "You Belong to Me" in 1952, couldn't resist rewriting the song's lyrics and cutting "I'm My Own Grandma." Though it managed to crawl into the top thirty, Jo's version thankfully died after just two weeks. Having learned her lesson, Stafford would never again record a novelty song.

After Jo Stafford's fling, logic would have seemed to indicate that "Grandpa" was a song that had very limited appeal outside of rural areas. But maybe because of his "country" Canadian background, Guy Lombardo, who had sold more than 100 million records, decided to give the tune another shot. In the early spring of 1948 the legendary bandleader released his Decca version of the recording. Surprisingly, this release of "I'm My Own Grandpa" crept into the top ten and languished on the charts for almost two months. But a year later, Guy would be taking very few requests for the unique song, and—for good reasons—"I'm My Own Grandpa" never replaced "Auld Lang Syne" as Guy's salute to the New Year.

In most cases in which a novelty song puts a group on the map, the group usually fades even before the song does. Yet for Lonzo and Oscar "I'm My Own Grandpa" was money in the bank not only in 1948, but for years afterward. Mainly because of Rollin "Oscar" Sullivan's musical and comedic talents, four decades later the group was still getting thousands of requests for "Grandpa" and other classic comedy recordings. The single was even revived for an Opry tribute album. And in spite of the fact that Lloyd George left the group just a year after the duo scored its biggest hit, the name Lonzo continued on strong through two other performers, Rollin's brother John Sullivan and David Hooten.

It is true that "I'm My Own Grandpa" was once thought to be one of the silliest songs to ever chart. Yet in the nineties the hit that was inspired by the writings of Mark Twain may have finally arrived in an era in which the concept will cease to be a novelty. In a day where mixed families, blended families, and special extended families are thought of as normal, how far can we be from having a lot of folks who end up being their own grandparents? When this finally happens, it will finally be obvious that Lonzo and Oscar were prophets, decades ahead of their time!

Jambalaya

*I*t is doubtful that old Hank Williams ever thought of himself as an artist. Yet a quick study of the body of his work proves that he was. The fragile marriage of words and music that usually gave a peek into the legend's life are not just poetic, but are usually filled with deep insights into the human soul. Out of a crystal-like union of lyrics and melody came a message that transcended all musical genres and sprang directly into a listener's soul. The songs that resulted from Hank's sweat were usually timeless, the meaning of each measured verse just as strong in each successive generation. Using no gimmicks, no plays on words, no sophisticated techniques, Hank wrote a plethora of pieces that became simple but profound testaments for every man or woman who heard them. As the years pass these songs remain fresh and haunting. Because his songs transcend time itself, it is as if they are suspended in eternity, just waiting to be rediscovered by each new generation. And they are, time and time again.

Inspired by waves of emotion that no one seemed to fully comprehend, Hank Williams created art. Using the tragic flavor of his own life, he wove together simple words and unadorned music in songs that seemed to have endless layers of substance. Foremost, he seemed to sense that he had a great deal to say, but very little time in which to say it.

The bandleader Mitch Miller once observed, "No matter who you were, a country person or a sophisticate, the language [Williams's writing] hits home. Nobody I know could use basic English so effectively."

Miller spoke of Williams as if describing inspirational beauty, and certainly Hank's songs were that. But much like Edgar Allan Poe, Hank Williams was seemingly possessed by forces which kept pulling him down into the depths of darkness. It was here, in the hopeless mire of booze and pills, that he sought refuge from demons only he saw and understood. Yet like Poe, there were moments in Williams's life when he pulled himself up to the sunshine. During these brilliant times he shared the anguish of his other world in songs.

As can be clearly seen when studying his brief life, Hank Williams by all accounts was a tortured soul. He was self-destructive, abusive, undependable, and tormented. Those who knew him talk more about the nightmares he lived than any moments of laughter and fun he experienced. But even in the midst of a catalog of hits that spoke of heartaches by the number, there were a few sets of lyrics which embraced something lighter than the blues—you just have to look hard to find them.

Hank stepped out of the shadows in the midst of a career boom to jot down the words to a novelty song (yes, even the Stephen Foster of the modern age lowered himself to writing a novelty number) about partying in Cajun country. Hank knew a great deal about partying, and over time he had grown familiar with Louisiana. One of the Creole dishes that Williams had eaten in New Orleans was called jambalaya. Using the recipe's name as the title for an idea that would become a silly little song, Hank grabbed other local bits of color such as the pirogue (canoe), crawfish pie, and gumbo, and mixed these mostly culinary delights into nonsensical bits of lyrics which had nothing to do with heartache and everything to do with fun. It was a big departure from the normal song fare of "Luke the Drifter."

Many feel that the melody Hank teamed with this lyrical effort was actually lifted from a tune entitled "Grand Texas." That song, by Chuck Guillory and His Rhythm Boys, was well-known to many folks in country music and had the Cajun feel and sound needed to propel Hank's lyrics. Whether the master "borrowed" much of the tune or was simply influenced by the same sources as Guillory will probably never be known. Interestingly, Hank, who usually employed three chords per song, and occasionally four, played this entire number with just two. In other words, it would be the easiest of all Williams songs to master on guitar.

"Jambalaya" was a song about the carefree life which Hank probably wished he could live. By 1952 the road and the booze had taken a heavy toll on the singer. He looked twenty years older than his age, his face was drawn, and his once lively step had been slowed. This novelty song about Cajun life, which had taken Hank several efforts to complete, represented an escape for the man. In the midst of all his dark nights, here was an ode to the sunshine.

MGM released the song late in the summer of 1952. When "Jambalaya" hit #1 on September 6, it knocked the first-ever #1 chart single by a female artist, Kitty Wells's "It Wasn't God Who Made Honky Tonk Angels," out of the top spot. Hank would hang on to #1 for an amazing fourteen weeks. It indeed seemed that, just as he himself did, his fans wanted Williams to enjoy life rather than drown in his misery. Many were hoping that this single signaled just such a turnaround.

"Jambalaya," which also became Hank's biggest pop chart hit, would be recorded time and time again. Maybe the definitive version belonged to Brenda Lee, but a host of other top acts, including Jo Stafford, put their spin on the Cajun classic. Yet of the millions who bought these or Hank's versions of "Jambalaya" and could sing all the words to the song, few knew or cared about the meaning of the song's anchor words: pirogue, gumbo, crawfish pie, or *ma chere amie-oh*. Those who loved this song were more caught up in its incredible upbeat sound than in defining its message. (Most folks weren't even aware that the title was the name of a food dish.)

Those who had hoped that this single would bring about a new, happier Hank Williams were soon to be disappointed. While "Jambalaya" was still in the top ten, Hank died of a heart attack while riding in the backseat of a Cadillac. The tortured genius had therefore failed to emulate his classic song about the carefree life on the bayou and had instead fulfilled the prophecy of the single of his released just after "Jambalaya": "I'll Never Get Out of This World Alive."

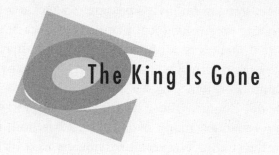

The King Is Gone

August 16, 1977, is one of those dates which will al-ways mean something special to baby boomers everywhere. It was on this day that millions of young men and women suddenly felt mortal. Around the world, time stopped. The man who was rock and roll to two genera-tions of teens died on the floor of his bathroom. It was a shock that shook the world almost as much as the assas-sination of John F. Kennedy had in 1963. Suddenly every-one was a lot older.

While many spent the remainder of August 16 listening to radio stations play Elvis recordings for hours on end, a struggling singer/songwriter from Fountain Head, Ten-nessee, got together with a close friend, Lee Morgan. For a while the two talked about what Elvis Presley had meant to their lives. Taking those thoughts, Ronnie McDowell and Morgan put them into an emotional musical tribute song to their idol. Once the duo completed "The King Is Gone," they realized the commercial possibilities of their song, pooled their resources, cut a demo, and immediately began to look for a Nashville label that would rush a ship-ment of the song to radio stations around the country while the nation was still in a state of mourning.

Most major labels simply couldn't move rapidly enough

to take advantage of the small window of opportunity which was going to be open for cashing in on Elvis's passing. So McDowell, who had been the lead singer in various local bands for a decade, sought out a smaller label that might just want to take a gamble that promised a possible large cash return. He finally found a company which would work with him: Scorpion.

With a label in hand, Ronnie, whose dark good looks and smooth balladeer vocal style reminded many of a young Elvis, did his best Presley imitation in the studio. The resulting single was a bit haunting, a bit hokey, and improbably sincere. As it turned out, of all of the rushed Presley tributes which came out in the weeks after the King's death, "The King Is Gone" was the best. The message about a man who treasured Elvis's contributions and style was solidly written, McDowell's voice was almost a clone of the late rocker's, and most important, the song was the first to hit the airwaves. Because it seemed genuinely heartfelt, and because Ronnie's was the first of the scores of quickly produced Presley offerings, Elvis fans everywhere flocked to stores to grab it.

"The King Is Gone" ran up the charts in the late summer and early fall of 1977, topping out at #13 on both rock and country charts. With his record selling into the millions worldwide, Ronnie McDowell put the tiny Scorpion label on the map. While enjoying his nearly overnight fame, the singer was also shrewd enough to realize that if he was going to last in the world of entertainment, he was going to have to quickly get back into the studio and come up with a follow-up hit.

McDowell had been going nowhere until he had cashed in on Elvis; Presley's death had literally given his career a chance to breathe. Yet the singer knew that while he had to be very smart in order to keep the millions of Elvis fans who had bought "The King Is Gone" in his camp, he also had to begin to build a separate career of his own that would allow him to establish a reputation as something other than a second-rate act who made a few bucks off a hero's death.

Ronnie's second single, "I Love You, I Love You, I Love You," sounded like a Presley classic. It was a broad and sweeping ballad, and Elvis would have probably loved to have sung it on a Vegas stage.

But the King didn't have the chance to cut it, and McDowell did. "I Love You" showed Ronnie's vocal range and power, which had only been hinted at in "The King Is Gone." With his follow-up record, McDowell laid claim to a style that was a great deal like Presley's, but because the material was fresh and new, the young singer could not now be accused of basing a career simply on the King's tragic demise. "I Love You" hit #5 on the country charts and brought McDowell a chance to move on to Epic Records in 1979.

Unlike so many who cashed in on a novel concept and then disappeared, Ronnie McDowell has carved out a niche by carefully using and building on the vehicle which gave him his first big break. And while it is true that Ronnie has never become a "major" country star like Vince Gill, over the course of a twenty-year career he has placed almost forty songs on the charts and seen thirteen of them jump into country music's top ten. During this time the singer has also managed to separate himself from his idol while keeping many Presley fans in his camp by having supplied new vocals for songs from several Elvis movies and a short-lived television show.

As a matter of fact, now that he is a player in his own right, the singer travels with Elvis's early band members and backup singers and spends a part of each show doing a tribute to the music of Presley. But in order to make sure that the audience doesn't forget who the living performer is, Ronnie never dresses like Elvis and always includes his own hits in each show too. Hence, McDowell proves to fans everywhere that he knows the King is gone and that, while he never wants to take Presley's place, he doesn't mind sharing a small bit of the earnings.

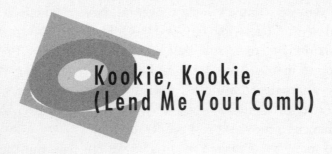

Kookie, Kookie
(Lend Me Your Comb)

They say that timing is everything. Nowhere can this statement be proven more true than in the novelty song market.

The year was 1958, Elvis was the King, James Dean was still revered as the greatest actor who ever died young, and the nation's teens had literally taken over the television and radio dials. Meanwhile, Edd Byrnes was just another young actor working odd jobs when he was asked to play a cold, cruel killer in the pilot for a series called *77 Sunset Strip*. ABC loved the two-hour movie that had been shot for the potential series and picked it up for the fall season. But in order to capitalize on the whims and buying power of America's youth, the network executives wanted the pilot's crazed murderer to be reformed and transformed into the show's cool dude. Thus, in a rehabilitation project that was never challenged by the penal system, Gerald Lloyd Kookson III ("Kookie") was born.

The new television series starred Roger Smith and Efrem Zimbalist Jr. as suave, sophisticated detectives, but it quickly became apparent that the main reason the *Strip*'s ratings soared each week was the impact made by a minor lead. This minor lead was played by the twenty-five-year-old Byrnes. And the reason he was so hot was that each week his character would invent a new slang version of an old expression, such as "keeping the eyeballs rolling" (translation—being on the lookout) or "piling up the z's" (catching forty winks). Cool beyond words, good-looking, and tall, Ed quickly became a pop icon before the term was invented and was just as quickly moved out of the show's parking lot and into the position of junior detective.

In the history of television only one other prime-time character would ever come close to Edd Byrnes's cult-hero status. And like Kookie, that other character began his tube life as a background player. Yet what the Fonz and Kookie had in common was what made them stars—they were lovable rebels who had good hearts, cool ways, and great hair. And it seemed that it was the latter attribute that kept Byrnes's character parked in front of the mirror for segments of every one of 77 *Sunset Strip*'s episodes.

Warner Bros. sensed that the teen power which Edd Byrnes had was something the studio needed to capitalize on in a big way in 1959. Reaching across the Pacific (actually, the back lot), the studio grabbed the perky Connie Stevens from *Hawaiian Eye,* had Irving Taylor fashion a song for Connie and Edd, and then put the hot duo into the studio for a recording session. These two "nice" kids were about to generate a sexual chemistry that would be enjoyed by members of both sexes.

When commissioned to write the song for Edd and Connie's recording session, Irving Taylor had to wonder what in the world he had gotten himself into. In Kookie's words, this seemed like a "koo koo deal." The studio wanted a song that was a "talker," not a "singer." Hey, Warner Bros. didn't even know if Byrnes could sing. Worse yet, it wanted to simply sell "cool" and "cute"; the quality of the material and its message were not important. Finally, the studio wanted the lyrics to include many of Kookie's favorite sayings. Taylor, who had written "Everybody Loves Somebody" and other love songs, had to put himself on a different planet and then review a year's worth of scripts to turn out such classic lyrics as "If you tune me out, Dad, I'm the saddest. Like I'm green."

But what the song's writer quickly discovered was that Connie, Edd, and he would soon be counting the pure green as "Kookie, Kookie" took off as fast as Byrnes's career had the year before.

Buoyed by the duo's appearance before hundreds of screaming teenage girls on *American Bandstand* (heaven knows how many millions more were screaming at home), the single raced up the charts. "Kookie" debuted in April and peaked in May, hanging on to #4 for two weeks and holding on to a top ten spot for six weeks. And even though the song would fade from the charts before the new television season began, Byrnes's cult-guru status was to continue strong for another four years as *77 Sunset Strip* held on to a top spot in the tube ratings war until 1963.

In part because it was an hour-long show, as well as the fact that it was shot in black and white, *77 Sunset Strip* never became a hot commodity in reruns. If the program had hung on in rerun heaven like *Happy Days* did, Kookie might well still be influencing new audiences of youth. But sadly, like Edd Byrnes, Kookie has faded as much as his jeans. So unless you witnessed the reaction of teenage girls to Edd Byrnes in the late fifties, there is no explaining why this silly song made such an impression on the nation's playlists.

Yet just as the TV program *Lassie* made the collie one of America's favorite pets, *77 Sunset Strip* made Kookie the model for the cool and hip American male. What Kookie said became part of the language and what he wore became the most important piece of a young man's wardrobe. Connie Stevens told him, "You're the maximum utmost," and he certainly was. He may have even been the ginchiest, too! Think about that the next time you look into the mirror and comb your hair.

Leader of the Pack

If you have read very many of the stories in this book you have probably noted that Jeff Barry and Ellie Greenwich are two song scribes who have helped generate millions in record sales while indulging in the basest of all teenage forms of musical expression—"bubble gum music." Yet in defense of the duo who composed such *classics* as "Tell Laura I Love Her," which was narrowly beaten out by "Teen Angel" in this book as the worst of the novelty songs about teenage love surviving tragic teenage death, the people who recorded Jeff and Ellie's songs were usually top-rate talent. Tommy James was good, Manfred Mann had more musical gifts than almost any other group of the mid-sixties, and of all the girl groups of the era, the Shangri-Las were among the very best, perhaps surpassed only by the Supremes. Yet the mere fact that these girls' career was *made* via a Barry/Greenwich record may have doomed them. If this is so, the songwriters cost fans a chance to see the magic that could have come from the world of Shangri-La.

The Shangri-Las would have been a novelty act even if they hadn't sung novelty songs. The quartet was made up of the two Weiss sisters, Mary and Betty, and Marge and Mary Ann Ganser, who just happened to be not only sisters, but identical twins. It was a publicity department's ideal gimmick, especially when the sisters were as pretty as the girls in this act. Certainly many of the boys who watched the high schoolers perform thought they had found their "Shangri-La" in the world of this quartet. Yet the best thing about the attractive, style-setting sister act was that they could really sing.

The girls began harmonizing at New York's Jackson High School in Queens. While still in school, they were "discovered" at a talent show by Artie Ripp of Smash Records in 1963. Their efforts for this label went largely unnoticed and the girls were quickly dropped. Lightning soon struck for a second time when the Weiss and Ganser sisters were noted by Gary Morton, who had ties to Kama Sutra Records. Working with the label and Jeff Barry and Ellie Greenwich, Morton came up with a song, "Remember (Walkin' in the Sand)." Then, after he had cut a demo, Gary also got the girls a second record deal with Red Bird. In the fall of 1964 the Shangri-Las had their first hit, as "Remember" hit #8 in the national top one hundred and #1 in New York. A lot of industry gossip at the time also had the four girls recording for Coral Records at this same time under the name the Bon Bons. If this was the case—and the question is still up in the air—the deception ended in 1964, and the sisters blended only for Red Bird for most of their remaining days in the business.

Sensing that it had a potential visual bonanza on its hands, Red Bird really began to publicize this "hip" group. And the fact was, these girls were as close to the cutting edge of mod fashion as were Motown's Supremes. Unfortunately, the Shangri-Las weren't going to get nearly the quality of material that Diana Ross and company got. This really became obvious when producer Morton insisted on getting involved in the group's total package and even worked with Barry and Greenwich on the girls' next single. Perhaps that was the reason for the warped inspiration that came out of the writing session.

Motorcycle gangs had been cool since the days of Marlon Brando and *The Wild One,* but the new Morton/Barry/Greenwich composition took this concept of a leather-clad, hog-riding gang leader to a new level. What must the innocent high school girl singers have thought when they first heard "Leader of the Pack"? Each of them had to have realized that recording this was not going to endear them to the parents of the teens who were going to purchase their product. They were undoubtedly also bright enough to know that this song was not even close to being art. And when the session began, and Morton insisted on having a motorcycle fired up and revving as the girls sang, the sisters must have realized that they were living out a joke that might backfire at any moment (actually, the motorcycle did on several occasions). It was said that Mary Weiss was so scared by everything that was going on in the studio that she couldn't sing at all and it took several takes for her to barely whisper the word "gone." Maybe it was the knowledge that this song might just kill her career that actually scared her. And what must have frightened her even more than the loud bike was that, like the movie producer Ed Wood when he made such films as *Plan 9 from Outer Space*, everyone at Red Bird was so serious about what they were laying down on the tape. It seemed no one realized that the joke they were creating was on them.

Released in October 1964, "Leader of the Pack" quickly became just that. The Shangri-Las actually pushed the Supremes out of #1 on November 28. It seemed appropriate that "Leader" actually celebrated Thanksgiving as the nation's top song—even many of those who bought the record admitted it was a turkey. Yet the bird did sell, not only in the United States, but in England and around the world. In fact, for the Shangri-Las it sold too well: They were quickly typecast as rigidly as Jerry Mathers, TV's "Beaver."

The real strength of "Leader of the Pack" was revealed in the months after it hit the charts. The Detergents, a group put together by Ron Dante of the Archies, sang a parody of the novelty song entitled "Leader of the Laundromat" that managed to hit the top twenty. Few novelty songs have made it to become nationally recognized standards, but only this one has managed to inspire a spinoff that was even more outlandish than the original. Sadly, it was a tribute that the talented quartet of girls didn't need, as it tossed even more of the laughter back at them.

The Shangri-Las never again challenged the Supremes, but it wasn't because of a lack of effort or talent. They performed on a bill with the Beatles, were featured on national television and radio shows, and toured the country. They also cut four more top forty singles, but "Leader of the Pack" had become their signature song and their albatross. This silly hit about a girl who meets a gang leader in a candy store, then loses him, was so much bigger than the Shangri-Las that fans soon lost interest in the girls themselves. By 1966, Red Bird and the group had both disappeared.

What would have happened if the Shangri-Las had recorded "Baby Love" and the Supremes had cut "Leader of the Pack"? Who would have been "gone, gone" then? Who knows?

The Lion
Sleeps Tonight

*O*n *December 7, 1959, most Americans stopped to remember Pearl Harbor Day. To properly memo-*rialize the "day which will live in infamy," people brought out flags, said prayers, and listened to speeches. While millions of others memorialized, Hank Medress and Mitch Margo marked the day by skipping school and singing with a sometime piano player named Phil. Phil just happened to be Mitch's older brother and was the reason the twelve-year-old got away with cutting class. That fateful day when three teens horsed around at a family piano laid the foundation for a group that would become known as the Tokens, and set in motion the process that would see the release of a song which many rock critics believe should also "live in infamy."

That first day of singing went so well that the group would continue to get together and eventually add lead singer Jay Siegal to the mix. Over the next year the group would begin to flesh out some of their original ideas in song, as well as create their versions of many of the era's hottest teen epics. It was probably no accident that the New Yorkers initially sounded a great deal like Dion and the Belmonts, but as Hank had once been in a group (strangely enough, called the Tokens) with the fabulously creative Neil Sedaka, elements of other styles crept into their harmonies as well. One of these was folk, and the folk group which seemed to inspire this set of Tokens the most were the Weavers. And it was the Weavers who would give the boys their biggest hit.

A chance meeting on a subway led to funding for a series of demos, and in 1961 the quartet landed a deal with Warwick Records and produced a charting song, "Tonight I Fell in Love." Yet in spite of their close harmonies and unique folk/rock style, the boys couldn't follow that modest hit up at their first label. To enhance both their status and their chances for more success, the Tokens moved on to RCA.

RCA didn't really know what to do with the Tokens, so it used them in studio work as background singers until the guys could come up with concepts that seemed strong enough to shake up the market. Already veterans of a couple of Dick Clark rock and roll tours, the four young men were itching for a real hit so that they could quit their day jobs. Yet when two releases in early 1961 generated no heat, the guys began to wonder if they were ever going to strike gold. The industry even joked that RCA liked the kids only enough to release "token" efforts, just to keep them under contract. But the boys knew that soon, without some kind of a charting single, their label would be forced to cut them loose. This was when the influence of the group's favorite folk group came back into the picture.

In the early fifties the Weavers had hit the charts with a tight but silly harmony cut entitled "Wimoweh." The boys had worked the old number up for their label, even though the song's lyrics were written in Zulu and no one had any idea what the native song meant; the Tokens simply liked the song's sound. So did their producers, but as RCA didn't sell a lot of products to Zulu tribesmen, they suggested that someone translate the words into English. When a linguist was called in it was discovered that "Wimoweh" had actually been "Mbube" in the original song and that the word had been somewhat butchered in the versions the Tokens had heard. "Mbube" meant "lion," and when the final English transcription of the African folk song was completed, the four Jewish rockers discovered that they had been crooning about a fabled lion hunt.

Along with RCA producers Hugo Peretti and Luigi Creatore, the
Tokens and several others sat down and reworked the lyrics to "Wimoweh," and the folk epic about a crusade to kill a big cat was
rewritten into "The Lion Sleeps Tonight." In the studio the new lyrics
were added as the lead lines, but the "Americanized" version of the
original song, including the repetitious "Wimoweh," was kept for
harmonies, thus making the Tokens' effort sound something like a
Zulu doo-wop party number. To a man the Tokens, who were extremely proud of their wonderfully close-knit harmonies and serious
recording efforts, were embarrassed by the final playback. They
begged RCA to scrap the whole thing and let them cut something
else. Producers Peretti and Creatore ignored their request for more
studio time, and ordered singles to be pressed and shipped.

At first disc jockeys agreed with the Tokens about the quality and
commercial prospects of "The Lion Sleeps Tonight." The cut was
treated as a B side, and it was the group's "Tina" that was first played
on radio stations. Yet beginning with DJ Dick Smith's show in
Worcester, Massachusetts, "The Lion Sleeps Tonight" began to earn
some airtime too. And much as Tommy James's "Hanky Panky" had
several years later, "The Lion" woke up in one local market, then
spread from station to station. Within weeks the offbeat folk/rock/
novelty number was receiving multiple spins at hundreds of outlets
around the country. By Thanksgiving it had entered the charts, and
a brief three weeks later "The Lion Sleeps Tonight" had knocked
"Please Mr. Postman" out of #1. The single which had at first embarrassed the Tokens was now the "King of the Recording Beasts"!

Unlike many hits which flukishly climb the charts armed with no
redeeming merits, "The Lion" did have something special to offer.
The lyrics that remained from the original African folk lyrics were so
strong that listeners couldn't help but get caught up in them. Much
like what had happened with "Blue Moon" and "Little Darlin'," teenagers, and even preteens, quickly learned the song's unusual harmonies and strange background words. And seemingly overnight,
millions who probably thought that Zulu was Zorro's younger
brother were droning out "Wimoweh" over and over again. And so

were the Tokens. Three years later they were still singing it to cheering masses when they opened for the Beatles in New York.

Though they would chart several more times and write or produce a host of hits for other groups, the Tokens themselves would be devoured by their beast of a rock and roll novelty hit. Blessed with far more talent than most groups of the period, the four New Yorkers couldn't ever escape "The Lion." It followed them every step of their musical careers. Yet while the bizarre nature of "The Lion Sleeps Tonight" probably did keep Hank Medress, Mitchell and Phil Margo, and Jay Siegal from ever hitting the top of the charts again, it also assured them that the Tokens would never be forgotten. Thanks to heavy rotation on oldies stations, as well as the song's constant use in movie sound tracks, the clear, clean harmonies of the Tokens are always around us and every new generation grows up singing "Wimoweh" over and over again. What that says about us as a society is in question, but it made the Tokens the most famous Jewish lads to team up with a lion since Daniel.

Little Darlin'

*A*t about the same time that Elvis was working as a truck driver for an electrical supply company, way up north four guys from the University of Toronto were forming a quartet. These friends were singing the show tunes and song standards of the previous generation while developing a sound that would someday put them into the mainstream of the new youth music called rock and roll. But in the beginning these very serious singers of very serious songs were going no place except to local talent shows, and their professional future appeared dim.

In 1954 the four guys—Stan Fisher, Ted Kowalski, Phil Leavitt, and Bill Reese—met a radio technician named David Somerville. Putting together a simple act that once again featured recognizable standards, the guys first performed at an Ontario church. The as-yet-unnamed group was well-received, and because of this the boys decided to seek out other bookings. Obviously, they needed a name. One of the members suggested the Diamonds, and though the quintet was still in the rough, they took a shine to the handle and adopted it as their own.

A year later the boys had progressed vocally to the point where they had been booked into gigs in the U.S.

and had caught the attention of Coral Records. An audition in the company's New York studio led to a record deal, and the Diamonds began to do what they would come to do best: cover other groups' songs.

Their association with Coral didn't pan out and produced no hits, but a few months after the label cut the Diamonds loose, Mercury Records caught them, thought they were a gem, and in 1956 signed them to a deal. They were interested in recording gospel music, but the label insisted they cut rock. In the studio the Diamonds were presented with a song that had been successfully sold in R&B circles by the black group Frankie Lymon and the Teenagers. "Why Do Fools Fall in Love" would become the Diamonds' first chart single, peaking at #12. By the fall they had placed five more songs on the *Billboard* lists. Then the cover magic fell flat and the group disappeared for almost a year.

Like so many white artists, including Pat Boone, the Diamonds had made a name for themselves doing "R&B lite." In other words, they were taking black songs and cutting safe new versions for the white market. The Canadian quintet had searched through the material of groups like the Clovers, the Cleftones, and the Willows for songs. In the Diamonds' defense, their versions of these cover tunes were at least equal to and often better than the originals. Yet as more radio stations opened up to black musicians, the Diamonds were being beaten to the punch by the originals. By late 1956 their gimmick appeared to be outdated. Mercury had about given up on them altogether when, in 1957, they stumbled onto the Gladiolas and what was to become their masterpiece.

The Gladiolas were a South Carolina group that had brought in Maurice Williams when their lead singer left. The group's first handle had been the Royal Charmers. In Nashville, a producer who was probably more familiar with country music than R&B asked the guys to sing the worst song they knew. They chose "Little Darlin'." Ironically, the producer passed on the Gladiolas' preferred stuff and recorded their "worst." When Williams had written "Little Darlin'," and when the group had recorded it, the song had had a somewhat serious feel. Sure it made little sense, and yes, the recording had seemingly used old coffee cans for drums, but it sounded as if Williams was really sincere about his love for his girl. Still, there was no driving bass vocal line, the production was terribly amateurish, and the lyrics took the song nowhere; thus there was little that distinguished this "Little Darlin' " from the rash of other equally bad doo-wop numbers that were flooding the market during this period. Hence, in its original form, one of rock music's most wonderful and best-loved songs would have died a quick death and then been buried in the tomb of the forgotten single. Thankfully, the Diamonds sensed that with a little reworking, this "Darlin' " was, if not a real gem, at least a good joke.

The new cover arrangement not only pushed this release to the top of the charts, but also nudged it over the edge into the realm of the crazy, strange, and bizarre. In an era when rock music was guitar-driven and four-piece bands were a must, Mercury brought in cow-bells, a piano, and a Mexican-sounding rhythm guitar lick, and sped the song's instrumental backing up to an almost frantic pace. The Diamonds, who had spent hours and hours learning the song before the session, were completely simpled-out when it came time to record the tracks. In sophomoric style and almost as a joke, the group laced the arrangement with exaggerated bass vocals and silly-sounding falsettos. No one took it seriously, and maybe because of this fact, for one of the first times in the history of cover music, an Anglo act actually took a risk and made a song wilder than the black version had been. Still, while it would probably make audiences laugh, there was no way that anyone in the group could conceive of its having much commercial possibility.

Mercury didn't really know what to do with "Little Darlin' "; executives there thought it had been recorded as a joke. The label considered burying the cut, but that seemed like a waste. After all, for the first time in almost a year the Diamonds had reflected real energy in a recording session. So, even while thinking that disc jockeys would laugh it out of the studios, the label released "Little Darlin'."

At best it was hoped that this number would put the Diamonds back on the bottom of the charts and pump some life into what seemed to be a dying group. Shipped in early 1957, "Little Darlin' " quickly surpassed expectations. Though no one could believe it, it was big from the start. Mercury quickly discovered that it had released the ultimate cruising song and teens all over America, as well as the rest of the free world, had learned its simple lyrics and unique vocal interpretations within weeks. On any given winter Saturday night in 1957, thousands of "cats" were singing "Little Darlin' " as they motored their rods up the strip. On street corners and in showers, too, this song was the new favorite. This Canadian white group was even making waves on the black R&B charts. In the country and in the ghettos, "Little Darlin' " was standing tall!

It had to have been its silly feel and the singability of the song, as well as the goofy arrangement, which made the Diamonds' version of "Little Darlin' " a monster hit. It would climb to #2 on the charts during a time when Elvis owned every playlist. It was the King's "All Shook Up," which stayed #1 for nine weeks, that kept "Little Darlin' " from peaking at the top position. Still, the single would hover at the second spot for two months, was a hit on the black charts as well, would remain a jukebox standard for years, and instantly made the Diamonds one of the world's premier rock vocal groups. A year later the Diamonds would strike major gold again with a revolutionary dance song that separated boys and girls, "The Stroll." But even though they charted several more times through the fifties and sixties and remained a touring group for years after the British invasion, it was "Little Darlin' " that remained the Diamonds' most requested standard.

It is indeed strange to believe that a white-bread group from Ontario that had gotten together to sing show tunes and gospel numbers in a barbershop style would find itself immortalized via a song that made little sense, had been kicked off with a cowbell, and contained such great lines as "Ahhhhhhh ya-ya-ya-yaaaaaaaa, Ya-ya-ya yaaaaaaaaa, Ya-Ya-Ya-Yaaaa-aaaa."

Yet everyone knows that a diamond's real potential is never revealed until it is cut, and that sometimes the cutting can produce a gem nothing like what had been expected. In the case of "Little Darlin'," the cut did just that, and the results are still causing facets of light to shine almost forty years after the fact. And thankfully, this silly song gave the world a chance to really get to know a group that was one of rock and roll's most talented vocal ensembles.

Louie Louie

*P*erhaps *no other song has ever created as much need-less controversy and misinformation as "Louie Louie."* In the paragraphs that follow we will attempt to dispel the myriad myths.

First and foremost, the tune's lyrics are not dirty, they are not filled with hidden meanings, and the song was not written as any form of demonic chant. Second, the state of Washington never did vote "Louie Louie" in as the official state song. And finally, the group which scored a hit with "Louie Louie" was not the same band which once backed Bill Haley on "Rock Around the Clock," nor were the guys who sang "Louie Louie" the quartet which became better known in country music as the Statler Brothers. Yet, while none of these onetime rumors contained any truth, the fact is that each of them did become a part of the story of "Louie Louie."

The first chapter in this song's misunderstood history began in 1956 when Richard Berry wrote and recorded "Louie Louie." Its simple lyrics were about a conversation between a man who worked at a bar and a customer who was obsessed with his girlfriend in Jamaica. No matter the extent to which the customer wanted to be with the woman, there was nothing in the song's words that could be taken as being dirty. Not surprisingly, the original cut, which was not at all in tune with the radio market of the day, died without making the charts.

The second chapter of this confusing and mixed-up story began two years later. In 1958 a number of Bill Haley's Comets formed a new rock and roll band called the Kingsmen. They cut a song for East West Records entitled "Week End," and managed to crack *Billboard*'s top one hundred playlists with their first single. This was the only time that the Kingsmen would ever hit the charts. The men who were the Kingsmen became the Comets again and were soon back with Bill touring England.

"Louie Louie" lay dormant until 1961, when it was recut by a Seattle performer named Robin Roberts. Robin was not the famed pitcher for the Philadelphia Phillies, nor was he very successful. But his "Louie Louie" was picked up by several local bands in the northwestern United States and became a college and lumberjack dance favorite.

In the early sixties another group called the Kingsmen began to get some work as folk/country/gospel singers throughout the Ohio valley. The quartet, made up of brothers Harold and Don Reid, Phil Basley, and Lew DeWitt, was a product of the southern church harmony tradition and would slowly work its way up the performing ladder, opening for Johnny Cash by 1964. Though these Kingsmen would have nothing to do with "Louie Louie," the rumor persists in some circles that they cut the first hit version of the song.

Finally, in 1963, a third bunch of guys named themselves the Kingsmen and began playing music in spots such as high school gyms and store parking lots. Perhaps it was because the song was so well-known at the local level, or maybe it was just because the rest of the show was not of very high quality, but "Louie Louie" became these Kingsmen's most requested number. Pooling their own resources, the five musicians made a homemade cut of "Louie Louie" in a makeshift studio and established themselves as local radio favorites. This cheaply made "Louie Louie" single got enough exposure in the Northwest to catch the attention of Wand Records on the East Coast. Wand thought enough of the Kingsmen's cut that the label bought the rights to it and released the song nationally. It actually appeared on the charts before the record company's executives met their latest act.

In its newest form "Louie Louie" would make its way up to #2 on the rock charts. Though it camped out at this spot for six long weeks, the single could never push either the Singing Nun or Bobby Vinton out of the top spot. Still, because of rumors that had started somewhere in the South, the song's lyrics managed to keep "Louie Louie" #1 in the news. Someone had decided that the song encouraged either drug use or premarital sex. The news media jumped on this rumor, played it up big, and suddenly P.T.A.'s and church groups were demanding that the single be banned. Even the FBI and the FCC got involved. Naturally, hundreds of thousands rushed out to purchase the single, just to find out what all the fuss was about. The fact was that while the lyrics were clean, the recording was so poorly produced that its words were muddy at best. Because of the dismal quality of the single's production, even more than three decades after the song was cleared by FBI top dog J. Edgar Hoover, today millions claim they know what the song's lyrics *really* mean. And the legend grows.

As "Louie Louie" was stirring controversy, the second group known as the Kingsmen were opening for Johnny Cash and were being asked to sing the song. There were even people who had turned out for the country music star's show just to hear this hot new rock band. As they didn't even know the song, this version of the Kingsmen opted to change their name in order to carve out their own identity. The name they chose came from a box of tissues. These four former Kingsmen would go on to sell tens of millions of records and gain international fame as country music's Statler Brothers. If they had stuck with the Kingsmen name, who knows if they would have even landed a spot on a record label.

The guys who had hit #2 on the charts as the Kingsmen were only able to follow the huge success of "Louie Louie" with two minor hits. By 1968 the group had broken up and gone their separate ways. Yet thanks in large part to the evil reputation of their hit single's lyrics, their record continued to be programmed and played. Rice University even picked the song up as a school fight song. Finally the old house

band song became so popular that in 1985 a resolution was introduced to make "Louie Louie" the official song of the state of Washington. Contrary to what many have heard, the resolution failed. It
seemed that the song's lyrics didn't fit with the image that Washington wanted to project. The tourist bureau couldn't figure out a way
to work "Oh baby, me gotta go," into anything but a campaign for
clean rest rooms at state parks.

Macarena

*B*y the time that the Macarena dance craze hit the United States, most of the world had already learned all of the very uncomplicated moves to the song that inspired it. Yet even two full months after the single had leapt up the charts, few of those from three to ninety-three who had mastered all the song's simple footwork could actually tell you anything about the tune's lyrics. So, it would seem that on Dick Clark's *American Bandstand* scale, "Macarena" would have registered a 100 for danceability, but a 0 for message.

Tony Bennett, who once left his heart in San Francisco only to discover that the organ had later been uncovered and restarted by the MTV generation, couldn't fathom why the "Macarena" had sold even a single copy. Bennett told *USA Today,* "What is that? I don't mind mediocrity, but that's insane." Tony was right—the "Macarena" was not only a long way from inspiring him, but the song probably wouldn't have drummed up much reaction from Joey Dee and the Starlighters either. Still, it did sell.

The fact is that dance songs have long been one of the best bets in the novelty market. Dances, especially the most modern ones, rarely have to make sense, so the lyrics simply pave the way for some fun footwork. "The Pony,"

"The Stroll," "The Frug," "The Bunny Hop," The Chicken," and hundreds of other choreographed bits of music existed mainly to get folks out on the dance floor. Having a clear vision as to what they were supposed to do, by and large these hot-selling songs limited their subject matter to the various steps needed to make the dance work. As Chubby Checker said when he began his signature piece, "I'm gonna do a dance and it goes like this." The rest of the song spelled out Chubby's step-by-step directions. And "Hokey Pokey" gave even more clear-cut directions than "The Twist."

During the disco craze more and more dance songs consisted simply of "normal" lyric lines placed into melody lines that lent themselves to movement. This theme held true when the country line dance craze hit Nashville as well. There were dances called the "Two-Step," but only rarely was there a song which coined a new dance craze. The song and dance moves had to have each other to survive, but they were often independent of each other at birth. The exception to the rule was "Achy Breaky Heart," which gave rise to the "Achy Breaky."

"Macarena," much like its country cousin, "Achy Breaky Heart," became a hit song due in large part to incredibly lucky timing coupled with incredible worldwide marketing. Around 1991 two writers, Antonio Romero and Rafael Ruiz, created a Venezuela club show with a young flamenco dancer, Diana Patricia. Captivated by the way that Diana's spirit and enthusiasm got people excited, Romero went back to his room and scribbled out the words to a new song idea. A year later, when the three again worked together, he and Ruiz were inspired by Diana anew, and finished the little ditty about a woman named Macarena. The duo then took the concept, reworked it, sold a demo, and released it in Spain. It was here that the dance steps originated that helped make "Macarena" a national sensation. With its Latin beat, simply choreographed steps, and a great deal of exposure in Spain, the dance single moved on, and in 1993 and 1994 "Macarena" swept South America, where having fun is a large part of each country's national attitude.

Because of its Latin beat, few believed that the song would have much of a chance outside of Spanish-speaking nations. But the team which held the rights to "Macarena" had seen tourists become caught up in "Macarena fever" on cruise ships and in local nightclubs. Based on this, they pitched the song as having international sales potential. Yet even Romero and Ruiz couldn't have guessed just how unlimited the number's potential really was.

From South America the dance wended its way around the world, making stops in Europe and Africa before then immigrating to the United States. Before it was released in America by the Bayside Boyz on RCA, the song's lyrics, about a young woman who, when her boyfriend leaves, goes on the prowl looking for a good time with his two best friends, were translated into English and recut. As if by magic, the heavily promoted and solidly backed single swept America even faster than it had conquered its native land, and became the nineties equivalent of "Hokey Pokey." Everyone was either doing the dance, laughing as they watched others do the dance, or pleading with someone to quit playing the song over and over again.

"Macarena" probably has hit pay dirt everywhere it has been released because of its infectious beat and its quickly paced harmonies. Yet even after the song had been played millions of times in the summer and fall of 1996, few of the hundreds of millions who had heard it at dances, football games, meetings, and political events could begin to repeat the lyrics. Only a handful of listeners even knew that the verses of the American version were being sung in English.

Most musicians attempt to put together classic melodies with thoughtful lyrics in order to make a timeless statement that can bring a higher level of understanding to the world. Romero and Ruiz seemed to have a better handle on what music is supposed to be. In its purest form it is not art or a voice of protest, it is an anthem of joy! In the case of the "Macarena," some fun which started in a small Latin nightclub led to a silly dance number that became the largest-selling non-Christmas release ever. Even the pope blessed the song for bringing the world together!

# Mairzy Doats

*M*ilton Drake, Al Hoffman, and Jerry Livingston were some of the most prolific and successful songwriters of the middle part of this century. Some of their combined and individual work gave us "Hawaiian Wedding Song," "Allegheny Moon," "Cinderella," "Ballad of Cat Ballou," "Wish Me a Rainbow," and "77 Sunset Strip." Yet the song for which the trio is most remembered, and which nearly everyone has sung, was not the title song of an Oscar-winning film or an Emmy-winning television show, it didn't make a statement, and no one really understood if it had any real meaning. Nonetheless, in 1944 it made a huge splash on the national hit parade and was a best-seller around the world.

"Mairzy Doats" became an institution during the Second World War. Bob Hope and Bing Crosby sang it to hundreds of thousands of troops at USO shows; those troops then took the song with them as they marched, as they waited for battle, and even as they attempted to survive the torture of enemy prison camps. In early 1944 the Merry Macs released the number on the Decca label, and it spent five weeks at #1. Others, such as Al Trace, the Pied Pipers, Lawrence Welk, and the King Sisters, also placed a version of "Mairzy Doats" on the playlists. During those trying days the song was as American as apple pie and baseball, universally loved by young and old alike . . . and yet made about as much sense as Gracie Allen.

Even though almost everyone from the oldest resident in a nursing home to an elementary school first-grader has sung the chorus of "Mairzy Doats," over the years many have never even heard the song's verses. It is the simple chorus which is still remembered. It is probably for that reason that five out of ten people cannot begin to explain what the title means. When asked, "What is a mairzy doat?" many people answer a flower, but everything from a girl's name to a certain kind of food is often included in the wide variety of responses to the simple question. The latter comes the closest.

When Drake, Hoffman, and Livingston put the song together they never intended to create a classic. They understood the needs of the times. By using a special blended spelling of the song's theme for the chorus, the team quickly put together lyrics that flowed with a lead line that was impossible to forget (one has to wonder just how much sleep has been lost because of not being able to get this tune out of one's head). What "Mairzy Doats" really meant was simply "mares eat oats." The verse also pointed out that deer also like oats, but that small sheep are satisfied with munching on ivy. With jive spelling and the lingo of the era, the simple song spelled the meaning out time and time again, but what meaning was that? It was at best a passable child's song; so why did it work so well and why has it lasted so long?

A lot of the reason that "Mairzy Doats" sold so well and became so special to so many was a matter of timing. Locked in the struggle of a lifetime, battling an enemy on two fronts, the people of the United States were in need of lightweight entertainment. With millions of lives on the line each day and most Americans having to sacrifice like they never had before, life was far too serious to spend much time listening to message songs. The nation didn't need tears, it needed laughs. And "Mairzy Doats" provided a bit of that needed escape. Those who heard it didn't have to think about a loved one five thousand miles away or be reminded of the neighbor who wasn't coming home. The song didn't remind a listener of anything that could bring them down or back into an often cruel reality.

"Mairzy Doats" also was so elementary that it could be learned instantly. This worked well for the many entertainers who were literally on the fly doing USO and live radio shows. Because of this fact, millions laughed and sung along with "Mairzy Doats" in hastily put together live performances each day. If the nation hadn't been at war, if performers such as Hope and Crosby had had more time to organize and learn shows, then something as simple and meaningless as "Mairzy Doats" might just have been left out altogether. But strange times call for special measures; thus everyone was doing the Drake-Hoffman-Livingston number.

Because everyone was doing "Mairzy Doats," everyone was listening to it and everyone was singing it. Even after the war the song was a staple of comedy sketches, variety shows, and sing-alongs on long family trips in the station wagon.

Though few know that it can trace its roots back to the Second World War, today "Mairzy Doats" is still remembered, and in an age when less than 10 percent of the population lives on a farm, the song is educational as well. After all, when a lot of city kids think of oats, they think of them only as a human breakfast food. They don't realize that livestock and wild animals eat oats too.

May the Bird of Paradise Fly up Your Nose

*N*ovelty songs are not reserved for one-shot, fly-by-night gimmick artists who discover a fad or hot news item and exploit it with some clever lyrics. The fact is that some of the best-known off-the-wall, idiotic, nonsensical numbers have been recorded by acts whose musical careers led them to awards, honors, and, in some cases, a place in a Hall of Fame (hey, even Sinatra and Presley recorded novelty songs). One of the best of the Hall of Famers who walked that fine line between oddball and honored legend was a four-foot-eleven giant of a man named James Cecil Dickens. As a matter of fact, this country music icon rode to fame on the strength of a joke.

From the day that he was born on a tiny farm in Bolt, West Virginia, Jimmy was different. He stood apart. Bright, curious, and musically inclined, this thirteenth child of a rancher graduated from high school with honors and in the midst of the Depression, when only a handful of young rural boys continued their education beyond eighth grade, won himself a spot at the University of West Virginia. But young Jimmy, who at the time was just four and a half feet tall and the butt of numerous campus jokes, was more interested in making a name for himself on a local radio station than he was in his classes, so he soon gave up on higher learning for a shot at entertaining on the nation's hottest medium.

Radio was the first institution in America that was truly an equal opportunity employer. None of the listeners at WMNN in Fairmont, West Virginia, or later at WLW in Cincinnati could have guessed that the young man with the big voice was scarcely bigger than the Munchkins who starred in *The Wizard of Oz*; all they knew was that Little Jimmy Dickens could sing up a Texas-sized storm. He was so good with a joke and a song that he kept moving up the radio ladder in a quick series of leaps and bounds, and by the middle forties he was a huge star in Saginaw, Michigan. In the days after the end of World War II, a twenty-six-year-old Jimmy caught the eye of Roy Acuff. The King of Country Music was interested in more than just the boy's great guitar playing and full, rich voice—Acuff knew a lot of folks who could do that. What Roy loved was the way the diminutive man worked an audience. His jokes came easy, his smooth stage presence belied his youth, and how he could make people forget their cares and laugh! Acuff was so impressed with Dickens that he invited the young man to join him on the Opry. From day one on that hallowed stage, Little Jimmy was a large success.

Soon after arriving in Nashville Dickens had landed a recording contract with Acuff's label, Columbia. In 1949 he released what was to become the first line in a long string of novelty song hits, "Take an Old Cold Tater and Wait." This single put Little Jimmy in the middle of a country music explosion that was being created by such stars as Eddy Arnold, Hank Williams, and Hank Snow. Teaming with Hall of Fame songwriters Boudleaux and Felice Bryant, the diminutive Opry artist created some mighty tall numbers on the country charts. Throughout the decade his music not only lit up playlists and jukeboxes, but his twin-lead guitar-driven road show sold thousands of tickets from coast to coast. He may have seemed the most unlikely of candidates for the job, but in his field, Dickens had become a giant.

By the mid-sixties, Jimmy, who hadn't cut a single which had made it inside the top ten since the fifties, was in need of a hit. Songs like "He Stands Real Tall" were well-written and nicely done, but they simply couldn't compete with the more pop-oriented sounds which were flooding the country music charts of the day. It seemed that the very music which had welcomed the young man from West Virginia to town had now evolved into something he couldn't do.

At about the same time that Little Jimmy Dickens was wondering if "real" country music had been lost forever, a disc jockey at KHEY radio in El Paso, Texas, was staying up late watching the flickering black-and-white images of Johnny Carson on *The Tonight Show*. With his interest in music and entertainment, Neal Merritt was probably more focused on what bandleader Skitch Henderson was doing than he was in what the host was saying, but as it turned out, it would be Carson who set the DJ's mind to whirling.

In an attempt at an insult, the show's host had said something about the "bird of paradise" depositing something in Skitch's beard. What happened next was lost on Merritt; he simply couldn't help thinking about all the funny things that could go with a bird of paradise haunting a man "evermore, evermore." With that in mind Neal drank a few beers, picked up a pen, and composed his countrified version of a Poe poem. When he was done his lyrics may have not challenged "The Raven" in style, but "May the Bird of Paradise Fly up Your Nose" was about to become about as well-known as Poe's bird.

Most strange, quirky songs never make it off the writer's desk; they are reserved strictly for family gatherings and drunken parties. But Merritt's composition was different. Because he had contacts in the entertainment field through his job, he found people interested in listening to "Bird." He sold the song's rights to the Central Songs Music Company, and he and the publisher began to look for an artist who could market this unique concept.

As the demo made the rounds, the song's subject—a penny-pincher's lack of generosity causes everyone he meets to curse him—caught the fancy of Little Jimmy Dickens. It was little wonder—this number seemed to be a perfect song for the man who had taken "Tater" and "A-Sleeping at the Foot of the Bed" into country music's top ten. And with the song's folksy, Roger Miller–sounding tune, Jimmy figured that it might just be different enough to be his ticket back into the big time. And even if it wasn't, he decided, it would still be a great song to feature on the Opry.

Columbia released "May the Bird of Paradise Fly up Your Nose" in the early fall of 1965. Surprising most critics, the single had raced within a few weeks into the country music top twenty. By Thanksgiving it would land at #1, thus becoming the only chart-topping song in Dickens's long and successful recording career. Yet if "Bird" had simply been a country music hit, the song's impact would have probably been written off and quickly forgotten by everyone except the regular Opry crowd. As it turned out, when Little Jimmy had latched onto this fowl, he didn't know just how big a bird it was going to be.

At about the same time as "May the Bird of Paradise Fly up Your Nose" was hitting the top of the country charts, the song somehow emerged on the pop playlists. In the midst of war protests, rioting in the streets, the British musical invasion, and the advent of the Motown sound, one of country music's most visible hillbillies found himself the owner of a rock music hit. A smiling Little Jimmy would ride the charts until Christmas, peaking at #15. But that was only a small part of the story. This strange alcohol-inspired song then began a life as a part of the very fabric of American expression.

The Dickens hit provided adults and children in both this country and abroad with a new way to express insults. And it seemed that everyone took part in it. From children to old folks, from teachers to lawyers, from housewives to presidents, millions were using the "Bird of Paradise" as a way to be funny and deliver insults at the same time. Within weeks of hitting the rock charts the "Bird" had become as overused as elephant jokes had a few years before. In a very real sense, the bird had become a monster. By 1966, the tens of millions who had laughed the first time they'd heard the song and the jokes that were spawned from it were now wishing that the bird of paradise would fly up Jimmy's nose and disappear forever. But it didn't!

Little Jimmy Dickens still performs his signature song on the Opry and at stage shows. His fans, as well as an endless supply of children, never grow tired of the song's irreverent message. As a comedy classic,

"May the Bird of Paradise Fly up Your Nose" ranks as one of the zaniest and best. But it was more than just another hit for Dickens. The small man with the big voice would have probably never gotten into the Country Music Hall of Fame without this number; his significant contributions during his first decade in country music would have probably been lost in the continual shuffle of new acts. But Jimmy was able to ride this "Bird" to the very top, and the song gave country music's shortest male star a chance not only to be appreciated in a big way, but to finally look down on everyone else. For a man who had spent his life looking up into people's noses, this would seem to be the most appropriate gift of all.

Monster Mash

In a dark 1940s Massachusetts movie theater a young boy sat glued to his seat, enjoying another of the classic Universal Studios monster epics. His eyes open wide, his body tense, the boy was more than a fan—he was almost a part of the films he viewed. There, up on a huge screen that shone in glorious black and white, Boris Karloff, Bela Lugosi, Lon Chaney Jr., and a host of other top horror performers were making a huge impact on this child who had gotten into the show without even buying a ticket. No one would have guessed then, even in their wildest nightmares, that little popcorn-eating Bobby Pickett would someday find his moment in the full moon's glow because of his love affair with Hollywood's creatures of the night.

Pickett was a movie freak because of environment. His father managed an East Coast motion picture theater, and Bobby got into all the shows free. In the youngster's mind westerns and dramas were all right, but monster movies were the greatest. Day after day, week after week, he would watch that genre's films over and over again, memorizing the dialogue until he could not only repeat the lines, but impersonate all the films' great characters as well. While this seemed to offer the boy little in the way of future employment opportunities, it did make Bobby the life of the party and the center of attention in school hallways.

After graduating from high school, Pickett spent time working in uniform for Uncle Sam in Korea. Upon his military discharge, spurred on by a dream that had been born in the seats of a darkened theater, he migrated to California to try to break into acting. To supplement his meager income working odd jobs, Bobby would enter talent shows and often win eating money by doing imitations of his favorite horror acts. Eventually the ambitious but as-yet-undiscovered talent joined a doo-wop group, the Cordials. There, as a joke, Pickett would perform the Diamonds' classic recitation bit in "Little Darlin'" using a Karloff-like voice. This unique version of an already strange song never failed to bring the house down and was probably the ticket that got the group most of its gigs. Yet by and large, Bobby was not nearly as enamored with music as he was with acting, and at about the time John Kennedy began to put his stamp on the nation as president, Pickett started to feel the urge to make a real stab at Hollywood.

Leaving the music business to devote his life to landing a choice acting role, Pickett almost turned his back on the black humor that had made so many laugh in nightclubs. Then, in the midst of the young man's auditions for television shots, Bobby's agent died. Suddenly, without representation and with no contacts, the actor found himself on the brink of failure and possible starvation. In his desperation he remembered something that one of the Cordials had said about the commercial prospects of using his unique Karloff bit for a novelty song.

Working around a classic doo-wop chord pattern—G, E minor, C, and D—Pickett sat down with some of his old music buddies and wrote out the words for a song. Originally the newly hatched concept had been called "The Monster Twist," but as "The Twist" was now fading from the dance scene, Lenny Capizzi, a close friend, suggested that Pickett center his theme on the latest dance craze, the "Mashed Potato." Thus came the mixed marriage between a spud and a freak.

Getting together with friends at the beach, Bobby and some of the members of the Cordials sang an a cappella version of "Monster

Mash" for a group of kids. One of those who was really turned on by the unique effort was a young girl whose father had made a name for himself in the novelty song business. Gary Paxton, whose "Alley-Oop" had made a chunk of change just a few years earlier, was now producing acts. When the beach girl introduced Bobby to her father, Gary flipped over the "Mash." The producer also thought it could be a hit. So Paxton brought Bobby into the studio of his Garpax Records company in early 1962. Their sole purpose was to create a song which was so unique that everyone would want a piece of it.

To "assemble" the various parts of this body of work, Paxton had resorted to tricks that had been employed by radio dramas just a few years before. Using chains, nails, glasses of water, and a host of other household items, he re-created the sounds of a mad scientist's laboratory. Then, assembling a team of good session players, including Leon Russell on piano, he placed Bobby at the microphone and told him to do his thing. Pickett, who had never been in a recording studio before, took a deep breath, and with Paxton and his people creating the right atmosphere and the musicians putting down the simply arranged tracks, did his best Boris. That first take was all Paxton needed; the song demanded no more work. It was perfect—or, as many were tempted to say as they listened to the playback, "It's alive!" Yet in actuality, the song was a long way from breathing.

Not having the resources for a national release, Paxton pressed a few demos and shopped them to the major labels. As was often the case with Frankenstein's monster himself, the song was viewed as either stupid or terrible and turned down time and time again. To put it another way, "Monster Mash" was simply misunderstood and therefore D.O.A.

As the rejections piled up, Paxton knew that he was going to need a strong bolt of luck to pump life into the orphan song. Logic should have told the producer to give up and let the project die a natural death. Yet Gary rarely considered logic when making business decisions, so he pressed a thousand copies of "Monster Mash" at his own expense and drove up and down the California coast dropping them off at radio stations. This simple act caused lightning to strike. Within a week Bobby Pickett had a regional radio hit and London Records had called and offered to step in with national distribution. Now the "Monster" really was alive!

As the records were pressed, Bobby was given the nickname Boris, and just as schools began their 1962 fall session his song was shipped to every distributor in the United States. Within two weeks "Monster Mash" was in the top forty, and on October 20 it hit #1. The "Monster Mash" had become a monster hit and was well on its way to becoming the "White Christmas" of Halloween.

"Monster Mash" would not only be revived each and every October on radio stations all around the world, but the single would reenter the charts in 1970 and hit the top ten again in 1973. Thanks in large part to Bobby's parody of the very films and stars he loved as a child, the song also seemed to create new interest in some of film's most wonderful mad scientists and monsters. Though Pickett never met the master, it was said that Boris Karloff had claimed the song as one of his favorites and had purchased several copies for himself and his friends.

Bobby Pickett would never make many waves as an actor; in that respect his performing career never took off. Still, the few lines he spoke on his first record would be remembered longer than most of the lines uttered by Clark Gable, Robert Redford, or Bobby's childhood monster idols. Almost everyone can quote, "I was working in the lab late one night . . ." Yet only one man had the good sense to bring those words to life in a monster song!

Mother-in-Law

New Orleans–based Allen Toussaint was a record producer/songwriter whose large contributions to rock and roll are often overlooked. Yet in 1996, due to the death of performer Jessie Hill, his name again surfaced as the man who brought the early sixties "classic" "Ooh Poo Pah Doo" to life. That novelty song would make it into the top thirty of *Billboard*'s charts and pave the way for Toussaint to push the Dixie piano sound that became his trademark.

Born in New Orleans's Gert Town neighborhood, Allen grew up playing piano and while still in school formed his own band. He worked at the famed Dew Drop Inn for a while, then was hired by Dave Bartholomew as a session player, where he provided the keyboard magic for some of the best New Orleans–based rock and roll recordings of the late fifties. By the time he hit his twenty-second birthday Toussaint had been hired to develop the sounds of a small record label, Minit ("Give us a Minit and we'll give you a hit").

Beyond being a piano player, arranger, producer, and the boy wonder behind Minit Records, Toussaint was also a songwriter. He was the creative force that had scribed "Holy Cow," "I Like It Like That," "Java," and "Yes We

Can Can." In the mid-seventies Allen would also pen what was to become one of Glen Campbell's biggest and best hits, "Southern Nights," as well as work with some of the biggest names in rock music. Yet though in the early sixties Toussaint was making a larger impact producing acts for Minit than he was scoring hits for the big stars, there is little doubt that he would have made a huge impact on popular music even if he hadn't met and signed a former preacher's kid.

Ernest Kador, born the son of a New Orleans minister, spent much of his early years a long way from Toussaint and the bayou. By the time he was fifteen, Kador, who had once sung in his father's church, was warbling the blues in Chicago nightclubs. Sometimes a solo act, other times a member of a quartet or vocal ensemble, Ernie, as his friends called him, even got the chance to be a part of the Moonglows and the Flamingos. Deciding that entertainment was his true calling, Ernest returned to his hometown and joined an early local rock and roll group, the Blue Diamonds.

Like Toussaint, Kador found himself working at the Dew Drop Inn. His smooth style and great rapport with the crowd made him a New Orleans favorite. With Little Richard and Fats Domino making waves on the national charts with their Dixie-style rock and roll, local record scouts soon signed Ernie to a deal. Yet Kador's stage style simply didn't translate to studio wax cuts, and his records for Savoy, Specialty, and Herald failed to score on the national charts. About the only thing that Kador earned for all his hard work was a new stage name, Ernie K-Doe.

It was as K-Doe that Allen Toussaint got to know the singer. Bringing Ernie into Minit's studio, the producer began to search through his best material, hoping to find something that would spotlight this young man's talent. Meanwhile, K-Doe, who was beginning to wonder if he was just marking time in the entertainment business, was attempting to put back together a rocky marriage, pay the bills, and still work enough club dates to keep his name in the local spotlight. This was a juggling act that was getting harder and harder to maintain.

One day while hanging out at Minit's offices, Ernie noted some scribbled notes that had fallen into Toussaint's wastebasket. Retrieving the scraps of paper, K-Doe read through the words that Allen had thought so little of that he had tossed them away. Immediately the singer realized that the songwriter's trashed lyrics described the central problem with his marriage and a good portion of his life. Allen might not have known it, but the woman from hell whom Toussaint had depicted in his failed composition was in reality Ernie K-Doe's mother-in-law. *I have got to record this*, Ernie thought has he rushed out to get the producer/songwriter's permission.

Even though he appreciated Ernie's enthusiasm and zeal, Allen by and large thought that "Mother-in-Law" was a waste of time. Yet because he needed a hit song for K-Doe so badly and hadn't found anything any better, he set up a time for a session. As the world would soon realize, it wasn't so much the singer that would assure this recording its status as a #1 hit, it was Allen's clever arrangement, a dynamite repeating bass line provided by Benny Spellman, and a concept that was played out on almost every one of the television sitcoms of the time—that the meanest women in the world had to be mother-in-laws. This had been such a long-running joke that it was amazing no one had thought of it before!

Ernie K-Doe hit the *Billboard* top forty for the first time almost six years after cutting his initial record. On April Fools' Day in 1961 (anyone dumb enough to insult one's own mother-in-law in public had to be considered somewhat foolish), almost every radio station in America was playing the song that Allen Toussaint had thrown away. By the third week in May, Ernie had a #1 hit, and strangely enough this seemed to get his mother-in-law off his back for a while. After all, he had made her famous.

K-Doe assumed that his success with this song would lead to a long list of other hits. Unfortunately, his three minutes of fame at Minit Records would be all there was for Ernie. Twelve weeks after landing in the top forty, his mother-in-law had used up her welcome and been shown the door. Sadly for the singer, she had earned the last laugh—by taking Ernie K-Doe with her!

# Mountain Dew

*I*n *theory mountain dew should be pretty much like the
dew in the valley. It should play havoc with suede*
shoes, become the active ingredient in the formula for a
cat's tracking up a recently washed and waxed car, and
serve to fairly accurately measure the humidity at seven in
the morning. In other words, wherever it may appear, fall,
or spring forth, dew should pretty much be dew. Yet in a
nation where "bad" said in just the right way can mean
good, it goes without saying that dew doesn't always
mean dew. Sometimes it means *dew*!

In the hills and hollows of the Carolinas, Tennessee,
and Arkansas, when a barefoot country boy would over-
hear a bunch of young men wondering where they could
find some mountain dew the lad would know there was a
party brewing. "Home brew," "moonshine," "white lightning," and "mountain dew" were all terms used to describe homemade corn liquor. Illegal, a source of
inspiration for thousands of church sermons, as well as a
source of income for thousands of regular church parish-
ioners, mountain dew gave birth to headaches, heartaches,
feuds, and stock car racing. It was to rural America in the
first half of this century what Al Capone's rum business
was to Chicago during Prohibition. Clear, potent, and vol-

atile, it was like nothing else. It was said to have a kick like a mule and the strength of a forest fire. Getting the mix of chemicals and brewing just right was as important a part of many families' legacies as knowing which grandpa had worn the gray in the Civil War. Moonshine was a hillbilly art form.

A musician from Asheville, North Carolina, Bascom Lunsford, had grown up not only hearing stories about home brew, but tasting a bit of the dew himself. He knew what it was, and what it could do, too. As brewing or possessing this form of alcohol was against the law, Lunsford also was well-aware of the unique methods of acquiring the "taste of the mountains." In most places home brew couldn't be purchased in a store, and small towns didn't have the private clubs where city folk often got their hard stuff. A still's regular buyers would therefore often leave notes and money under rocks, in hollow trees, and beside streams, then come back an hour or so later and find the money and note gone and a glass jug of pure liquid delight or misery (depending upon your perspective) left in its place. The buying transaction was simple, clean, and not unlike many of today's inner-city drug deals. Yet during the twenties and thirties, most of the same folks who wanted the G-men to gun down Capone and his bootleggers saw little but humor in farmers' hiding stills in the woods. To almost everyone except the preachers and the revenuers, home brew was considered about as serious an offense as going five miles over the posted speed limit.

Calling his ode to the glories of moonshine "Mountain Dew," Bascom sang the number at small-town shows, as well as every year before a big crowd at a folk festival in his hometown. It was there that Scotty Wiseman first heard it. And it was in Scotty's hands that "Mountain Dew" would be distributed to a thirsty public.

Wiseman was the male half of the team of Lulu Belle and Scotty on the radio show *National Barn Dance*. A guitar and banjo player, Scotty had drifted to WLS radio in Chicago, where he had been signed for *Barn Dance* and then been teamed with a young female singer, Myrtle "Lulu Belle" Cooper.

Lulu Belle, who was one of the first successful country female comedians, had been named the "Radio Queen" in 1936. She and Wiseman became even more popular once teamed, appearing not just on large road tours but also becoming a featured act in several Hollywood films. Married in 1934, Lulu Belle and Scotty had released numerous records (the duo's "Have I Told You Lately" is a classic) and were huge stars by the time Wiseman discovered Bascom's tune.

Wiseman reworked the song for a novelty bit to be used as part of his and his wife's act. Then came a hurdle which he hadn't anticipated. Even though Vocation Records allowed the duo to record the number in 1939, WLS radio, then owned by the Sears Department Store Company, wouldn't let the duo sing the song on the *Barn Dance*. It seemed that the station felt the lyrics about drinking and breaking the law to do so were not appropriate for the American public. Without airplay on the nationally heard weekly show, "Mountain Dew" couldn't get the exposure or the kick it needed, and the record fell flat. Just as with moonshine itself, a buyer had to *know* where and how to shop for Lulu Belle and Scotty's new song.

In Nashville the Grand Ole Opry didn't turn its nose up at Lunsford's ode. Rather, acts like Grandpa Jones and Roy Acuff made it a regular feature of their programs. Just off radio play and live work alone, "Mountain Dew" quickly became one of the best-known novelty songs in the country music industry. Still, the number was collecting more dew than cash. Not one of the many who'd recorded it had placed it on a national playlist. (It may seem hard to believe now, but country music radio at that time wouldn't allow songs about either drinking or cheating. If that was still the rule, country's top forty would have to be reduced down to the top four!)

Visiting Chicago, Bascom Lunsford got a huge kick out of Lulu Belle and Scotty's record. He couldn't wait to take it home and play it for his friends and family. But the writer also sensed that his song wasn't going to run up much of a tab at the record sales bar. Bascom therefore sold all rights to Scotty for a bus ticket back to Asheville. At the time, this seemed like a sober deal.

After World War II "Mountain Dew" became such a country music standard that Wiseman began to get healthy semiannual royalty checks. But as Scotty looked at the sales contract for the song, which had been scribbled on hotel stationery, he began to feel a bit hung over. In an action that some would find so strange that they wondered if it wasn't taken under the influence of the song's subject, Wiseman phoned the publisher with instructions to give half of the tune's royalties to Lunsford. While few questioned the integrity of this move, some wondered if a "fifth" wouldn't have been a more appropriate share. But Scotty felt that the jug should be shared equally, and it has been ever since.

Even though almost everyone in country and out of country music knows some if not all the lyrics about the still around the bend and Aunt June's perfume, it wasn't until 1981 that "Mountain Dew" finally tasted the charts as a single. Willie Nelson, who knew the song's subject ever so well, took Bascom's comedic work into the top thirty that year. To be precise, the hit status of "Mountain Dew" was assured by Nelson with *Billboard* measurement of "21 proof"—not very potent to hill folk, but still good enough be called the real thing by the families of Lunsford and Wiseman, who have now been sipping on the profits for half a century.

The Movies

*I*n 1955 Harold Reid joined Lew DeWitt, Phil Balsley, *and Joe McDorman and performed before a handful* of people at a Methodist church in tiny Lynhurst, Virginia. This performance was the debut of a group that would eventually come to be known and loved as the Statler Brothers. In the mid-fifties, long before they considered "Whatever Happened to Randolph Scott" or remembered "Elizabeth," the guys were called the Four Star Quartet and their most requested song was "Have a Little Talk with Jesus." Slowly at first, the four high school friends would add more gospel standards to their act and build themselves into one of the area's best-known local gospel groups. But there wasn't much money to be made at Sunday services or church socials, so by 1960 the group had dissolved. Missing the good times with friends and the opportunity to harmonize, Reid re-formed the quartet as the Kingsmen a year later. Harold's brother Don replaced McDorman, who had left to find a real job in the real world.

While the Kingsmen generally performed the religious standards, financial concerns necessitated their singing any kind of music that would put money in their pockets. So while the Kingsmen were a straight gospel quartet on Sunday, during the week they performed country, pop, and rock music at conventions, dances, and banquets. And the more they played in the secular world, the more interested the guys became in developing their sound to fit the songs that people requested.

The Kingsmen's gospel role models were the Blackwood Brothers; in rock the guys could emulate the sounds of the close-harmony doo-wop groups such as the Crew Cuts; but in country there were no groups to look to for inspiration. Except for a very few harmonizing family acts, hillbilly music relied heavily on lead vocals, with groups only being used for chorus accompaniment. Having no pattern to follow, the Kingsmen simply worked out their own arrangements of songs that were written to be sung as solos.

The Kingsmen might have never found the warm Music City spotlight if it hadn't been for Johnny Cash. Cash first caught the group in 1963. As he watched them work a small-town crowd, he was impressed with not only their sound, but their ability to charm a country audience. A year later when Johnny put together one of the first big country music package shows, he thought of the Kingsmen again.

Cash already had the Carter Family signed to tour with him. He had also persuaded his old Sun Records buddy Carl Perkins to come along. Yet he needed something else to bring a big-time show to small-town America. That something, he reflected, might be a quartet that could do gospel and easily turn a country standard too. To evaluate his theory, Cash booked the Kingsmen as his opening act for a one-shot deal. After seeing the crowd's enthusiastic reaction, Cash asked the quartet to join him. Within days the guys were playing before thousands instead of hundreds.

Being on the road with Cash provided the four young men with enough money to quit their real-world daytime jobs. It also presented them with a new problem. In Virginia everyone knew who the Kingsmen were. Now they were performing in front of people who didn't know them personally and who assumed that they were the rock group that had just scored with "Louie Louie." In order to separate themselves from the other Kingsmen, the group picked a name off a tissue box and became the Statler Brothers.

Late in 1965 the group hit the charts with "Flowers on the Wall."

A few more hits followed for Columbia before the Statlers moved to Mercury in 1970. With "Bed of Roses," the quartet established itself as the premier country music singing ensemble and reeled off scores of top country hits, most of them written by the singers themselves.

As Lew, Don, Phil, and Harold grew in stature, they also grew in talent. Taking an almost Norman Rockwell–type view of life, they began to "paint" songs which touched not just the buying public's fancy, but its heart, too. Capitalizing on this talent, the Statlers began more and more to reflect the very fabric of the warmest American memories. Through a string of hit records the quartet energetically and creatively posed many musical questions. In "Whatever Happened to Randolph Scott" they critiqued the state of violence and sex in modern movies. "The Class of '57" looked back on dreams that didn't happen for a bunch of high school kids who thought they could change the world. "Do You Remember These" echoed the theme of better days and simpler times. Yet while all of these songs had a novel quality about them, each of them was filled with too much thought and soul-searching to be considered a novelty song. So by and large the Statlers had evolved into being a serious group rather than a country music version of rock and roll's the Coasters.

In 1978 the four men combined their extensive knowledge of movies (their touring bus showed old films as they traveled from date to date) with their magical ability to compose lyrics. What resulted was a single entitled "The Movies." The song was the inspiration of Lew DeWitt. DeWitt masterfully blended movie titles into a running dialogue that played out almost like the old sneak peeks shown during Saturday matinees. This time the sneak peeks were mainly clips from Hollywood's Golden Age. Employing a technique which was somewhat like the child's game of "follow word," Lew would link *Citizen Kane, The Caine Mutiny, Mutiny on the Bounty, Bounty Hunter,* and so on. Over the length of his piece he included almost a hundred titles, everything from *Thunderball* to *The Sting.* Even *The Creature from the Black Lagoon* made the final cut.

Just as country music's great traveling hit from an earlier era, "I've Been Everywhere," had done, "The Movies" struck an instant chord with fans. Infectious, it not only got people singing along, but also created scores of discussions about which movie from which era really was the greatest of all time. A top ten song the year it was released, "The Movies" was followed by a wave of Statler hits that combined lively tunes with Norman Rockwell stories centering on real people and real places. The two best of these were probably "Do You Know You Are My Sunshine" and "How to Be a Country Star."

Today the Statlers continue to be a "novel" group in a fashion that is not unlike that of Ray Stevens. Yet unlike the zany Stevens, even when the Statlers jumped into the realm of gimmick material, there was a facet of them that was still connected more to warm memories than to outrageous situations. Because of their tendency to inspire smiles rather than belly laughs, the group has evolved into the very thing which their song "The Movies" described: a one-of-a-kind classic.

Mr. Custer

*How about this for a wonderful song premise? Take thousands of angry Sioux Indians, bring them to-*gether in a desolate part of the Black Hills, toss in an egomaniacal army general and some stupid planning, then laugh with glee as the Indians blast several hundred of the United States' finest to bits in a few minutes. To top it off, set it in the early summer of 1876 and have the singer/ narrator die just before the end of the song. What American teenager wouldn't be drawn to a composition like this?

A trio of writers—Fred Darian, Al Delory, and Joe Van Winkle—thought that Custer's last stand at the Little Bighorn was somehow the perfect fodder for a humorous novelty song. It was Al Delory who could claim most of the responsibility for this almost criminal bit of inspiration. He was the one who had first pictured himself as a trooper studying Custer's plan and begging the famous, and at this time lionized, general to give him the day off, whining, "I don't want to go." From this premise the song about a trooper who didn't want to die was written.

For lead writer Fred Darian, completing a concept like this one was a long way from writing "The Impossible

Dream." That song captured the essence of never giving up, of giving it your all in the face of huge obstacles, and of doing something that everyone else believes is undoable. Yet, even though the trooper wanted no part of the battle, in a very real way, "Mr. Custer" represented just that. It was an "Impossible Dream" in several fundamental ways. The first was who in their right mind would record it. The second was who would release it. And finally, the song's lead character was set up in a situation that was impossible. Is this dreaming big or what?

Once "Mr. Custer" found its way to some type of conclusion, the trio needed a volunteer to mount up and take the reins on a demo which probably no one would want to buy anyway. Knowing that few, if any, top acts would sign up for this kind of perilous duty, the songwriters began to look around the building where they worked. In a darkroom filled with the smell of chemicals used for developing and printing pictures, they found a funny fellow named Larry Verne. Possibly the harsh chemical fumes had gotten to the young man's brain, because he agreed to go to a session and help the songwriters out.

"Mr. Custer" was in reality little more than a fleshed-out idea when the day for laying the tracks on the demo rolled around. Showing up for his assignment, Verne discovered that the team had about as many solid plans as Custer himself had had on June 25, 1876. And in truth the songwriters were still trying to finish the verses and had not thought a great deal about what they wanted their final arrangement to sound like. Plus, just as Custer might not have had a clear concept of how good or bad his troops were, Darian, Delory, and Van Winkle didn't even know if Larry Verne could sing. The only thing they had gathered about Mr. Verne was that he was funny. And at this point "funny" was much more important than musical talent.

When the demo was finally hashed out and sewn together, the songwriters shopped it. Every major label in the business turned it down, with exclamations that "Mr. Custer" was the worst song they had ever heard. Weeks turned into months, and even minor independent labels, which would often take almost anything on the chance that they could produce a successful enough record to sell distributing rights to one of the "big boys," ran from the song as fast as the song's narrator wanted to run from George Custer.

The trio of struggling songwriters refused to give up. They recut another demo and shopped it some more. At first it looked as if Del-Fi, the label which had put Ritchie Valens on the map, might take it. After a few weeks, though, execs there shipped the demo back, wondering what they'd seen in it in the first place.

In retrospect, many might wonder why so many labels passed on a concept that seemed to have some solid satirical merit at the very least. The fact was that most producers thought that a song about a soldier wanting to bail out of a battle with one of the nation's most revered military heroes would be an abhorrent thought to most people of that era. Laying down your life for your country was a concept that wasn't just some distant image of forgotten wars; hundreds of thousands of men had done just that within the past twenty years. Therefore, poking fun at a coward who didn't want to do battle seemed almost un-American. Also keeping this song out of the saddle was the fact that history had yet to paint Custer as the ego-possessed fool that he was, and history had also failed to allow the public to understand much, if anything, from the Indian point of view.

The newest demo for "Mr. Custer" had been cut in the New Era studios of Herb Newman. Newman, who probably recognized just how big a fool the general had been and knew that there was little glory in being stupid, liked what Verne had done with the song. He opted to put out a few copies and took one to a Los Angeles disc jockey, Bob Crane. Crane, who was a few years away from poking fun at World War II via a starring role in *Hogan's Heroes,* liked what he heard too. When the DJ put "Mr. Custer" into rotation, the lines lit up. Within a few weeks tens of thousands of orders were coming into New Era Records.

Larry Verne, who had never held any job for too long, was taken out of the darkroom and put on the road. Dressed liked a member of the 7th Cavalry, he hit all the major cities promoting his record. His off-the-wall sense of humor, combined with his lack of concern about making a fool of himself, matched the mood of the recording itself. When the record finally sold enough copies to hit the charts in the fall of 1960, it seemed that the joke was on all of the labels who had turned "Mr. Custer" down. In a very real sense, each of those record companies had discovered that the nation really was in a "New Era."

"Mr. Custer" surprised everyone by climbing into the top forty the first week in September. Over the next few weeks it made steady progress in the face of attacks by some of the military establishment and various patriotic groups. Three weeks later the single had joined songs like "My Heart Has a Mind of Its Own," "The Twist," and "It's Now or Never" in the top ten. Certainly this trio of songs, all of which would earn #1 status, were appropriate playlist mates for "Mr. Custer." After all, the song's trooper did know in his heart and mind that he shouldn't follow the order of "Forward ho!" Verne's character also knew that if he didn't find a way to twist out of this situation, he would be lost. And finally, if he didn't find a way to get out now, he knew he would never have a chance to get out of anything again.

On October 10, more than seven decades after the death of General George Custer had been the #1 story on the front pages of the nation's newspapers, Larry Verne returned a new Custer to #1 status. For Verne, his burst of fame would be short; Custer, in fact, would have a longer tenure on the western plains than Larry would have in the music business. Yet Verne's "Mr. Custer" would give him a shot at "The Impossible Dream" that its lead songwriter would write about, as well as put a spotlight on a DJ who wanted to live his own "Impossible Dream" by making it as a television actor. All things considered, when viewed in the context that it finally shouted out the fact that Custer had been a fool, this was one really bad novelty song that did have its really good historical points.

My Ding-a-Ling

He was born in St. Louis in the middle of the flapper era and would grow into a young man who would cause a flap in the fifties by bringing his brand of "race" music to white middle-class America. A guitar-playing, duck-walking songwriter, Chuck Berry was probably the resonant voice of the nation's teenagers for the first four years of rock of roll. The style he developed, the songs he wrote, and the music he played had a profound effect on not only those who danced to his records, but on those who would shape youth music for generations to come.

Chuck gave the world such great teenage anthems as "Sweet Little Sixteen," "Maybellene," "School Day," and "Johnny B. Goode." It would be hard to envision the rock and roll revolution having taken place without Berry. His records were crisp, fresh, unique, and filled with everything that mattered in the culture of the time, including high school crushes, making out in the backseat, fast cars, great music, and school activities. With all that Berry gave to the sound that literally took over the world, it seems more than a bit sad that he only managed one #1 single and that this record caught Chuck not at his greatest, but at his most vulgar.

No one had ever accused Chuck Berry of being a saint.

Even when the former hairdresser finally made it into the music business, his lifestyle was deemed inappropriate to serve as a youth role model. Still, with the powerful New York disc jockey Alan Freed serving as his mentor, Chuck's records took off on white charts at a time when a majority of black acts were limited to R&B playlists. Yet just when Chuck was hitting stride, a rape charge, trouble with the IRS, and a host of other incidents not only got the singer blacklisted by most radio stations, but also sent him to prison. By the time he had served his sentence, the Beatles, an act he had inspired, had taken over his turf and Chuck was limited to appearing at smaller venues and essentially playing his old hits over and over again.

By the early seventies a renewed interest in the roots of rock and roll had led to Chuck's being spotlighted in everything from jazz festivals to symphony concerts. It was at a 1972 concert in front of the Arts Festival of Lancaster, England, that a ribald Berry decided to sing a little ditty whose meaning was not hidden behind double entendres.

"My Ding-a-Ling" could trace its roots back to the beginnings of what has often been labeled race music. Many of the early rock and roll hits had originally been sung as R&B standards. Some of the best known of these standards had two sets of lyrics. The first was for a crowd that demanded clean standards. The second and often more popular set of words was used when performing before audiences who relished a good dirty joke. When Chuck performed "My Ding-a-Ling" for the Brits, he hit below the belt. He gave them the muddy version of a song he had once recorded in a vastly different manner.

"My Ding-a-Ling" hit a not-so-innocent nerve with rebellious youth at the English show. The raucous crowd love it. Chess Records, which had been linked to Berry since the beginning of his career, had taped the concert and decided that this bit of audience excitement should be exposed to the public. Worrying little about offending anyone (this was the period when Americans were enjoying watching *All in the Family* push the limits of what had once been considered good taste), the label released the number about a man who was in love with the part of his anatomy which defined him as male. Sadly, millions were seduced.

Singing about sex put Chuck Berry where he had never before been—at the top of the charts. His "Ding-a-Ling" knocked Michael Jackson out of #1 (the irony of this would not be realized for another generation). It seemed that as the country sang along to this rude and totally uncreative ditty, all the prophets who had once proclaimed that rock and roll music was a complete and total wasteland void of any sense of morals or taste had been proven correct. And many fans believed that Chuck Berry had sold out.

Yet to judge Berry on this one mistake would be like judging Elvis by all of those throwaway numbers he performed in his movies. It wouldn't be fair. What "Ding-a-Ling" represents is the low end of the novelty market and the low end of Berry's career, while most of Chuck's other youth anthems represent the real message and glory of the music which he helped to define. So in the end, forget about Berry's bad little "Ding-a-Ling" and remember him when he was really (Johnny B.) good.

Na Na Hey Hey
Kiss Him Goodbye

*H*ave you ever been singing a song and couldn't re-member all the words, so you replaced the un-known lyrics with "Na na"? If you have, you have a good idea as to how a good deal of the lyrics for Steam's only hit were created.

In 1969 Paul Leka had moved from a production job at Circle Five Productions to the New York office of Mercury Records. While at this new label, Paul had gotten a recording contract for a good friend and former band-mate, Gary De Carlo. The producer had cut four sides of stuff with his new artist when Mercury asked for a single to try out on radio. Feeling that all the songs which had been already cut were too strong to just throw away as a B side, Paul called Gary back into the studio to cut some-thing so bad that no one would want to listen to more than a few seconds of the song. The producer felt he needed to do this so that no disc jockey would possibly be confused as to what Mercury felt was the hit side.

To accomplish this goal, Paul got in touch with friend and writer Dale Frashuer and inquired if in his old ma-terial he had anything that was dismal enough to be con-sidered a complete piece of garbage. As the ultimate insult Dale pulled out a song which he and Leka had written eight years before called "Kiss Him Goodbye." It was short, contained nothing of redeeming value, and could be put together with a limited amount of effort and money. In other words, it was perfect for what they needed.

After a bit of studio work, Paul determined that "Kiss Him Goodbye" needed a chorus. So while he worked out a melody line, he sang the traditional "Na na" in the places where he needed words which had not yet come to him. Just for a laugh, either Dale or Gary then chimed in with "Hey hey." Soon, the running joke worked its way into a rough cut of a B side.

De Carlo, Frashuer, and Leka had planned on coming up with some lyrics for the final cut to replace "na" and "hey," but as it was late and this was supposed to be a trash side anyway, they simply blew it off. They let "Kiss Him Goodbye" ride with a chorus that really hadn't been completed and didn't make much sense.

A few days later, after a couple of promotional copies had been pressed, Mercury determined that "Na Na Hey Hey Kiss Him Goodbye" had real potential on its own. Leka was dumbfounded when he discovered that the label wanted him to release the song as an A side for his new artist. When the producer said "No no" to "Na na," the label suggested that the single be shipped on its Fontana imprint using a new name for the recording artist. That way Gary De Carlo would not have to be associated with it, and the company could still use the song that its production staff liked so well. So, given no opportunity to bury the cut, Leka searched for a name for this "new" group.

As he walked the streets of New York City, Paul had often noted steam rising from manhole covers late at night. This observation led to the inspiration behind the name Steam. Besides, Leka had thought as he went back to work on the promotional plans for his friend's serious releases, what self-respecting DJ would play "Na Na Hey Hey Kiss Him Goodbye" anyway?

The fake group's Fontana single hit the charts in November of 1969 and in just six weeks climbed past the Beatles' "Come Together" to hit #1. Mercury, now caught up in promoting its new but nonexistent group, called on Paul to put together a band. Gary and Dale having other things on their agendas, Leka auditioned several groups before finding one in his hometown of Bridgeport, Connecticut. Turning out a batch of new material, Paul then quickly slapped together an album and put Steam on the road. Though the single had become a major hit, the hastily formed band quickly ran out of steam. Yet while the group never had another hit, Steam did chart exactly one more time than Gary De Carlo ever did.

Steam and "Na Na Hey Hey Kiss Him Goodbye" would have probably been forgotten altogether if not for America's love affair with sports. Baseball stadium musicians began to use the phrase "Na na" whenever an opposing team's pitcher was knocked out of a game. Then football and basketball crowds began to chant it when the visiting team looked as if it was going down to defeat. Finally even college and high school bands began to play the song. By the advent of ESPN, it seemed that at any sporting event held anywhere in the United States, fans could be assured that they would hear two songs, "The Star-Spangled Banner" to start the contest and "Na Na Hey Hey Kiss Him Goodbye" to close it.

It is incredibly ironic that in a time when trash talking in sports has been elevated to an art form, a song which was recorded as nothing more than a throwaway record has become the theme song for fans who want to hurl one last bit of trash at a lesser opponent. One has to wonder if it is only because these rabid groups can't remember the words to any other farewell chorus.

One's on the Way

*L*oretta Lynn's life is one of the best chronicled in country music history. Her millions of fans can recite her story line for line and verse for verse. Her humble beginnings, her early marriage, her days spent raising children when she was still a child herself, her first tentative steps into country music, her close friendship with Patsy Cline, her rise to superstardom, and the Hollywood movie made about her life are the major elements of Lynn's stranger-than-fiction biography. Much like George Washington, Davy Crockett, or Babe Ruth, this daughter of a coal miner has somehow stepped beyond her life's station to become something more than what she ever was or intended to be. At the same time, Lynn had never ceased being the real person who escaped poverty at about the same time she first appeared on the Opry. Bigger than life, the star is also seen as the representation of the everyday blue-collar women.

Loretta was born in Butcher Hollow, Kentucky. She married when barely a teenager and began her career by working local talent shows, fairs, and honky-tonks. Her husband, Mooney, served as manager, driver, promoter, and baby-sitter during her early lean years. The couple often drove from town to town just visiting with disc jockeys and passing out her first record. Within a year of this mostly personally financed promo tour, Lynn had been signed by Decca, and America's latest Cinderella tale was born.

Simple, direct, homespun Loretta's rise to the top of the country music charts wouldn't come overnight. In the beginning, she was as much trapped in the restrictive times as any other female singer. She was the decoration on a man's show. She was expected to let men make her decisions. She was asked to believe that the gal singers just weren't as important as their male counterparts and that they would never sell as well. This is the way Nashville was, and it was the way most insiders expected it to remain.

While other female acts might have acquiesced to these unwritten rules, Lynn didn't. Soon she was defying the men and picking her own material, writing her own songs, and building a fan club that would rival and eventually surpass that of all the mighty men on Music City labels. Carefully, but boldly, she stepped out and demanded not only to be heard, but to have a real voice. Once people began to listen, she took up a banner that would make her one of America's best-known women.

Via hard work, from 1962 through the middle of 1966 Loretta became one of the dominant female singers in Nashville. Her concerts slowly built into lovefests and reunions. Fans who had seen her ten times would return again, not just to hear her sing, but to stay afterward to visit with the star. The "Blue Kentucky Girl," as some were calling her, was affecting country music's faithful at the grass roots. She wasn't on a par with the successful male stars, but she already had seen more chart action than Patsy Cline.

As her fame grew, so did Lynn's assertiveness. She might not have had much formal education, but she had a lot of common sense. She knew that she could identify with the women who made up her audience and bought her records a lot more than could the men who were running her career. Against those males' advice, she began to write songs that verbalized the woman's view. Subtly at first, she began to sing about abusive relationships, cheating, scheming, drinking, and lying. As her confidence grew, so did her courage. By mid-1966 she was both loud and bold, and her messages were no longer veiled.

Still, Lynn remained under the thumb of the Wilburn brothers, a country music act who had discovered Loretta when she was hungry and signed her to a deal that gave them a piece of every song she wrote. Tired of being tied to this unjust agreement, in the early seventies Lynn stood up for herself and all women by essentially going on strike. She was not going to write any more songs just to have some man who was doing nothing get a lion's share of the profit from her talents.

This stand placed Lynn's Decca producer, Owen Bradley, in a bad position. Lynn's fans had come to think of the singer/songwriter as their idol. Her lyrics spoke not only *to* these women, but *for* them. To have Loretta record just anything was unthinkable. Her next single had to have a message, like all her songs. And even though the superstar was not going to write another song until she was legally free of the Wilburn brothers, her next release also had to sound like Lynn. This combination of the singer's stubborn will, her producer's problem, and her fans' expectations paved the way for not only Loretta's biggest hit, but for a unique marriage of talent between Music City and *Playboy* magazine. That in itself makes this song a novelty!

Shel Silverstein, who had written such classics "A Boy Named Sue," had penned a song some years before for Jeannie Seely. Seely hadn't liked it and her producer—the same Owen Bradley—had pretty much forgotten about Shel's effort. Now, faced with the prospect of having nothing ready for Loretta, the producer recalled the old number. Digging out the demo, he listened to the song's quirky message and decided to pitch it to Lynn. She loved it!

In retrospect, the humorous "One's on the Way" probably worked only because of its singer. It is the story of a woman who has been pretty much kept barefoot and pregnant by her husband. On top of this, the husband spends his time on the road, thus giving the woman no help with her motherly duties. Because Loretta had so many children and was now the voice of women who were demanding that men quit taking advantage of them and begin to share in household duties, "One's on the Way" worked. And when country music's version of a women's libber ended the song with the off-the-wall comment, "Gee, I hope it ain't twins again," females all over the country knew exactly where she was coming from.

In early 1975 millions of women moved Loretta and her new song into country music's top spot. And at concert after concert they saluted the woman who had been brave enough to not only think about all the ways her man had taken advantage of her, but to voice those concerns in a song. Here was a woman who didn't want to be pregnant again, and she had basically told it right out! From now on it would be her choice. Wouldn't those fans have been shocked to have discovered that the writer of "One's on the Way" was not Lynn, but one of *Playboy* magazine's top contributors! (Yes, that is exactly where Shel had gotten his first big breaks.) More than likely, Silverstein's and Lynn's definitions of "babe" were very different.

This marriage forced by circumstances hadn't really pushed Lynn in a new direction. It had long been Loretta Lynn's passion to shock and wake up her often conservative and downtrodden fans. Recording one of Shel Silverstein's songs was just a way of keeping with that tradition, and in the process making millions not only smile, but think. Not many novelty numbers can make that claim; then again, not many country music stars wore invisible bunny ears while talking about women's rights either.

Pistol Packin' Mama

*A*l *Dexter is a member of the Songwriters' Hall of Fame, and with his long list of compositions that* have racked up millions in sales, he should be. There were few acts in the forties who turned out better western songs than Dexter and his Troopers.

A product of the oil fields of East Texas, Dexter lived his early years as a honky-tonk warrior. By day he would toil at hard labor and by night he would party with members of his crew. Eventually Al took to tending bar and singing songs. It was during this musical period that he hired on a pretty young woman to help out at night at one of his honky-tonks. Dexter had seen his newest employee in the company of a regular patron on several occasions and knew her to be friendly and outgoing. She was attractive too, so Al figured she would be good for business. As it turned out, the barmaid lasted longer at the honky-tonk than even Dexter himself. Yet just because they had parted company for the time being didn't mean they were not going to come together again in a big way down the road.

Among other things, Al Dexter has long been recognized as the first songwriter to actually use the term "honky-tonk" in a song title. He did so in the mid-thirties with a regional hit, "Honky-Tonk Blues." The fact that most hillbilly stations wouldn't play the single because of the word "honky-tonk" and the glorification of the honky-tonk lifestyle bothered the writer little. He and his band were too intent on making a living off those who came to dance at honky-tonks to be bothered by folks who called in complaints to radio stations.

But the days of Al and his Texas Troopers scraping by with few fans knowing who they were would change for good when the barmaid came back into Al's life.

In 1942, forty-year-old Al Dexter was sitting in an East Texas honky-tonk trading stories and drinks with friends when a familiar woman walked up to him. Even though she was bleeding from several scratches on her face and arms, wore a scared and wild look in her eye, and sported a mop of hair which appeared as though it had been caught in a wind machine, Al immediately recognized the lady as the pretty girl who had once tended bar for him in Turnertown. After she caught her breath, Al inquired as to what was the matter. He wondered what had put this lady in such an unkempt state.

It seemed that the man who had introduced Al to the young woman the year before had not been her innocent boyfriend. Rather, the barmaid and the bar patron had been having a long-term affair behind the patron's wife's back. When the wife had finally discovered their honky-tonk liaisons, all heck had broken loose.

The wronged woman had charged into the bar—the same one Al had poured drinks at—with guns drawn, seeking her retribution. Sensing the danger, the barmaid had ducked out the back door, run through a barbed-wire fence, and in her fear-motivated haste fallen several times in a rocky, thorn-covered field before finally catching a ride away from the scene. Still, she knew that her adversary was on her trail, and as she explained to Dexter, the other woman's guns were drawn and ready for action. So she needed some help.

The bloodied barmaid wanted Al to talk the wronged wife into putting her pistols down. As the two of them waited for the other woman to show up, Dexter kept wondering, *How do you talk to a lady with a gun?* The line which came to his mind was, "Lay that pistol down, babe."

The woman never showed up and Al didn't have to find out if his reply would have worked in real life, but within a few weeks he sensed that it would work perfectly in a song. Changing the premise to a man being chased by his gun-toting wife, Dexter scribbled out the words to "Pistol Packin' Mama."

The song's quirky lyrics were buoyed by a bright, up-tempo lead that belied the seriousness of the situation the words presented. And even though the singer was unable to talk Mama into laying the pistol down and was shot dead at the end of the final verse, the fact that this cheating, lying, scheming wretch was finally getting what he deserved seemed to bring a smile to almost everyone's face. Now if Al could make five verses and a chorus of a man begging for his life and then being executed funny, wasn't that a signal that this was the work of a songwriting genius? Time would prove that Dexter was just that!

None other than Bing Crosby and the Andrews Sisters picked up Al Dexter's ode to a cheating man and cut "Pistol Packin' Mama" in 1943. This classic team would take the single to #2 on the popular charts. Yet this high-scoring effort would finish a poor second to Dexter's version. Al's "Pistol Packin' Mama" would linger on the charts for more than two-thirds of the year, sell 2 million copies, keep the sheet music factory running low on ink and paper for over a year, and hold #1 for two months. In the process "Pistol Packin' Mama" would become one of the three biggest songs of the decade.

Seen in today's more enlightened context of domestic violence, the spiraling use of guns in solving family disputes, and the overall recognition of the seriousness of a situation in which one uses a firearm to threaten another person, "Pistol Packin' Mama" seems anything but funny. Yet to understand how this novelty song had rung so true in its time, consider that the top box office stars in Hollywood were often cowboy idols and that almost every American child had at one time been given a cap gun with a holster as a Christmas present. And finally, how many times had the public laughed at someone like Bob Hope being brought to his knees in a movie by a gun-toting wronged former girlfriend?

In a very real sense, humor is not so much universal in nature as it is topical. "Pistol Packin' Mama," a novelty classic in its time, would probably receive very little play in today's market. The violent message in its lyrics would doom it from many playlists. Ironically, that almost happened when the song was released, too. Yet the things that would have gotten it banned in its day, cheating and drinking, would not even be considered a problem now.

Country songwriter R. C. Bannon, whose "Only One Love in My Life" hit the top of the charts for Ronnie Milsap in the eighties, was also once inspired by what he witnessed in a honky-tonk. This time the setting was in Washington State rather than Texas, and this jilted lover didn't bring a gun. But unlike Al, R. C. could never figure out how to work this weapon—a chain saw—into a humorous ode about cheating.

The Purple People Eater

*M*GM *was the company that gave the world such great movies as* Gone with the Wind, Lassie Come Home *and* Manhattan Melodrama. MGM was the home of Gable, Harlow, and Taylor. MGM was the studio whose movie musicals have been called the finest ever produced. And it was MGM that gave the world . . . "The Purple People Eater."

Sheb Wooley was born in Erick, Oklahoma, in 1921. There must have been something in the water in Erick, because Roger Miller also came from this rural community, and from the minds of Wooley and Miller sprang forth some of the most off-the-wall songs ever written.

Sheb was just eleven when he talked his father into trading an old shotgun for a guitar. A few years later the teenage Wooley formed a band and was performing at dances throughout the area. Then, just when his musical career appeared to be warming up, Sheb got married and at nineteen left the dust bowl for California. There he settled into a job as a welder. Yet deep in his soul there was an itch to perform and a need to write down all of his ideas. This itch and this need led him to Nashville just after the end of World War II. When the front doors of Nashville's music row didn't respond to the handsome Okie, Wooley fed his family by working the airwaves as a disc jockey.

By 1950 Wooley had pretty much given up on the idea of becoming a country music singer, so he packed his bags and returned to the West Coast. There, using some of his old contacts and the skills he had learned on the ranch as a boy, he found work in the movies, gradually moving his way up from bit parts to supporting roles in epics like *Giant* and *High Noon*. When television westerns hit the big time, Sheb was right there, ready to saddle up and ride onto the tube too. Still, even as he spent weeks and weeks in the saddle, he never gave up on his music.

One evening the actor was visiting with close friend Don Robertson. Don, whose songwriting credits included some of the greatest ballads of the era, told Sheb a riddle that Robertson's son had recently told his father. By sharing the humor Robertson may have wanted to show Sheb just how strangely kids' minds work, but as it turned out he gave the Okie much more than just an insight into child psychology.

"What has one eye, one horn, and flies and eats people?" Don asked.

Sheb shrugged his shoulders.

Robertson laughed. "A one-eyed, one-horned, flying purple people eater!"

The rather dense gag should have died there, but for some inexplicable reason it didn't. Throughout the night Sheb kept coming back to the concept behind the feeble attempt at comedy. In his idiosyncratic mind Wooley somehow sensed that this would make a great song. He even tried to persuade Don to write it with him that night. Robertson, who had a knack for knowing a good song idea when he heard one, didn't think this one would fly. So he declined. Still, even after he returned home, the actor kept picturing the image of the flying monster. Finally he picked up his guitar and a pad and pencil and scribbled down what even he thought was undoubtedly the worst song he had ever written.

Once he had exorcised the monster song from his soul, Wooley returned to acting. One of the things he did was a part for a TV pilot called *Rawhide*. His role was that of a serious trail scout. After the production wrapped, Sheb had some time on his hands. As he waited to find out if CBS was going to add the show to its fall schedule, he auditioned some of his most recent ballads for MGM Records. The buyers were not impressed. After about an hour of singing just about everything he had written, the music honchos inquired, "Is that all you've got?" Against his better judgment Sheb admitted it wasn't. He told them that he had one more song, but that it was the "bottom of the barrel." And that was when the purple beast first reared its ugly head in public.

Much to Wooley's surprise, the president of the MGM record division loved "The Purple People Eater"; he thought it was one of the greatest things he had ever heard. Other, more sensible heads considered this piece even worse than the ballads Wooley had just sung, but because the man in charge liked it, MGM allowed Sheb to record a demo.

In the studio, the songwriter pulled out all the stops. To create a bizarre voice for his monster he used a fast-playback technique that had just been employed by David Seville. He also added other unique audio effects and his own slightly tipsy-sounding booming bass voice to tell the story. Sheb eventually used everything but the kitchen sink. The final product was completely over the edge, off-the-wall, and utterly juvenile, and most of those at MGM were horrified that it had been created in their studios.

"Kill the monster now!" the angry executives cried. "Kill it before it grows and ruins us all!" Yet the president still loved it. So in spite of the sales department's threatening to not promote the record and the A&R men's updating their resumes, the label shipped "The Purple People Eater" to the masses. And just when all those who had worked on the project were denying that they had had anything to do with it, the public adopted the monster like a lost little kitten.

"The Purple People Eater" was released two months after David Seville's cult classic, "Witch Doctor." Logic would have dictated that there was room on the charts for only one of these creations at a time. Yet this was the middle of the cold war, and people were spending millions on backyard bomb shelters, still driving DeSotos and Ramblers, and watching thirty different horse operas each week on network television. This was also the era when Hollywood was making millions turning out flicks about giant spiders, locusts, and crabs. So, evidently, logic was in short supply.

As "Witch Doctor" came down from #1, "The Purple People Eater" rose up the same charts. (The Everly Brothers' "All I Have to Do Is Dream" was the only thing that prevented Elvis's worst nightmare of having back-to-back novelty songs take control of *Billboard*'s top spot.) Yet what was even more incredible than the fact that the American public would make a one-eyed, one-horned monster #1 at all was that the song stayed on top for six weeks!

At the same time that his novelty song hit #1, Sheb Wooley hit the trail—not to promote his monster hit, but rather to film his new television series, *Rawhide*. Not having Sheb around to promote the song meant that the MGM public relations department—whch just months before had balked at the idea of working for "The Purple People Eater" at all—was now frantically pushing everything from T-shirts to lunch boxes. Before this alien hysteria had ended, 3 million records and countless spin-offs had been sold.

MGM had once boasted that it was the cream of the Hollywood crop. The studio had proudly declared that it had more stars on its payroll than there were in the heavens. In 1958 it added a one-eyed, one-horned purple character to its long list of megastars. And while Sheb's creation wasn't exactly *Gone with the Wind*, when the millions of dollars in profits that "The Purple People Eater" created came pouring in, frankly, MGM really didn't give a . . . !

 The Race Is On

With the exception of Eddy Arnold, no country music artist has spent more time on the charts than George Jones. The Texas native first sang in church, but he would find his fame and fortune far away from a sanctuary pew. By the time he returned from the war in Korea, George had taken up performing in clubs and at dances throughout southeast Texas. An old-fashioned honky-tonk stylist, Jones had a much more traditional sound than many of the performers of his day. With a phrasing style that was closer to Webb Pierce than to Hank Snow, Hank Williams, or Bob Wills, George caught the eye of H. W. "Pappy" Daily, a Houston record executive, in 1954. Daily took the twenty-four-year-old singer under his wing and groomed him for stardom. It didn't take long.

In 1955 Jones scored with the first of his more than 150 chart appearances. The song, released on the small Starday label, started as a regional Texas hit before catching on to the *Billboard* playlist in late 1955. "Why Baby Why" would spend fifteen weeks on the national charts, peaking at #4 before being replaced by another Jones offering, "What Am I Worth."

Jones's success on Starday earned him an invitation to

join the *Louisiana Hayride*. The Shreveport radio show was then at its peak. Elvis had just left the show to go on to international fame. Johnny Horton, Faron Young, Jim Reeves, and a host of other up-and-comers were either in the midst of a long ride on the show or had just been invited to Nashville. This was the stage upon which unknowns became big stars overnight; there was magic in Shreveport, and Jones took full advantage of it. With his energy and unique sound, George would quickly become one of the *Hayride*'s most popular draws.

When rockabilly took over country music, Jones made a living with a string of top ten honky-tonk songs. Yet he didn't break out and register a major hit until he signed with Mercury. Taking a number that had been written by the Big Bopper, J. P. Richardson, Jones recorded his first #1, "White Lightning." Two years later he would follow with an even bigger hit, "Tender Years." If the singer had never recorded another song, these two monsters would have established him as one of the era's best country acts. As it was, they were simply the foundation for much greater things.

By 1964 George Jones had charted more than forty times. He was one of country music's most recognized stars and had a style that was all his own. Yet in spite of all of this success, the singer was still in need of a big record. He hadn't had a #1 since 1962's "She Thinks I Still Care."

As he had grown into a major star, George had evolved into a singer of serious songs. His almost "whining" style lent itself to pleading ballads filled with pain and heartache. But he and his United Artists label also recognized that "the Possum" had slyly grinned his way through several novelty-type numbers early in his career. So when they heard the demo of a new Dan Rollins song, they felt that they had found a formula to shake up the charts again while reestablishing Jones's humor as well.

Dan Rollins had been living in Arizona, where he had become a regular at the two-dollar window of the Turf Paradise horse track. The songwriter loved betting on the ponies and really thrived in the environment that surrounded each day's activities at the track. Yet by and large that venue didn't appear to be a promising one for working on a career as a songwriter; it was hard to write lyrics on the side of a racing form. After watching his share of winners and losers and trying to develop a system which would allow him to pick the right funny-named filly over the wrong funny-named nag, Rollins got caught up in an idea for a song about losing at love. Using a track announcer's cadence, he penned lyrics about a race for passion. In his number, the irony was that love always caused so much pain and misery that the "winner loses all."

Tree Publishing bought the rights to "The Race Is On," and soon after it did, the demo found its way into George Jones's hand. Jones took to the horse racing song and fit it to his own style. Both the singer and his label sensed early on that this song was no gamble. Released in the fall of 1964, "The Race Is On" would spend more than half a year on the country charts. It would also cross over into pop and help pave the way for George Jones to become one of country music's longest-running and most successful acts.

Twenty-five years later, country/pop group Sawyer Brown revived the Don Robbins song. This time, with the help of the magic of video, "The Race Is On" ran strongly again. While Jones's version made the song a big hit and a favorite oldie request, Sawyer Brown's cut seemed to prove that a great gimmick, crafted into an even greater song, can make a funny idea timeless. With its multiple wins run on tracks far different from one another during wildly diverse eras, "The Race Is On" is one of the few novelty songs to earn the status of "musical thoroughbred." And, when the conditions are right, don't bet against this novelty song becoming a winner again with another jockey in the saddle.

She Can't Find Her Keys

"***W**hen Ricky Nelson invented the whole 'Bubble Gum Teen Idol' thing it got a lot of television* producers to thinking,"* remembered Paul Petersen, the star of the beloved ABC family icon *The Donna Reed Show*. "Suddenly those associated with our show were licking their chops hoping to be able to do the same thing with us."

In retrospect, it is surprising that it took ABC so long to decide to use Paul Petersen and Shelley Fabares as recording artists. The audience who tuned in each week to watch them act out the parts of Jeff and Mary Stone numbered in the millions. And more important, what each of these two teens said and did was reported in every television news publication in the country. The fact was that Paul and Shelley were already teen idols, and not exploiting their recording talent in the way that had been done for more than five years with Ricky Nelson was wasting a good deal of the teen stars' earning potential for the network and the production company.

Tony Owen, *Donna Reed*'s executive producer and the star's husband, finally made the decision to have the two kids cut a few records in early 1962. Even as Tony made the calls to put the deal together, the two child stars were not consulted about whether they wanted to go into the studio and record. When the duo was finally "given the script" for this new facet of their careers, Shelley, who believed she had no musical talent, was apprehensive, but Paul was not.

"I relished the opportunity to do the teen idol thing," Paul remembered. "Shelley was upset. She didn't want to do it. The fact was she was a bit scared by it all, but I never met a microphone I didn't like. I was ready. Of course the fact that I never considered the recording business an art form helped me have a positive attitude about the whole experience as well."

Columbia television execs secured producer Stu Phillips of New York to meet with Petersen and Fabares. Phillips, who would go on to become one of television's most important musical directors and composers, brought with him a briefcaseful of demos.

"Stu had been told by Tony Owen to find songs which fit the image of our show," Paul explained. "And that was wise. So Stu had dug through a lot of different demos before bringing them to our meeting. The ones which he had chosen were picked out with an eye to working them into the television show. When written into the script either Shelley or I would be singing them as a part of a show's plot."

One of the songs which Phillips had chosen for Paul was a novelty number about a girl's not being able to find her keys in her purse. The music producer saw it as the perfect plot device. Paul's character of Jeff Stone could be dropping a girl off after a date, the young woman could then dump what seemed like hundreds of items out of a handbag while looking for her house key, and Jeff could sing about this comedic situation to the millions of Americans who had tuned in to *Donna Reed* that week.

"In my mind it was a stupid novelty song which I hated from the beginning," Paul recalled. "I could just picture myself getting stuck with a Stan Freberg reputation [Freberg was a popular parody song artist of the era]. Yet even I had to admit that it was perfect for the show." Besides, like Shelley, Paul had no real choice in the matter anyway.

With a degree of trepidation, Petersen cut "She Can't Find Her Keys," as well as a host of other songs which Stu Phillips had found for him. Shelley was almost dragged into the recording studio to lay down her part of "Johnny Angel" at about the same time. Both singles would be introduced to the public via a "music" segment of *The Donna Reed Show*.

To complete Tony Owen's marketing concept, Colpix Records had been signed to distribute Paul's and Shelley's records. The label already had landed the Marcels, who would sell millions of copies of "Blue Moon," and teenage movie heartthrob James Darren, who would find huge success when he cut "Goodbye Cruel World." With this quartet of "made-for-the-teen-market" artists in house, the publicity push began.

Everyone except for Shelley, who simply wouldn't sing in public, hit the road promoting their product and performing before huge crowds. Paul sang in front of screaming teenage girls on *American Bandstand* and then made his way across the United States as a part of the Dick Clark Summer Tour. Thanks in large part to his promotion work, and the fact that he had a pretty fair voice, Petersen jumped ahead of other television stars turned singers such as Johnny Crawford (*The Rifleman*), Lorne Greene (*Bonanza*), and Richard Chamberlain (*Dr. Kildare*). As a reward for all of his hard work, "She Can't Find Her Keys" jumped into the top twenty and Paul's follow-up single, "My Dad," made the top ten.

Of the several songs which Paul cut and that were used on his show, "Keys" remains the most memorable. As the singer/actor himself opined, "It has become a classic because it is real." The song uncovered and exposed men's complete lack of understanding of not only how women pack so much stuff into a purse, but how it is organized. It is still a fact of life that only males who are very ignorant or very brave will attempt to find something in a woman's handbag. "She Can't Find Her Keys" used comedy to tell this story from a man's point of view, and by doing so touched millions who had actually lived this adventure. It was a great novelty concept which became a hit thanks to the help of the television publicity machine.

Sadly, a problem much greater than finding keys in a crowded bag was being played out at the same time Paul's songs were climbing the charts. It seemed that while Petersen, Fabares, the Marcels, and Darren were selling millions of records for Colpix, the company could never manage to show a profit. No matter how much money singles like "Keys" and "Johnny Angel" seemed to generate, when the accounting department sent out royalty statements, the teenage stars who kept the label afloat were always informed that they owed the company money.

"Colpix sold tens of millions of records," Paul explained. "And when the final accounting was completed I ending up owing them $27,000 and Shelley $40,000. Can you imagine that? I never got a royalty check, and we were told we couldn't audit the books."

Paul Petersen, who survived teenage superstardom and the experiences of being a child actor to go on to a successful life in the world of writing, never forgot all those other child actors who had been scarred forever by everything from unfair accounting to exploitation by parents and the studio. For more than two decades, when these teens would find themselves without work and discover that the millions they had made had been spent or stolen, Paul would step in and find help. In 1990, as he saw conditions become worse rather than better and when the cases of abused child stars had grown to such numbers that he could no longer manage to help each one individually, Petersen formed an organization which reached out not only with aid and spiritual guidance, but also with legal help. Today, A Minor Consideration is at the forefront of making sure that child actors are protected while they work and paving a transition into the real world for these once famous faces when the entertainment business has finished with them.

Paul Petersen is only remembered by most of the public as a former teen idol and onetime television star. Yet for thousands of child actors who were ripped off by the entertainment industry, Paul is the one man they can trust and on whom they can depend. When they are searching for answers, Petersen is there, and unlike the subject of his famous novelty song, he doesn't have to ransack a big bag to find a key to unlock a door that will lead to help and understanding.

Short People

*B*rilliant, incredibly talented, courageous, one of the best pop songwriters of all time, a member of an extraordinarily gifted family—and this overview simply *begins* to describe master scribe and performer Randy Newman. His bio makes him sound like an entertainment giant, and in many ways he is, so it is all the more strange that a man like Newman should be most remembered for a song that helped give real meaning to the phrase "politically incorrect." Yet this is the real "short" story of Randy Newman's strange claim to fame.

Essentially, by focusing more on social and political satire than on love songs, Randy has drawn an artistic impression of himself and his work that still causes many to overlook his incredible writing talents. But who is to really say that just because "Mama Told Me Not to Come" was one of the definitive rockers of its time, "God's Song" wasn't one of the definitive theological musings of its time as well. Facts are facts, and Randy Newman could in fact write about *anything and everything,* and always do it well. His problems were created because most of what he chose to record himself contained messages that were just a bit controversial. It seemed that he gave his "bland" stuff about love and parties to other people.

A college dropout, Newman made his first tiny mark with a Warner Bros. album released in the midst of the sixties social revolution. *Randy Newman* bombed. Yet those within the music community who happened to obtain one of the few copies that weren't destroyed fell in love with the bizarre messages Newman set forth in his debut product. Many thought that Randy's writing was as clever and rich as Mark Twain's. In truth, there were also those who believed it was appropriate that Randy was being marketed by the same folks who produced *Looney Tunes*. Because, after all, who in their right mind wanted to spend real money on lyrics that were wrapped around the world's freaks and forgotten souls?

Four years and two albums after his initial failure, Randy was still not clicking with the radio stations or the general public. Yet he was still shaking up his few loyal fans with messages they were hearing nowhere else. Where else could you hear a song like "Sail Away," which told the story of a slave trader selling a bill of goods to African natives? It turned heads and stomachs, as did "Rednecks" a year later. Those who listened to Randy thought he was good, but many probably also considered him a bit daft and completely uncommercial.

Though he was failing to obtain cash register success as a singer/songwriter, Newman was eating pretty well, as he was writing for a host of talented performers. His list of success stories ran from Judy Collins to Three Dog Night, and scores of his songs were generating big royalties for both the artists and the writer. This allowed him the freedom to continue to plug away on his own projects at Warners and not be dropped by the label. And his writing was the only reason that in 1977, after five false starts, Newman finally managed to reward Warners for its faith and loyalty with a "little" hit of his own.

Randy Newman wrote "Short People" as satire. The song was supposed to make people realize how badly they treated anyone who didn't live up to a certain standard set forth by a rigid society. Thus the writer thought that he was actually revealing prejudice, not taking part in it. Yet as soon as the single was shipped, those who were "vertically challenged" demanded that the song be banned. "It's offensive," they declared, reacting to the song's lead line: "Short people have no reason to live." Of course, the mere fact that a large percentage of the population was rallying against "Short People" meant that another larger and "taller" section of the population was laughing *with* it. Tall people thought it was great!

Newman couldn't believe that anyone was actually serious about wanting "Short People" banned, and so on a tour to promote his live shows and his new album, the singer jokingly spoke of the insecurities of those who had been offended. Surprisingly, he soon discovered that this joke was taken seriously too. He needed police protection as he faced numerous death threats. From there on, the more he opened his mouth and tried to explain away the song's meaning, the more he became convinced that he couldn't win for losing. Everything he said angered everyone under the height of five feet six (Newman had declared that to be the magic cutoff for "short"). Ironically, this anger had finally made Randy Newman commercial.

Disc jockeys loved "Short People," and Newman's ode raced up the charts in late '77. By January of the next year Randy and his single had moved past country music's favorite short person, Dolly Parton, and camped out at #2. "Short People" would hang on to this rather lofty perch for three weeks, only being kept from #1 by the Bee Gees' "Stayin' Alive." Still, not everyone was amused by Randy's joke. Even newspaper columns rallied against the message Newman had sent out. It seemed that while millions loved and laughed with Randy, millions of others wanted to do him in.

"Short People" gave the writer his only trip to the top forty. For Randy, the hot spotlight was a rather uncomfortable place, so he chose to make himself small and disappear. Yet unknown to most of those who had come to either love or hate Newman for declaring that diminutive folks didn't have much reason to exist, after his "short" stay on the charts the writer began one of the most creative periods of his life. Working behind the scenes, Randy composed the sound tracks for a slew of award-winning films, including *The Natural, Toy Story,* and *Ragtime.* By doing the musical work in some of modern

Hollywood's most loved motion pictures, the colorful Newman was following in the footsteps of his uncles, Alfred, Lionel, and Emil. Between them the brothers won nine Oscars for musical scores. And just for the record, the elder Newmans had not only composed for feature-length films, but for "shorts" as well.

Smoke, Smoke, Smoke
(That Cigarette)

One of the most creative forces in country music history was born in Rosewood, Kentucky, in 1917. Merle Robert Travis, the son of a poor banjo-playing mine worker, grew up in the middle of coal country. He lived most of his youth in a rented house that had no running water or electricity. The Travises' landlords and best friends had been slaves until after the Civil War. Life was hard, times were tough, and the only real joy the Travises could afford was the music they made on hand-me-down instruments. Yet it was this life of poverty, as well as the humor that kept many poor families from becoming spiritually bankrupt during these times, that would buy Merle not only a ticket out of the mines, but a chance at international fame as well.

By the time he had reached the age of eight, Merle was plucking a five-string and a homemade guitar. After local Pentecostal meetings the boy would stay late just so Ike Everly (Don and Phil's father), one of the church's finest guitar pickers, could teach him new chords. Young Travis soon mastered the Everly style of thumb and finger picking and began to add to it. Long before he left school in the eighth grade, Merle was known as one of the area's best string men.

In a peculiar irony, the Depression actually improved Merle's life. By enlisting and working in the Civilian Conservation Corps, Travis made enough money to purchase a Gretsch guitar. Teaming with other members of his CCC troop, Travis formed a band and worked the streets for nickels and dimes. This eventually led to a radio job in Evansville, Indiana. By World War II the guitar player had moved up to WLW in Cincinnati. In less than a decade he had escaped the mines and was making good money playing music. The boy who had once been lucky to get patched-up hand-me-downs was now purchasing suits off the rack and driving his own car. Then the marines called him.

Merle continued to play music during his service stint and after the war secured a West Coast music job with western star Tex Ritter. By the middle of 1946 Travis was recording for Capitol and on his way to producing a long string of hit records. The biggest, *Divorce Me C.O.D.*, held #1 on the country charts for fourteen weeks.

Travis was a songwriter of such magnitude that he couldn't even record all of his own efforts, and a lot of the other top country acts sought out his material. One of these, Tex Williams, was in need of a hit in a big way. A recent addition to the Capitol Records stable, Williams had once been the lead singer for the highly successful Spade Cooley band. Swing artist Tex (who was born in Illinois) was gifted with a smooth voice and a great deal of stage presence, and Capitol sensed that he could be a major star. What the label felt Williams needed was a great Merle Travis tune to pave the way for bigger and better things.

The inspiration for the single which would make Tex Williams a brighter recording star than even Merle Travis had come from Merle's father. The elder Travis had always believed that cigarette smoking led to a host of bad habits, including laziness. A foreman in the mine, the elder simply couldn't get his men to work very long before they had to take a break and light up. Recalling all the ranting which he had once heard about the evils of cigarettes, Merle quickly penned a song for Williams.

"Smoke, Smoke, Smoke" truly was a song ahead of its time. Fifty years before presidential candidate Bob Dole got himself in trouble by saying he didn't believe cigarettes were addictive, Travis wrote in his song that anyone who smoked was a "nicotine slave." The songwriter also pointed out that smoking put a stop to everything and that if he had the chance, "I'd murder that son of a gun [the man who invented cigarettes] in the first degree."

Mixing smoke with romance, work, and poker games, the inventive Travis gave Williams a song with which both smokers and nonsmokers could identify. Funny, not meant to be taken seriously, but still pointing out just how much those who lit up were doomed to waste a good deal of their lives and their pocket change repeating this habit time and time again, Merle created a song perfect for Tex Williams's voice and personality.

Capitol Records released "Smoke, Smoke, Smoke (That Cigarette)" in the summer of 1947. Not only would Tex Williams's record go on to become Capitol's first million-seller, but it would top the country charts for sixteen weeks. It would also cross over onto the pop side and rule that playlist for another month and a half. It was the biggest seller of 1947 and was such a strong number that it reappeared on the country or pop charts six more times in the next four decades, recorded by five different artists. Along with "Sixteen Tons," "Smoke, Smoke, Smoke" would become one of Merle Travis's biggest hit songs and pave the way for his induction into the Country Music Hall of Fame.

In the wake of recent reports indicating that everyone from the AMA to the government itself covered up the long-term effects of cigarette smoking for decades, the message of "Smoke, Smoke, Smoke (That Cigarette)" may now seem a bit out of date. While the song did claim that cigarette smoking was addictive and wasted a great deal of productive time, the lyrics also stated, "I don't reckon they'll harm your health." Millions would die proving this statement wrong. As a matter of fact, the subject of Tex Williams's hit single would eventually come back to haunt the singer himself. Lung cancer, the result of Williams's own habit of stopping every once in a while for a smoke, killed him in 1985. In light of Tex's and millions of others' deaths and the fact that teen smoking is at an all-time high, maybe someone should cut a new version of Travis's old song called "Don't Smoke, Don't Smoke, Don't Smoke (That Cigarette)." Now there's a novel idea!

Snoopy Vs.
the Red Baron

*T*he year was 1966, one of the most violent and heated times in modern American history. President Lyndon Johnson was watching his contributions to the "Great Society," in the form of the War on Poverty, be dismissed and forgotten in the wake of a war where thousands of Americans were dying in rice paddies as other Americans protested on college campuses. Never before had there been such a huge gap between parents and their offspring. They called it a "generation gap," and it had laid a channel across the nation longer and wider than the Mississippi River. The Beach Boys may have been beating back the British invasion with "Good Vibrations," but in all honesty there simply weren't very many good vibrations anywhere.

Rock music was in a transitional period. The Motown sound was hot, especially the female trio known as the Supremes. The made-for-television group, the Monkees, were also charting regularly. Stevie Wonder, Johnny Rivers, and even Frank Sinatra were showing up from time to time too. But the Beatles were still the definitive group, and they were leading the rock world to the more acid sounds that would soon control youth culture. It was a time for music with a message, and lost in the mix were the simple songs of teenage love, hot cars, and surf. America's youth thought they were simply too mature for those juvenile considerations.

It would seem like a strange time to have drawn inspiration from the comic pages. It would seem the wrong time to have issued a single glorifying the acts of war. And yet in late 1966, Laurie Records released a song that embraced both the themes of war and the funny pages.

Charles Schulz had been making the country both laugh and think in his comic strip *Peanuts* for a decade. His characters, led by the eternal klutz Charlie Brown, the insecure Linus, and the selfish Lucy, were all members of a neighborhood gang of kids who were losers a great deal more than they were winners. America took these losers to their hearts in a big way. And in simple messages taken from even simpler story lines, Schultz taught moral truths at a time when America was in search of answers and values.

A background character whom readers quickly took to their bosom was Charlie's beagle, Snoopy. Snoopy would never be confused with Lassie or Rin Tin Tin. He was a dog who thought a great deal more of himself than he did of his master. He also lived the adventurous life, at least in his imagination. There, while sleeping on top of his doghouse, he roared into the skies piloting a World War I airplane and seeking out the sky's most legendary ace, Baron Manfred von Richthofen.

There really had been a flying ace Richthofen who had become known as the Red Baron and had shot down more than eight enemy planes during World War I. So there was no arguing that the Baron really had ruled the skies of Europe during the First World War. Then Richthofen had run into a Brit named Brown. The English flier had brought the Baron down and with that act turned the tide of the war in the skies in the Allies' favor for the duration. Yet in Snoopy's mind, the war and the Red Baron were still out there, and it was his job to race into the clouds and seek out either death or victory in a face-to-face battle with the "Bloody Baron."

Songwriter Phil Gernhard couldn't help but notice the amount of merchandise that was being generated via the *Peanuts* comic strip.

He also couldn't help but observe that a great deal of it showed Snoopy flying through the skies on his doghouse dressed in a long scarf and a World War I vintage flier's cap. Inspired, Gernhard, who was also a record producer, scribbled down some words and music about the dog's most memorable battle. He entitled it, "Snoopy Vs. the Red Baron."

Gernhard had been trying to score a hit for an Ocala, Florida, group called the Royal Guardsmen. The quintet consisted of Barry Winslow, Chris Nunley, Tom Richards, Bill Balough, and Billy Taylor. Like many rock groups of the era they were a guitar-driven band that also used an organ. Initially, Gernhard had brought the men into Laurie's music studio to cut straight material. But the Guardsmen's first release, "Baby Let's Wait," had not made it onto any top forty charts. Looking for another opportunity to give the group a break, the producer began to consider the five for his novelty number about Charlie Brown's dog.

During the days when Gernhard was fiddling with Snoopy, National Guardsmen were seen as the enemy by many American youth. And as this was a period during which teens were burning draft cards and retreating to Canada to duck military service, it should have seemed a poor time to have a group with a military-sounding name cut a song that glorified battle, war, and even death. Logic should have told Gernhard to hold the song. But the producer ignored all of those signs and brought the Royal Guardsmen back into the studio to lay down the tracks on the Snoopy epic.

Released in early winter, "Snoopy Vs. the Red Baron" took off like a jet. The week before Christmas saw the song land in the top forty, at #30. Two weeks later, on December 31, 1966, the single was resting at #2, topped only by the Monkees' "I'm a Believer." For the next four weeks the two songs would hold those positions and the Guardsmen would be on their way to network television appearances and national tours.

The momentum created by a novelty concept is often hard to sustain, and "Snoopy" only flew for eleven weeks on the playlists before spinning out of sight. Despite a follow-up, "The Return of the Red Baron," that managed to climb into the top twenty some three months later, the Royal Guardsmen were also soon grounded. Though they had a solid sound and some genuine talent, everyone thought of them as little more than vocal members of the Snoopy fan club. They couldn't get a break. Their hit was simply much bigger than they were, and the star of their hit was even bigger than the hit itself. So the very thing that made them, destroyed them.

A Christmas album got the group some airplay in late 1967. Naturally, the number which sparked that play was "Snoopy's Christmas Song." But though they continued to perform and work in the studio, they only appeared on the playlists one more time, in 1969, with a reissue of their first release for Laurie, "Baby Let's Wait." As the old proverb says, "He who lies down with dogs often is ignored forever," and so it was with the Royal Guardsmen. (Then again, the dog seems to have done pretty well for himself!)

Why, in the face of Vietnam, did "Snoopy" fly so well? The answer may go a bit deeper than that it simply rode the crest of a comic book sensation. Snoopy's war was against an enemy that had brought the nation together, not torn it apart. The beagle's battle was one that had been fought for something which United States citizens understood and believed in. Deep down, both young and old were seeking something that the battle in Vietnam did not seem to provide—a war with moral value. Snoopy was fighting in just such a war, and just as the nation had fifty years before with her doughboys, we supported him. But Snoopy never went to Vietnam. It seemed that this was a war that even he couldn't win.

The Streak

*R*ay Stevens is one of the most gifted musical talents to ever grace the stage of the Grand Ole Opry, the Hollywood Bowl, and Carnegie Hall. He is a little bit country, part rock and roll, and a touch of blues and gospel. In life the man who was born Henry Ragsdale in Clarksdale, Georgia, and who often plays every instrument used in his recording sessions, is often deadly serious, but onstage he is usually more off-the-wall than Jonathan Winters. Turn on a spotlight and the sly grin appears and he seems to find a laugh behind every note, yet as he works by himself in the studio one senses that the very genre which has made Ray Stevens famous has also vastly limited his ability to use his incredible wealth of God-given talent. Though few know it, this is an often quiet and introspective individual, a deep thinker with a deep thirst to create.

Born in the years just before World War II, Stevens drifted to Nashville after studying music theory and composition at Georgia State University. First signing with Capitol Records in 1957, Ray moved on to Mercury in 1961. His first cut for the new label, "Jeremiah Peabody's Poly Unsaturated Quick Dissolving Fast Acting Pleasant Tasting Green and Purple Pills," gave him a #40 single. It also seemed to set in motion a pattern of novelty songs which would take him to the top of the charts on several occasions over the next three decades.

"Ahab the Arab" was Stevens's first huge comedy hit. Several other chart busters followed, including "Harry the Hairy Ape" and "Gitarzan." The latter earned Ray his first certified Gold Single. A dozen years into his career Ray was so defined by his comedic talents that he was rarely taken seriously. Yet in 1971 Stevens seemed ready to shrug off his comedic collar when he released what would become his first #1 single, "Everything Is Beautiful." He followed that with a fresh arrangement of the old pop standard "Misty." By 1973 Ray Stevens had almost reached his goal of becoming recognized as a serious entertainer. Then he got another quirky idea.

As is often the case with performers, Ray spent so much time on the road doing shows that he was often out of touch with fads which were sweeping the country. It was while he was on a long plane ride that he picked up a paper and read a report of a naked man dressed in sneakers who had been seen racing through a crowded store. Stevens, who had often composed songs about bizarre characters, was amused that anyone would think that running nude was a joke. Still, he was shocked a few days later when he discovered that thousands were doing just that every night.

Even though he had promised himself that he was going to play things straight, Ray simply couldn't stay away from the idea of a song about a guy who took great delight in "streaking" in front of other folks. Through several writing sessions, Stevens fleshed out his idea, then got dressed and raced over to Barnaby Records to cut "The Streak."

Ray was not alone in realizing that the latest fad was ripe for musical commentary. Scores of other streaking songs were being produced in almost every part of the country. Fortunately, Barnaby quickly turned around Stevens's "The Streak" and Ray beat the other folks to the punch. The loony single, which would undo all the work Ray had put into trying to get the world to take him seriously, was shipped in April. It moved from #84 to #19 in its first two weeks on the rock charts and took the #1 spot away from Grand Funk's "The

Loco-Motion" on May 18. "The Streak" would hold the top spot for three weeks. On the country side Ray would claim a strong #3 at about the same time.

It now seems a shame that "The Streak" was written and produced before the advent of video and MTV. There is little doubt that Ray's creative mind could have done wonders with his biggest hit in the video format. As it was, the images Stevens conjured up through his song's crazy lyrics painted pictures that probably made many a churchgoer blush. And the song was so good that if that person listened to a radio, he or she had the opportunity to blush time and time again.

"The Streak" did a great deal to charge Ray Stevens's career and wit. Over the course of the next few years he scored again and again with such musical laughfests as "Shriners' Convention," "Would Jesus Wear a Rolex," "Mississippi Squirrel Convention," and "I Need Your Help, Barry Manilow." His concerts, videos, and television appearances cemented his wacky and wild image and seemed to engrave in stone Ray's stage persona. Now, with more than two dozen novelty hits under his belt, Stevens can lay claim to being the most creative funnyman in music. Yet, one wonders if the often introspective genius who has made millions laugh would have passed on writing his biggest hit if he had known that no matter what he wore once he'd penned it, he would never be taken seriously again.

Take This Job and Shove It

If there ever was a country music star with an attitude, it was Johnny Paycheck. In the 1970s, his run-ins with the law, his barroom brawls, and his greatly publicized drug problems, as well as his lack of respect for authority, made him Nashville's equivalent to many of the rap acts of the 1990s. Born Donald Eugene Lyle, the singer had already performed under a number of different handles and been in trouble a few times before joining the navy in the late fifties. His time in uniform didn't go smoothly either. Lyle's enlistment was cut short by a court-martial and a sentence in the brig. Drummed out of the navy for his lack of responsible behavior, the singer migrated to Nashville in 1959. Famed producer Buddy Killen listened to Lyle, liked what he heard, and signed him to a deal with Decca. Killen also gave Donald the name Donny Young.

Donald Eugene Lyle had little more success under the name of Donny Young than he'd had when he'd toured in his younger days as the "Ohio Kid." Soon Decca lost interest in him, and the singer was forced to knock on door after door looking for a new deal. To supplement his income while he waited for a record deal, Lyle worked with a number of different bands. But his temper and often bizarre behavior meant that he never held any job for very long. To put it mildly, he was a pain in the neck who spent as much time telling people where to stick it as he did doing things the right way. Nevertheless, he always found someone willing to give him just one more chance.

In the mid-sixties Lyle renamed himself after a boxer, Johnny Paycheck. He also earned a short contract with Hilltop Records. It didn't take long for that stint to play out. Another label stepped up and signed the singer in 1966, but Paycheck's time with Little Darlin' Records was also unproductive. By the early seventies, he had seemingly used up his chances in Music City, his writing revenue had dried up, and he packed his bags. Bitter, Paycheck caught a ride to Los Angeles and got involved with drugs.

Johnny was literally rescued from a life as a skid-row bum by producer Billy Sherrill. In 1971, Billy got Paycheck a deal with Epic, and the singer finally produced a major hit, "She's All I Got." It would have seemed that this bit of good fortune would straighten Johnny out. Yet a year later Johnny got in trouble with the law again, over bad checks. So even during the good times, it seemed, the singer would find ways to bring himself down.

After a five-year dry period, Paycheck produced two top ten records in 1977 and seemed ready to once again become a viable force in country music. Yet probably because of his unpredictable behavior, Epic didn't spend a great deal on publicizing the now forty-year-old performer. More often than not, Johnny had embarrassed his label. Because of this, the relationship between Paycheck and Epic was at best an uncomfortable one. Many even thought the label was looking for an excuse to drop Johnny altogether.

In order to really establish himself as a major force and keep on solid ground at Epic, Paycheck needed a song that not only fit his outlaw image, but would also earn a #1 status on the charts. The man who stepped to the front with the answer to this need understood Johnny only too well.

David Allan Coe had spent over half of his life behind bars. He also was often consumed by the same kind of anger which had plagued Paycheck's career. Coe, whose career is more completely documented in *You Never Even Call Me by My Name,* was just as likely to tell someone to go to hell as he was to shake their hand. And like Johnny, David seemed to play up this outlaw image every chance he got.

Coe had used the new song's title line when explaining to people what he would do if he ever found himself working as a fireman. Employing this sentiment as the song's title and the hook for his chorus, David used his own belligerent attitude for the song's style and message. In the end, what Coe finally fashioned was a song that spoke directly to the millions of men and women who were tired of slaving away at jobs they hated. In three minutes he summed up millions of hours of frustration for millions upon millions of both blue-collar and white-collar employees. He had also summed up both his and Johnny Paycheck's view of life.

Johnny had been losing money and opportunities by telling people to shove it for years. Now, with this song, the singer could use his anger to speak for millions of others. Besides, "Take This Job and Shove It" seemed like the perfect vehicle for a man whose name was Paycheck.

The attitude needed to sell the lyrics of "Take This Job" came straight from the heart. This was *his* song, Johnny felt, and it was also a song he had lived out more times than he cared to remember. This had been his attitude when he had been booted out of the navy and ushered out of numerous recording studios. Now, in a bit of irony that didn't elude the singer, he was getting to shout at the top of his lungs, "Take This Job and Shove It," and by doing so getting to make some real money for both himself and his employer.

"Take This Job" jumped onto the country music charts in late 1977 and by the first week in January had hit #1. The Paycheck release would hold the top spot for two weeks and remain on the playlists for eighteen. Just as "Convoy" had become the truckers' national anthem, "Take This Job and Shove It" became the theme song for all of the world's disgruntled workers. It also became the inspiration for a movie by the same name. Yet the man who sang the song never really stopped to enjoy the rewards of his work.

After "Take This Job and Shove It," Johnny Paycheck would never again top the charts. Within five years he not only didn't have a record label, he was fighting several battles in court. Faced with charges of slander and libel, as well as disorderly conduct, Johnny again consoled his pain with booze and drugs. On December 19, 1985, the singer stopped at a bar in Hillsboro, Ohio, got into a fight, and shot a man. He was sentenced to seven years in prison. And for perhaps the first time in his life, Johnny Paycheck was faced with a situation where he couldn't say "shove it" and walk away.

Teen Angel

Of all the songs which are regularly played on oldies-formatted stations, "Teen Angel" is the one the current generation finds hardest to fathom. Today's kids can't imagine any girl being stupid enough to race back into a car about to be hit by a forty-ton locomotive just to save her boyfriend's class ring. Besides, most of them point out, why wasn't she wearing it in the first place? If it wasn't important enough to already have on her finger or around her neck, then it certainly wasn't worth a return trip to a death trap. And in all honesty, today's kids are right!

So, of all the teenage "death" songs of the rock and roll era, "Teen Angel" ranks ahead of "Running Bear," "Patches," and even "Tell Laura I Love Her" as the most inane. Yet this didn't keep the MGM single from becoming not only a #1 record, but one of the most remembered songs of the sixties or any other era.

The song was sung by a young man who seemed destined to make his living as a singer. The product of a large Oklahoma family, this preacher's son had often been turned over to a baby-sitter because his older siblings, the Dinning Sisters, were recording and radio stars. In the forties, Ginger, Lou, and Jean placed four songs on the charts for Capitol, two of which went top ten. The sisters' version of "Button and Bows" was even certified gold. Hence, the Dinning family had experienced the sweet taste of entertainment glory.

Mark's baby-sitter was as impressed with the Dinning musical success as the brother was. Clara Ann Fowler, a local beauty, would leave Oklahoma, change her name to Patti Page, and become the most successful female recording artist of all time. (How much of this was due to Page's personal drive and how much was due to the Dinning inspiration is open to debate.)

With the success of the Dinning Sisters and Patti Page, it came as no surprise when the Dinning boys, Mark and Ace, formed a group of their own in the early fifties. Who knows how far they would have gotten if the army hadn't called for Mark. At that point Ace must have drifted back to the family farm, because he never charted as a Dinning.

It was while he was in the service that Mark affirmed that he was going to follow in his sisters' footsteps and become a part of the entertainment field. And with rock and roll opening up new territory for young male acts, Mark's 1957 release from the service seemed to be perfectly timed for the young man to accomplish his goal. But a majority of the talent scouts who heard the young man weren't impressed. To most of the folks in Nashville it seemed that Dinning was just one of thousands who thought he was the next Elvis and wasn't!

Wesley Rose, the son of the man who had discovered Hank Williams, finally rescued Mark from oblivion. Impressed with his good looks, sincere manner, and singing voice, the publisher went to work landing Dinning a record deal. The company that would eventually sign the young man was the same one that had taken Fred Rose's advice and placed Hank Williams under contract a decade before. MGM would soon find that it hadn't signed the second coming of "Luke the Drifter," but the signing wouldn't be a complete waste of time and money, either.

For a couple of years Mark played rock and roll, but without much success; he didn't produce anything that hit the top forty. He might never had made an impact if one of his sisters hadn't gotten involved. It seemed that Jean, who had dropped out of music and was now married, had read an article about the need for positive role models among American youth. At this time, many preachers were basing sermons on the belief that rock and roll was creating a nation filled with juvenile delinquents. The author of the magazine story had suggested that good kids should be called "Teen Angels" and recognized for their proper conduct. One look at the popular catchphrases of the time proves that this concept never took off—but it did give Jean an idea for a song.

Jean, writing under her married name Surrey, composed her morbid classic of teenage love in one night. She would later play it for Mark at a family get-together at their folks' home. Mark used his parents' tape recorder and cut a simple version of "Teen Angel" in a plaintive, direct manner at the kitchen table. Jean then had a few demo 45s made from that rough cut. One of these cuts made it to Acuff-Rose publishing in late 1959.

Wesley Rose liked the demo on "Teen Angel" and turned it over to one of the world's best songwriters, Felice Bryant. Felice and her husband had written most of the Everly Brothers' early hits and knew the youth market very well. Felice also liked the song's hit potential, but suggested a few changes in some of the lines. Rose and Dinning agreed to the rewrite and took this slightly changed version to MGM. Needing a hit for Mark, the label took a chance that "Teen Angel" might have wings and put him in the studio for a session.

Even before MGM shipped "Teen Angel," there was talk about the single's being blacklisted. Many felt that the fact that the teenage girl dies in such a tragic, idiotic, and senseless manner might turn off radio programmers (a few did refuse to air the single). Death was a taboo subject in many markets, and certainly it was the theme of death which drove "Teen Angel." Nevertheless, MGM shipped Dinning's "Teen Angel." As the song hit the charts on January 4, 1960, the label was assured that it had made the proper decision. But as the record really began to take off over the next two weeks, its success shocked even those at the company who had actually liked the morbid song in the first place.

It took just three weeks for "Teen Angel" to make it from its top forty chart debut to #1. In that brief period of time, Mark Dinning went from being a nobody to appearing before screaming, and in some cases crying, teenagers on *American Bandstand*. For fourteen weeks the singer and the song hung on to the national playlists and became a small part of the history of the "teen idol" era of rock and roll. Then "Teen Angel" died.

His sister's song had finally given Mark Dinning something he had wanted since his early childhood—a hit—but "Teen Angel" might also have doomed his chances for any further musical success. It seemed that the young man was so identified with this tragic and stupid song about a girl who loved a twenty-dollar ring more than she did life itself that he was never taken seriously as an artist. For Dinning, "Teen Angel" might just have been the devil in disguise.

 Tennessee Birdwalk

*I*n 1970, "Tennessee Birdwalk," a comedy number centering on birdbaths and "fowl" underwear, put a young married couple on the map. This madcap special would also prove to be the only time that the duo was able to wing its way to the top of the charts. But getting a chance to fly in rare air, if only once, is something which both of them had dreamed of all of their lives. So for Jack Blanchard and Misty Morgan, being forgotten today is better than having never been noticed at all.

Jack Blanchard was born in New York just months before the United States entered World War II. By the time he left high school, the young man had played in a couple of bands and dreamed of making his niche in show business. Proficient on several instruments, Blanchard worked his way to Hollywood, Florida, in the early sixties and began to entertain nightclub patrons with both his songs and his comedic skills. Though no one was predicting that the young man would make it big in Music City or L.A., he was at least able to make a living by his own rules.

Like Jack, Misty Morgan was also born in New York, only she made her first appearance on earth during the final days of the Second World War. A child prodigy, as a teen she took her vocal talents and piano skills and hooked up with several different live shows. While in her early twenties she migrated from Ohio to Hollywood, Florida, and found a spot performing in a nightclub just down the street from the one where Jack worked.

As a result of Misty's auditioning for Jack's job, the two got to know each other and began to date. One thing led to another, and Blanchard and Morgan fell in love and got married. Logic should have suggested that the two musical talents team up, but at first they didn't. It took more than five years of Misty's working alone and Jack's singing with his own band for the two of them to decide to try music as a duo.

During the late sixties Blanchard's band had broken up, his dates had dried up, and he and his wife were in danger of losing what little they had. Things had gotten so bad that the couple had been forced to work in a department store over the Christmas holidays. With Jack playing Santa and Misty his pretty little elf, they had earned enough to stay afloat. But it had taken teamwork, so in the interest of eating, they opted to keep the team together at home and on the job.

A Florida radio personality caught the couple's new musical act at a local club date and sent a record scout their way. Impressed with the couple's musical harmonies and onstage high jinks, Rickie Johnson of little-known Wayside Records signed them to a contract in 1968. Within just a few months, Jack and Misty had hit the charts and vowed to never play Santa and his elf again.

Jack's comedic skill was what had really impressed promoter Johnson, so he urged him to compose songs which drew on his unique outlook on life. The reason Rickie sought the ridiculous rather than the deep was his need to turn a quick profit for his small company. The fact was that for a label like Wayside, it was far easier to get stations to play a novelty song than it was a serious love ballad. Hence, they wanted something closer to "Tip-Toe thru the Tulips" than "You Don't Bring Me Flowers." Added to this was the fact that the only duet teams making any kind of noise in country music at this time were the results of the molding of two successful solo acts into one. At this point Jack and Misty simply didn't have the drawing power of Porter and Dolly or Conway and Loretta.

The song which Blanchard brought to the studio that seemed to best meet Rickie Johnson's needs was "Tennessee Birdwalk." To the folks at Wayside the song's lyrics sounded like something that might have come from the mind of a Roger Miller or Ray Stevens. Some could even picture it being used as the story line for a Warner Bros. cartoon. Still, they had to wonder if a simple number about a "modest" bird in his underwear and the trouble that seemed to follow him everywhere would fly in the contemporary country market. How many people would care about a hapless pigeon?

What made "Birdwalk" unique enough to assure Wayside that it was worth the risk of spending money to produce and promote it was the almost monotonous melody line and the straightforward harmonies which Jack and Misty employed when performing the song. They didn't sound like anyone else on the market, and the couple's deadpan and serious style was perfectly suited for the song's nonsensical message. Rickie figured that this marriage of the senseless and the serious might just be bizarre enough to interest programmers and fans alike.

Wayside shipped "Tennessee Birdwalk" to radio stations in early 1970. The song made the charts in February and two months later hit #1. Surprising everyone at the label, the single then took off on the pop charts too—spurred on by its rapid rise to the top in Nashville, rock stations picked Jack and Misty up in late March, and by the middle of May the duo had reached #23.

Wayside assumed that it had dialed the right combination and that Jack Blanchard and Misty Morgan were about to become the biggest things to hit the country comedy scene since Ray Stevens. The label therefore hurriedly shipped out a novelty follow-up to "Birdwalk," this time using a slightly larger beast to earn laughs and sales. Unfortunately, "Humphrey the Camel" couldn't ride to the top of the Music City–based charts and barely made a blip on *Billboard*'s rock top one hundred list. It seemed that what was funny a first time couldn't generate as many laughs on the second, third, fourth, or even ninth try. And the couple's attempts at recording straight songs of love and passion failed as well.

For Jack Blanchard and Misty Morgan, their time in the spotlight was brief. And as country stations rarely go back and pick up songs to program into an oldies format, it is likely that most of those who have turned country music into a multibillion-dollar business have never even heard of the couple. Yet for a few folks who tuned in to "Tennessee Birdwalk" in the early seventies, spotting a lonely bird splashing in a birdbath will always create a smile and bring back the memories of the simple harmonies of a couple whose name they just can't quite seem to remember.

They're Coming to Take Me Away, Ha-Haaa!

*I*t was one of the fastest-moving songs in the history of *rock and roll. It sold five hundred thousand copies dur-*ing its first week of release. It was so hot that it debuted on the rock charts at #50 and the very next week had already climbed to #11. On August 13, 1966, it moved to #3 and seemed ready to roll the #1 "Summer in the City" right off the charts. Then, for reasons that mystified millions, the nation's hottest song simply disappeared; one day it was there and the next it had been taken away. *Very strange!* Then again, "They're Coming to Take Me Away, Ha-Haaa!" was a very strange song and touched on some very strange emotions.

In his late teens Jerry Samuels had spent some time in a mental institution. Unlike many who spoke of terrible days locked in rooms with screaming lunatics, Jerry felt that the period during which he was "locked up" had been very rewarding. A natural observer of people, Samuels spent a great deal of his spare time at the mental institution (and he had a great deal of spare time there) watching what was going on around him. What he and those who became his friends there often noted was just how much there was at which to poke fun and laugh. Samuels would later say that it was laughter, in fact, that had enabled him to survive those days.

By 1964, Jerry was living in New York and had managed to use a combination of creative juices and his keen observation skills to carve out a niche in the world of music. A recording studio engineer, he was also finding success as a songwriter. One of his compositions, "The Shelter of Your Arms," had been cut by Sammy Davis Jr. and had found a place in the top twenty. Things were certainly looking up for the man who had once been considered a bit off the mark. But the happily married and up-and-coming Samuels couldn't completely forget his past. It wasn't the dark days at the mental facility which haunted him, however; it was the many wonderful people who had shared with him their humor and unique outlooks on life during those days.

Taking pen in hand, Jerry put together a song that embraced the period in his life when everyone he knew was unafraid to make fun of themselves. This carefree attitude of acceptance and laughter was a long way from the "normal" world Samuels toiled in now. Now, those who weren't "crazy" seemed too busy to even smile, much less laugh. And how seriously they took themselves as they walked along city streets or shopped in stores. *Where is the fun?* the writer begged to know. *Where is the joy and the laughter?*

It took a few months for the young man to finish his ode to the insane. When Jerry was finally satisfied with the strange number, he popped down a few dollars to put his music and words on a demo record. It was 1965—the Beatles were ruling the charts, the country was still dealing with the loss of JFK, the civil rights movement was turning the nation upside down, and Vietnam was becoming a regular fixture on television newscasts. And in the midst of all the confusion and craziness, Jerry Samuels was shopping a song about a man who had lost his mind simply because his girl had deserted him. In a logical time, who would have given "They're Coming to Take Me Away, Ha-Haaa!" a second look? But 1965 was hardly the most logical of times, and there were many people who indeed thought that this new, rapidly changing world was driving them closer to crazy every day.

Warner Bros. immediately saw the commercial potential of "They're Coming to Take Me Away, Ha-Haaa!"; it bought the rights to the demo and didn't even bother recutting it. The simple and rather crude recording that Jerry had made was deemed good enough for radio standards. But rather than release it under the writer's real name, the label suggested that Jerry come up with a professional handle. Grabbing on the standard Hollywood image of the mentally ill, Samuels chose Napoleon. After all, in the movies there was always at least one guy who walked around asylums thinking he was the famous French general. It seemed to make sense that if a crazy man knew there were other crazy men who thought they were Napoleon, then that crazy man would need to set himself apart, so Jerry added the Roman numerals for the number fourteen after Napoleon. When Warners released "They're Coming to Take Me Away, Ha-Haaa!" the crazy-sounding Napoleon XIV was listed as the recording artist. To have even more fun the label recorded the song backwards and put it on the B side of the "legitimate" version. No one ever stopped to consider that there were individuals who might just take this record seriously.

Most Americans immediately loved Jerry Samuels's latest composition. Most could see the humor in a song about a man who had gone so crazy that there were men in white suits coming to get him. Former mental patients seemed to really love it. Yet many who worked in the mental health profession felt that this song was cruel and smacked of prejudice. Petitions were signed, newspaper stories were written, investigations were demanded, and the noisy minority got "They're Coming to Take Me Away, Ha-Haaa!" banned after just five weeks in the top forty.

Having the song pulled from under him might have been the best thing that could have happened to Jerry. The crowds who listened and raved about the song at live shows were a bit more crazy than those who had been locked up with the songwriter. Many of them were cruel, and rather than seeing the humor in the hit, they were more interested in tearing down the performer and anyone else they deemed as crazy. As Jerry was disguised as Napoleon XIV, no one knew just what he looked like, and this was probably in his best interest. Some of the teenagers might just have tormented Samuels and the others who had been hired by the label to lip-sync the record while dressed up as Napoleon at live shows; they might have even attacked them. As Jerry would find out, it was the real world that was filled with crazy people.

"They're Coming to Take Me Away, Ha-Haaa!" was really meant as a salute to survival, but the story behind the funny song was lost on those who should have known better. As Jerry proved, it usually wasn't the patients in the institutions who took life too seriously, but rather those who treated them. Maybe the ones who had Jerry Samuels's song banned should have been taken away. Maybe over time, the pressures of being so serious got to them and they were. Ha-haaa!

Tie Me
Kangaroo Down, Sport

*I*n the late fifties Rolf Harris was a broke Australian living in England and dabbling in music; then he and his brother came up with the idea of a song that combined some of the images of their native land with a sound known as calypso that was sweeping the world. Harris figured that if he could mate a kangaroo with something that sounded like Harry Belafonte, he could tear up the charts and have the fans hopping. So, using a unique Caribbean beat and every native Australian animal he could remember, Rolf scribbled twelve verses of something he called "Kangalypso." He then tried out his new composition in his club act.

During this period the world was buying records like "Witch Doctor" by the millions, so it would have seemed that fans and record labels alike would have been jumping for Harris's calypso-flavored Outback, off-the-wall epic. But in fact, the first time he sang "Kangalypso," Rolf was almost booed off the stage. And when he previewed the new tune for a record producer, he was met with absolute disdain. The singer just assumed that the Brits didn't fathom the real depth of an Aussie's sense of humor, so when he returned home he brought out his "old friend" and found a live audience for his song about a dying man. He discovered that people, and kids especially, loved it.

In 1961, Harris made a demo of the record, now known as "Tie Me Kangaroo Down, Sport," and shipped it to a label in Sydney. The company liked it, tried it on a radio station, received hundreds of requests to replay it, and then released it. Within a month Rolf was no longer a starving artist—the singer/songwriter had the #1 song in his homeland. The single would end up selling pretty well in the rest of the United Kingdom too. In Canada it hit the charts, in Great Britain it went into the top ten, and it was even rumored that the Queen Mum loved it. Yet in the United States it was ignored for two years.

In 1963, just before America fell under the spell of Beatlemania, folk music was impacting both rock and country music. Epic Records sensed that Rolf Harris's Australian hit might just have a shot, so it contacted him and obtained the U.S. rights to "Tie Me Kangaroo Down, Sport." Shipped in June, the song immediately became a cult classic. In an era when the surf sound was the defining influence on youth, a song from a land with more beaches than anywhere else "wiped out" the competition. "Tie Me Kangaroo Down, Sport" jumped into the top ten the first week in July and peaked at #3 seven days later. It would continue to hold America in its pocket and hop around the top forty for nine weeks. The easy-to-sing-along-with classic would become the most beloved import from Down Under until Olivia Newton-John hit the charts more than a decade later.

Rolf Harris, whose entire career now revolved around the wobble-board sound that he had created in "Kangaroo," couldn't follow up his silly smash hit. But the song did create a rash of imitations. The best of these jumped onto the country charts in late 1963, as Arthur "Guitar Boogie" Smith and His Cracker-Jacks parodied the parody with "Tie My Hunting Dog Down, Jed."

There was little doubt that Rolf Harris owed a great deal of the success that "Tie Me Kangaroo Down, Sport" had given him to the millions of children who not only made their parents purchase a copy of it, but then memorized all the ditty's words and sang them in

schoolyards all around the world. It seemed that these kids were absolutely fascinated with kangaroos, dingoes, koala bears, and almost
everything else Australian. Capitalizing on this fact, Harris returned
to England and starred for years in a children's show on which he
featured not only "Tie Me Kangaroo Down, Sport," but a host of
other classic kids' compositions inspired by the stories of the land,
animals, and people from Down Under. In other words, Britain finally
paid for having rejected Rolf and his unique song in the first place
by having to hear it on television stations every week for years.

Tip-Toe thru the Tulips

When Joe Burke and Al Dubin sat down and wrote the words and music to "Tip-Toe thru the Tulips," Herbert Khaury hadn't been born yet. But the combination of the songwriters' work and Herbert's stage persona would not only plant this bunch of "Tulips" on the map five decades after it was written, it would also lead to one of television's most bizarre moments.

For decades Burke and Dubin churned out hundreds of songs aimed for musicals on both the Broadway stage and Hollywood films. Because many of the musicals of any era often use songs that have no meaning for the plot, the singer, or the audience, the writing team was not limited by the common views of life and love. No matter how strange the inspiration or how unusual the circumstance, Burke and Dubin were free to go with it. Hence the origins of epics such as "Crazy as a Loon," "Muchacha," "What Has Become of Hinky Dinky Parlay Voo," and an honorable mention for this book, "It Looks Like Rain on Cherry Blossom Lane."

But the two writers also had a hand in some of the great songs of this century. Imagine show business without "Forty-second Street," Busby Berkeley not having his "Honeymoon Hotel," or a cowboy not being able to serenade his sweetheart with "Along the Sante Fe Trail." In their era Burke and Dubin were master tunesmiths, and there is little doubt that during the Great Depression their work lightened up many a movie patron's darkest days. At their best they were geniuses, and on their off days their songs were a lot of fun.

At about the same time that Burke and Dubin were supplying the golden age of the silver screen scores of great tunes each year, Herbert Khaury was being born in New York City. Like the two writers, Herb had been bitten by the entertainment bug early on, and for as long as he could remember the boy planned on making it big as a singer. More than three decades later, having changed stage names and performing styles more often than many people change suits, Khaury was still an unknown and unappreciated club act in Greenwich Village. He probably would have remained that way if not for a bit of luck and the advent of the hippie age.

Trying to fit in, the incredibly pale and toothy Herb grew his curly locks well past his shoulders. Trying to stand out, the large and soft-bodied Khaury changed his name again, this time to Tiny Tim, and played a ukulele as part of his act. Finally, in perhaps an ill-begotten attempt to imitate either Frankie Valli or Lou Christie, the performer began to sing in a grating falsetto. This combination of look, sound, and downright weirdness was spotted by a network talent (we use the term loosely in this case) scout and earned the performer, now almost forty years old, a chance to have it socked to him on television's most off-the-wall series, *Laugh-In*.

Laugh-In was hip, cool, and on the edge, all the things which Tiny Tim was not. Yet for some reason the singer fit in with the bizarre cast of characters who made up the laugh troupe for the highly rated NBC show. Not only did the audience love making fun of TT, but other show business professionals, such as Johnny Carson, saw the opportunity for some sure laughs by hooking up with Double T as well.

During his on-screen interviews with Johnny, Tiny Tim came off as a cross between the slowest kid in school and the world's biggest wimp. He just seemed like the kind of guy that bullies loved to beat up. Carson's deadpan expressions coupled to Tim's idiosyncratic statements made for classic TV. For that reason, Tiny Tim was invited back time and time again.

Reprise Records, the home of none other than Frank Sinatra, was captivated by the cult following that TT was generating via *Laugh-In* and *The Tonight Show*. The label offered the performer a contract and put him in the studio. Ukulele in hand, Tiny Tim cut his most requested number, none other than Burke and Dubin's "Tip-Toe thru the Tulips." Tiny Tim's version was much different from the one that had been used in *Gold Diggers of Broadway* or the single that Nick Lucas had taken to the top of the charts in 1929. When judged strictly from the standpoint of royalties generated, it was a much better one, too!

Tim's trembling falsetto quickly joined the Stones and the Beatles on the charts. It was a true novelty rendition of a true novelty song (who could or would ever tiptoe through tulips?), and millions rushed out to purchase the single, and later the album. And in developments that even Mr. Ripley wouldn't have believed, Tiny Tim suddenly found himself not only on *Billboard*'s top twenty, but appearing before thousands on the concert trail too. Then, as if things couldn't get any stranger than having women swoon at the feet of an overweight, homely, pale, middle-aged man singing in a weak, high-pitched vibrato, Tiny Tim announced that he was going to get married to the love of his life, a much younger woman he called "Miss Vicki."

Tiny Tim's actual wedding ceremony took place on *The Tonight Show*. Tim was so excited by the prospect of his honeymoon with the woman he claimed was as "pure as the driven snow" that he almost hyperventilated on national television. Somehow, Johnny Carson kept the boy from fainting dead on the set, and the couple was able to walk through the tulips that decorated the stage. But this highly rated moment in the nuptial spotlight would be Double T's last hurrah.

By 1970 Tiny Tim was history. His gimmick had grown old. He made another brief overhyped appearance to announce the birth of his daughter Tulip, then faded away altogether. As he departed he probably took with him all chances of the Burke/Dublin composition's ever being recorded again. "Tip-toe thru the Tulips" will now always be considered Tiny Tim's song. And with his mark on it, who else would want it!

Toot, Toot, Tootsie!
(Goo'Bye)

If you were to ask someone today, "Who is the world's greatest entertainer?" you might have a flurry of votes for Michael Jackson, the late Elvis Presley, Frank Sinatra, and maybe even a few for the likes of Madonna, Garth Brooks, or Barbra Streisand. If this same question had been posed in 1930, almost 100 percent of those responding would have named Al Jolson. For the first half of this century Jolson was the only man known as "The World's Greatest Entertainer."

The road to earning the title of entertainment's best was not an easy one for this Russian immigrant. He went to work on vaudeville's stages at an age when most are beginning high school. From his youth his life was filled with long days spent mastering intricate comic routines and dance steps. Day after day he traveled, performed, slept, traveled and performed some more. The boy's life was a hard one which was dedicated to one thing alone: earning the appreciation of each night's audience.

By the time Al hit the age of twenty-five in 1911, he was a Broadway star. A year later Victor Records made him a recording sensation as well. Using "The Haunting Melody" from the musical *Vera Violetta*, the label released the first Jolson single in 1912. It topped the pop charts in the spring for two weeks. Jolson followed that #1 with a series of four Victor hits before switching to Columbia in 1913. His first major release for his new label, "You Made Me Love You," topped the pop charts for seven weeks. Over the course of the next few years the man who was quickly becoming the nation's favorite vocalist hit #1 again with a wide variety of recordings, including "I'm All Bound Round with the Mason-Dixon Line," "I'll Say She Does," and "Rock-a-Bye Your Baby with a Dixie Melody." By the time Jolson scored again with "Swanee" in 1920, he was the biggest thing on the American stage.

Jolson is best remembered now as the man who wore white gloves and painted his face black in order to imitate the appearance, look and style of the Negro minstrel. While certainly Al used this effect to project his music, he did not need a gimmick; he was in all ways a consummate performer. Those who saw him on the Broadway stage or heard him on records and later via radio have a much different image of Jolson than those who look back at his career with an eye for the politically correct. Though he made millions of dollars, he never made any easy money. He worked hard for every penny he got, and no crowd was ever cheated by a Jolson show. Al was a hard-working performer who would not leave the stage until he had given everything he had. He didn't just wow crowds, he inspired them.

Even though almost any songwriter would have sold a portion of his soul to have Jolson cut his tune, most of the entertainer's new material came directly from his Broadway shows. Thus, when taken out of the context of the production a great deal of what he recorded seemed to make little sense. Some of his singles didn't tell much of a story even when viewed as a part of the show. Yet that didn't stop them from being hits. What Al realized early on was that to be a commercial success all a song needed was a catchy tune coupled to easy-to-remember lyrics. Thus, when Gus Kahn, Ernie Erdman, Ted Florito, and Robert A. King composed the score for the Broadway production of *Bombo*, they included several numbers which fit the special Jolson hit formula. One of these was a nonsensical ditty called "Toot, Toot, Tootsie! (Goo'Bye)."

Broadway songwriters knew long before rock and roll or country music were even conceived that a good hook and a clever lyric were far more important than a carefully crafted story line. Hence, they produced countless songs which were simply written for audience appeal and commercial potential. Songs like "Toot, Toot, Tootsie!" were never meant to stir the heart or be timeless classics; they were meant to bring a smile and generate revenue.

When Jolson cut "Toot, Toot, Tootsie!" for Columbia he was convinced that folks were going to like it; after all, the crowds had left the theater already humming the tune. Al realized that not only would the record generate royalties, but it would also help sell more tickets to the show in which the song appeared. "The World's Greatest Entertainer" didn't earn the title by not knowing how to promote Al Jolson, and this song did a great deal to promote Al and his latest Broadway show.

"Toot, Toot, Tootsie!" hit #1 in 1923 and held the top spot on the charts for a month. A host of other acts rushed out to cover the Jolson hit, and a few, such as Ernest Hare and Billy Jones, achieved modest success with it. Yet by and large the single would have probably suffered the same fate as most of the other comedic show tunes which Jolson cut if not for the arrival of a new medium.

In 1927 Al Jolson starred in a Hollywood feature called *The Jazz Singer*. The movie would use "The World's Greatest Entertainer" to trumpet the studio's newest piece of technological wizardry—talking motion pictures. With Jolson and his music being featured, the studio seemed convinced that millions would turn out to view its latest advance. And indeed, with Al kicking off the picture with his trademark "You ain't heard nothing yet," the film became a huge hit.

The Jazz Singer's importance to Hollywood and film history is without precedent. Hence, the songs which were used in the picture still echo in listeners' heads each time the movie is viewed on television or at film festivals. This is a huge reason that while most of the novelty and comedic numbers of the vaudeville age have disappeared or been forgotten, "Toot, Toot, Tootsie!" has remained a part of our musical landscape. But the bit of Hollywood magic that would assure "Toot, Toot, Tootsie!" a place in every American generation's psyche would not take place until just after World War II.

In the late forties Hollywood decided to make a movie about Al's life. Jolson was played by Larry Parks. The biographical film rekindled an interest in Al's career and music. The singer even managed to return to the stage and gain a short-term record deal. At the same time, in a move that seemed at the time to be more parody than tribute, Warner Bros. took advantage of the revival of "Jolsonmania" and wrote a cartoon that centered on a frog that sang "Toot, Toot, Tootsie!" in the Jolson style. With hat and cane, this green minstrel kicked back and forth in front of millions of moviegoers. The bit was so successful that Mel Blanc, who had done the frog's voice, even cut a recording of "Toot, Toot, Tootsie!" that was released by Capitol. Though not as big a success as Blanc's Woody Woodpecker, the single still generated considerable record sales and appeared on the national hit parade's top thirty. So, just as talking pictures had brought Jolson's sound to millions of new fans, another even younger generation first caught a bit of Al's style, as well as one of the songs which made him famous, through a singing cartoon frog. And today they are still watching that frog (which is the symbol and spokesperson for the Warner Bros. television network) sing its heart out again and again on television.

Most of the fans of "The World's Greatest Entertainer" have died. *The Jazz Singer* is still shown, but more as history than entertainment. Al's records are not programmed on the radio, and only through Larry Parks's acting in *The Jolson Story* do modern audiences get to sneak a peek at what made the real Jolson so successful. But "Toot, Toot, Tootsie!" survives, in large part due to Mel Blanc's frog. And if that animated amphibian occasionally gets a few folks to take a look back at the man who inspired the parody, it is worth its place in history. After all, "Toot, Toot, Tootsie!" is one novelty song that offers the key to a gold mine of treasured performances from another time. And if "Toot, Toot, Tootsie!" is the only song you have heard by Jolson, then, to use his own words, "You ain't heard nothing yet!"

Travelin' Man

Ricky Nelson's "Travelin' Man" in and of itself was not much of a novelty song. There is a long list of traveling songs—including "I've Been Everywhere, Man," "You Belong to Me," "Road to Morocco," and "On the Road Again"—which sold the adventure of going from spot to spot just as well as "Travelin' Man." What made this song one of the rock era's most novel was not its rather normal theme, but instead the way in which it was introduced and "sold" to the public. This special bit of marketing put Nelson and his hit single light-years ahead of the oncoming media revolution.

Ricky Nelson might just have been the first real teen idol. Put before the public's eye since childhood via television's *The Adventures of Ozzie and Harriet,* Ricky had grown up from precocious child to good-looking adolescent in front of millions each week. It seemed that almost everything in his life was shared with America. And by 1957, when young Nelson had gotten turned on to the music of Elvis Presley and persuaded his father to allow him to put together a band, this facet of Ozzie's son's life would be played out dramatically via the tube as well. A few months after learning the guitar, Ricky appeared in a segment of *Ozzie and Harriet* singing his version of a Fats

Domino song, "I'm Walking." Within days thousands of letters flooded the studio begging for more Nelson songs.

Signed first by Verve and then by Imperial, Ricky would use his popular all-American image and the new rock and roll sound to reel off a host of best-selling singles, which were always introduced via a concert segment at the end of the ABC television show on which his family starred. It was a formula that worked well for seventeen singles. Then, in 1959, kids seemingly quit buying Ricky's product and turned instead to the host of new teen idols who appeared almost daily on *American Bandstand*.

For two years Ricky had problems cracking the top ten, but because of his exposure on *Ozzie and Harriet,* the young man still attracted enough of a fan base to keep Imperial Records happy. Meanwhile, across L.A., Jerry Fuller was stuck in a park waiting for his wife when an idea struck him for a song. Fuller, who would go on to write a host of top ten singles, pulled out a map and put together an ode about a man who had a girl in every port. To find towns which would work as rhyming words in his composition, Jerry used the world map. When he finished with his "Travelin' Man," he felt sure that he had just written the next hit for the smooth-singing Sam Cooke.

Using an unknown Glen Campbell and a couple of other friends to cut a demo, Fuller pitched the demo to Cooke's manager, who was not impressed. There could be little doubt that if Cooke had gotten the chance to record the song, "Travelin' Man" would have become one of his bigger hits. Yet if Sam had cut Fuller's composition, there would not have been the novelty value that would come from Nelson's treatment.

Cooke's manager's office happened to be next door to the office of Imperial Records. As the wall which separated the two businesses was not very thick, a great deal of "informal spying" went on between the two companies. One of Ricky's band members had been visiting at Imperial during the same time "Travelin' Man" was being previewed next door—and the Jerry Fuller song soon "found" its way out of a trash bin and into the hands of the television star–turned–recording artist.

The final cut which Ricky Nelson gave Imperial Records was a straightforward treatment of a rock and roll ballad. As Nelson did not have the natural vocal talents of Sam Cooke, the version which Jerry Fuller heard Ricky sing was probably not as awe-inspiring as the writer had imagined it would be when he'd written it for Sam. But how Nelson chose to introduce the new single to the public would soon get the scribe's blood pumping.

For four years Ricky had stood in front of a curtain with his band and introduced his latest recording to television audiences. Now this once successful formula had gotten old. It was also being used in a similar fashion by a host of others, such as Shelley Fabares and Annette Funicello, via their own television outlets. In order to set "Travelin' Man" apart from the singer's own past efforts, as well as from those of others who were now using television to introduce music product, the producer of *Ozzie and Harriet* chose to spend some time filming Ricky with beautiful exotic women in the very places mentioned in the lyrics. In actuality stock footage and the studio back lot were used for Hawaii, New York, Germany, England, and the other foreign locales, but when spliced together with the song's story line, the film appeared authentic. Judging from the letters written to the network demanding repeats of the short film, as well as the immediate record sales response ("Travelin' Man" was the top-selling debut record for the week of April 24, 1961), the new approach worked even better than anyone at Imperial and ABC would have thought possible. The minifilm had created a major hit.

Though the video of Ricky Nelson traversing the world via his "Travelin' Man" song might seem simplistic today, in 1961 this mini-movie was revolutionary. Ricky was meshing rock and roll and video in a new way to sell product, and no one had done anything quite like it before. The mere fact that "Travelin' Man" produced Nelson his first #1 since 1958 signaled that the ploy had worked. There can also be little doubt that this bit of film magic helped to get the single's B side noticed and put into heavy rotation as well. "Travelin' Man"/ "Hello Mary Lou" became a huge double-sided hit.

What is worth noting about "Travelin' Man" is therefore not the actual single as much as the novel concept of making a minimovie to go with a song's lyric line. This bit of marketing would give a fore-taste of the real future of the music industry. Of course, few picked up on this potential at the time; even Nelson didn't try to film another minimovie around one of his songs. But even if he didn't realize it then, Ricky had managed to put together the first rock video. This little video effort started the revolution which would lead to MTV, CMTV, VH-1, and hundreds of thousands of music videos being used to plug story lines into song lyrics and put them in front of millions of customers via television. Since he introduced it in 1961, Ricky Nelson's unique concept has done a lot of successful traveling.

Walk Like an Egyptian

*S*ome songs owe their credit to timing. Others lay claim to originality. Some simply hit with a unique sound that resounds in the listener's mind. A few even find success due to the fact that they are stupid. And then there are those very few which hit on all those things.

It is doubtful that the Ohio native Liam Sternberg had King Tut on his mind when he first came up with the concept of walking in a manner that was suggested by the hieroglyphics drawings on the walls of the tombs of ancient Egyptian monarchs. Yet the mere fact that the world was somewhat caught up in a "love of mummy" craze probably had a great deal to do with the success of the song whose lyrics were penned by Sternberg some days after first thinking of them while crossing the English Channel.

When he finished what appeared to be a "dance" concept, Sternberg sold the song to Peer Southern Music Publishing, which shipped the demo tape out, coupled to another one of Liam's compositions, "Rock and Roll Vertigo." "Walk Like an Egyptian" was included as a throwaway, the B side which was supposed to be piggybacked to "Vertigo" to insure more royalties for the publisher and the writer. And indeed, most of those who heard the dual demo viewed "Egyptian" as just barely up to B side standards. But when the producer for a West Coast all-girls band heard it, he thought that there was something magical about the silly concept. David Kahne could sense that in a live show and on video, this song might just come off as a unique offering. He pitched it to his ladies, the Bangles.

The Bangles had initially consisted of sisters—Vicki and Debbi Peterson, Susanna Hoffs, and Annette Zalikas. The ladies had been brought together by a classified ad placed by Susanna hoping to find other young women who were interested in creating a "female Beatles"–type group and sound. After meeting and discovering a mutual drive to perform, the quartet took on more of a Beach Boy sound. Employing vocal quirks and unique harmonies, the four continued to evolve to the point where they were writing much of their own material. When they produced their first single, the girls, now called the Supersonic Bangs, were dreaming of instant success. Instead they discovered that no one wanted to pay good money for their "Getting out of Hand."

After working local clubs, the quartet toured with acts such as Cyndi Lauper. Changing their name and sound, they reworked their look and modified their name a few more times. Finally, over supper, the four decided to go back to a new version of Supersonic Bangs and give music one last big shot. As the Bangles, the quartet finally garnered enough local interest in the Los Angeles area to earn a contract with Columbia in 1983. For three years they floundered. Zalinkas grew tired of the strain and left the group. She was replaced by Micki Steele, who had just run away from the Runaways. Finally, in 1986, when it seemed as though Columbia was about to give up on them, the Bangles hit the big time with a top ten single, "Manic Monday." But their following release flopped. Then, just when the label was wondering if it had signed a one-hit wonder, the group discovered the Sternberg song.

Several years before the Bangles went into the studio to cut the latest "Egyptian" novelty number, Steve Martin had scored with a very weird song called "King Tut." Martin's tune made no more sense

than most of his antics on *Saturday Night Live,* but "Tut" did prove
that millions had a special place in their hearts for anything having
to do with mummies, pyramids, and strange ways of walking.

With the U.S. caught up in the midst of museums devoting entire
wings to Egyptian studies, it seems amazing now that the concept
was not revived until the end of 1986. Someone should have realized
that there was a king's ransom out there waiting for the creative soul
who could resuscitate the musical image of the mummy. Yet until the
Bangles latched onto it, it seemed that even Liam Sternberg's light-
hearted view of this era was going to be passed by. Then, just as so
many explorers had accidentally stumbled into ancient treasure-filled
tombs, producer Kahne fell into "Walk Like an Egyptian."

In the studio Kahne liked Sternberg's demo, which he had called
"offhanded," so much that he changed the arrangement little for his
act. Yet while the simple yet catchy production and the girls' singing
made the song stand apart from anything else on the market, "Walk
Like an Egyptian" was not a hit simply because of the work in the
studio. Rather, this was a release that showed the real power of cou-
pling a unique song to a hot theme, and while its message may have
made little sense, the lyrics had been expertly wrapped around a tune
that was so easy to remember and so hard to dislike that everyone
from toddlers to senior citizens got into it. The video, complete with
images of the ancient Nile, played everywhere, and the Bangles suddenly were caught up in a storm of popularity. The album which
contained "Egyptian" went double platinum, the Bangles tours sold
out, and when they sang their theme song, everyone joined in.

"Walk Like an Egyptian" served also to help electrify the interest
of young people in King Tut and other exhibits from Egypt's colorful
and important past. While this fascination in all things Egyptian was
certainly already at a fever pitch among the educated elements of
society, the Bangles' single drummed up a curiosity about King Tut,
Cleopatra, and other past rulers in teenagers who had previously
shown few interests outside of zit cream and slumber parties. It was
ironic that it took a novelty song to wake up these kids' minds, which
had remained untouched by teachers, television specials, and reams

of feature articles in newspapers and magazines. (Never mind that millions of brain-dead teens seemed to actually believe that the real ancient Egyptians walked at weird angles.)

"Walk Like an Egyptian" would hit #1 in late December and remain there through most of the first month of 1987. It would be the most successful song ever for the Bangles. In 1989, after just one more #1, "Eternal Flame," the Bangles broke up and went their separate ways. Most of the quartet's work was forgotten by the next decade, but there was no doubt that this throwaway song that had been meant for a B side would assure the four women a spot in music history, even when rock itself is considered ancient.

Though it unquestionably is a bit bizarre, some might wonder if "Walk Like an Egyptian" really deserves a place in a book about novelty numbers. Consider this: Would the song have cracked the charts if Liam Sternberg had called it "Walk Like an Italian"? No; in this case only the novel inspiration of a real mummy would do!

We Love You, Beatles

The names of the classic sixties girl groups easily roll off the tongue of even the most casual rock and roll historian. Who could forget the Supremes, the Ronettes, the Vandellas, the Shirelles, and the Carefrees. The Carefrees? Who the devil are the Carefrees, you ask?

One of the least remembered girl trios of the sixties is the Carefrees. And there is good reason for that: In the entire span of their careers, this quaint little group spent all of one week on the charts. That week was April 11, 1964, and for those brief seven days Lyn Cornell, Betty Prescott, and Barbara Kay were famous for singing a ditty that was filled with as much creativity and charm as the 1930s "classic" "It Looks Like Rain on Cherry Blossom Lane" (whose title contained every one of the song's lyrics).

The week before the Carefrees made their lone appearance in *Billboard*'s top forty, another British group had controlled each of the top five spots on the charts. With "Can't Buy Me Love" topping the playlists, and "Twist and Shout," "She Loves You," "I Want to Hold Your Hand," and "Please Please Me" following in order, the Beatles were riding the crest of something the American press was calling Beatlemania. As timing is everything in rock music, the London International Record Company couldn't help but congratulate itself on its wonderful stroke of luck in getting the Carefrees' new release to the States just in time to capitalize on the success of the Beatles. However, the real inspiration for the Carefrees' number was not the Beatles, but Elvis.

One of the most successful Broadway musicals of the era spoofed Elvis Presley's early career, his induction into the army, and the way teenage girls swooned every time he moved his hips. In order to keep this account supposedly fictional, the King's name had been changed to Conrad Birdie. Just prior to the invasion of the Beatles, Hollywood had taken *Bye Bye Birdie* and adapted it for film. Using Ann-Margret, Janet Leigh, Dick Van Dyke, and even Ed Sullivan in starring rolls, the movie drew millions of patrons to view the film version of the Broadway musical which they had heard so much about.

Bye Bye Birdie was flooded with great musical numbers. The production values of both the Broadway play and the movie were extremely high. But in the midst of the action a simple little ditty appeared almost as a joke. This thankfully short burst of song poked fun at the way millions of young women had bought into the Elvis phenomenon. The small bit of satire was never meant to be taken seriously, nor was it written to become the centerpiece of the musical score. Yet when people left their seats to go home, they didn't spend the rest of the week singing "A Lot of Livin' to Do," "Kids," or "Put on a Happy Face"; the song they couldn't quit humming was "We Love You, Conrad."

For the millions in 1963 and 1964 who couldn't get the inane "We Love You, Conrad" out of their heads, *Bye Bye Birdie* became as big a curse as the chorus of "Achy Breaky Heart" would become in the early nineties. Any thoughts of anything associated with the movie gave many people the "I can't stop singing 'We Love You, Conrad' fever." It was reported that thousands even thought of the song when they would catch a rerun of Janet Leigh showering in *Psycho*. After a while it seemed that the only good thing about "We Love You, Conrad" was that it had never been released as a single and therefore had not been put out over the airwaves.

Unfortunately, that was about to change.

The Carefrees were brought into their London studio to work on a single based on "We Love You, Conrad"—only instead of Conrad, the trio inserted the name of the Fab Four. As if it wasn't enough for Americans to have to face the fact that seemingly every other song being played on the radio had been released by the Beatles, now they had to listen to a mediocre English trio warbling "We Love You, Beatles" in between spins of "She Loves You" and "Can't Buy Me Love." It was enough to drive millions insane!

The mere fact that "We Love You, Beatles" made the top forty and sold several hundred thousand copies shows just how badly American youth had been caught up in Beatlemania. George, John, Paul, and Ringo had cast their spells on millions. This huge wave of affection and adulation would dramatically change everything from the entertainment industry to fashion for years to come. And the novelty which the lads from Liverpool created would still hold fans' attention and interest thirty years later. Thankfully, "We Love You, Beatles" and the Carefrees have not been remembered or treasured as deeply, and one can only pray that London International is not planning on coming out with a *Carefrees Anthology*.

Welfare Cadillac

*Many of the critics who make a living analyzing such
things view a host of top novelty songs as more*
social commentary than comedic relief. Certainly this has
been true with many of the tunes which have hit the country music charts. Merle Haggard established himself with
several "novelty" hits in the sixties and seventies which
embraced the themes of God and country. "Okie from
Muskogee" helped define the voice of what was to become
known as the silent majority. Charlie Daniels also
wrapped himself in the American flag on occasion. His "In
America" expressed the growing anger of many of the nation's citizens toward foreign and domestic efforts to de-
fame the United States. Many will even argue that Tom
T. Hall's lyrics were often fraught with messages of things
which needed to be addressed by society. "Harper Valley
P.T.A." can easily be seen as a song about the state of
society. Yet by and large, just as is so on the rock side of
the ledger, in country music novelty efforts' symbolism
have usually given way to laughs. If the message is lost in
the process, so be it.

But when Guy Drake penned a hit about one of the
nation's most troubling problems, the symbolism was

more than obvious. Everyone who listened to "Welfare Cadillac" had an opinion about the song and its subject.

The late sixties saw much of the nation reeling with contempt for former president Lyndon Johnson's noble attempt to lift the poor out of poverty. While LBJ's "Great Society" was getting food and other necessities to millions of needy people, the program was filled with loopholes which allowed millions more who didn't need aid to take advantage of the system. Newspapers and television news reports constantly spotlighted families who were getting government checks while living a rather lavish lifestyle, but rarely touched on those who had used these same programs to save themselves from hunger and disease. These controversial reports, combined with many other misconceptions about who was on welfare, paved the way for what would become known as the "angry white male" vote.

Guy Drake, a former high school teacher and onetime leader of a country music swing band, was living in Greenville, Kentucky, during these troubled times. Surrounded by poverty and joblessness, Guy knew firsthand America's poorest poor. Yet he also sensed that a song which tapped in on the excesses of Johnson's Great Society might just play to the grassroots country audience. So, taking pen in hand, he fashioned a story about a man who had figured out a system to take advantage of the government in a big way. The scribe felt his song had commercial possibility because rather than having turned the lyrics into a dark bit of social commentary, he had ingeniously wrapped his tale in humor.

Guy Drake's "Welfare Cadillac" was the story of a man who fed his kids with handouts while driving the nicest car in town. Although it went almost exclusively for laughs, Guy also outlined a way for a man to get the most out of the poverty programs of the time. The giveaways which Drake included were for peanut butter, cheese, various other food commodities, clothes, and school supplies. The song's narrative also pointed out that the more kids a family had the more programs to which it could apply; thus the man and his wife in this song needed to keep producing children. The songwriter also got across the point that getting a job was not in the subject's best interest because it would mean that the free ride would stop and the family would be forced back into a life of having to just scrape by.

Thinking he had a surefire hit, Guy Drake traveled to Nashville to push his new song. He was not greeted with much charity. Record company executives didn't see how the song could fly. One after another, the labels turned "Welfare Cadillac" down. Finally Drake cut the song himself for an obscure company, pressed a few demo copies, then proceeded to drive from town to town handing them out to radio stations. It seemed a bit ironic that the man who was peddling "Welfare Cadillac" was going to have to depend upon the goodwill and welfare of disc jockeys to have any chance of breaking even on his effort. After more than a month of door-to-door sales pitches, he received a bit of on-the-air charity, and when Guy returned home he discovered that his song had made it onto the country charts. It would camp out in the top one hundred for almost four months, climbing as high as #6. Surprisingly, this very country ode would show up on the rock charts as well.

"Welfare Cadillac" took country music fans on a ride to laughter by pointing out the extremes of a system designed to help the poor. But many had concerns about what the song's effect would be on the national effort to ease the burden of poverty in America. On the surface "Welfare Cadillac" may have been a singing joke, but underneath it was rife with rage. A lot of the "angry white males" who made up a large percentage of the country music market of that era saw this song as more factual than fictional. These men also felt that welfare was a program which took away their opportunities to get ahead and gave those chances to lazy people who had no ambition to work for a living. Some even believed that the song was a stab at African-Americans, and that it thus fueled the fires of racial hatred.

Yet if those who had latched onto "Welfare Cadillac" as a symbol of protest had read between the lines of Guy Drake's song, they might have seen a picture of a family just lucky to be treading water. Yes, this family did have a really nice car—but they had nothing else. Their home was a wreck, their clothes were hand-me-downs, and the food that came through the government programs was bland at best. Cadillac or not, this was not a way that anyone would want to live.

"Welfare Cadillac" worked because America was having problems figuring out how to help those who were down-and-out. With the rural landscape giving way to a largely urban society, the family farm just couldn't support the average family anymore. But even in the face of terrible times, Guy Drake also accurately pointed out, everyone wanted to cling to something that showed they had a piece of the American dream. In this case, the family may have been living in the poorhouse, but at least they had figured out a way to drive there in style.

Although Guy Drake could have purchased a few Cadillacs off the royalty checks from his hit song, as it turned out the vehicle which put him on the charts wouldn't run too long. "Welfare Cadillac" was Drake's only trip on the *Billboard* charts as a solo artist. It seems that LBJ's programs outlasted the singer/songwriter's Music City career.

When You're Hot, You're Hot

*I*f *Jerry Reed were not such an outlandish character and didn't seem to treat so much of his life as a joke, he* might just be recognized as one of the most talented all-around entertainers to ever carve out country music hits. The Atlanta native is a solid songwriter, a strong comedic actor, one of the music business's most original and inventive guitar players, and a great live performer. Yet for most of his career critics and fans have been too busy laughing at Reed's outlandish antics and sidesplitting stories to really take note of his incredible talents. Hence, even though he has earned high marks in a wide variety of pursuits, he has also spread himself so thin that folks have looked through his huge body of work. Many have argued that the entertainer should stick with just one facet of his interests, work to grow that facet, and magnify it to its full potential. But Jerry will have none of that. If there are three doors at the end of a hall, the curious man wants to see what's behind all of them, and so it is with his career.

Jerry Reed Hubbard arrived in Nashville in the mid-fifties when Music City was struggling to figure out what musical direction it was going to take. Rockabilly had recently brought with it a host of talented southern boys steeped in electric guitar, heavy bass lines, and drums, and they had invaded country music like Hitler had Poland, taking no prisoners along the way. Elvis, Jerry Lee, Sonny James, and others were knocking the traditional Nashville acts off the charts. Many of the movers and shakers in country music saw this youth movement as the wave of the future, and were beating the bushes for new talent. Hubbard, just out of high school, seemed to fit the bill. He impressed the talent scouts at Capitol with his voice and style and earned a record deal. Over the course of the next three years he would cut a number of rock and country efforts for the label, but experienced little success. His only real brush with fame came when Gene Vincent covered one of Jerry's compositions, "Crazy Legs."

After a stint in the army, Reed returned to Nashville and toiled well out of the limelight. Most folks felt he had the talent to be a star, but few could sense what it was they needed to do to lead him to the spotlight. Jerry might have been forgotten altogether if it hadn't been for Chet Atkins. The master guitar player guided Reed to RCA and began to produce his records. And just as Atkins had done with Elvis in the fifties, rather than mold Reed into the prototype country star, Chet simply pushed Jerry to be Jerry. His allowing Jerry to grow in his own way would lead to Reed's chance at stardom.

"What are you, Jerry?" the singer was asked again and again.

"I'm just a guitar man" would come the reply.

A 1968 Jerry-penned song became the backbone of one of the most stupendous hours in the history of network television. Elvis's NBC comeback special's most elaborate production sequence was built around Reed's explanation of who he was, a simple little "Guitar Man." The song not only helped push the special's ratings through the roof, but raced up the pop charts, returned Presley to the rock map, and sent the King back to Reed for another song. The second single was "U.S. Male," a novelty hit that cemented a special bond between Elvis and Jerry and prompted RCA to take a firmer interest in the young man from Atlanta. To capitalize on this interest Reed wrote a musical thank-you to the King, "Tupelo, Mississippi Flash." And that song became the singer/songwriter's first "minor" hit.

A tour and appearances on Glen Campbell's network television series got Reed some national recognition. A duet guitar album with Chet Atkins did much to enhance the respect Reed deserved as an instrumentalist. But what really aimed the spotlight his way was an offbeat number about a one-armed alligator trapper from the Louisiana swamps, "Amos Moses."

"Moses" established Reed as the latest in a long line of country funnymen. Yet to fully build a career off this image he was going to have to do what Ray Stevens had done—spin off a series of novelty hits that were as creative and humorous as his first. In 1971, at the age of thirty-six, Reed did just that. He became one of the hottest commodities in the entertainment world by simply noting one of the most accepted of humanity's unwritten laws: "When you're hot you're hot, but when you're not you're not."

The concept for a song that talked about everything from crap games to run-ins with the law had come to Jerry when he had messed up a line during the filming of a television show. His timing off, the singer had simply shrugged, "When you're hot, you're hot." That observation provoked thought about other times and situations where he had been hot and cold, and thus inspired the witty lyrics to the song which would anchor his career.

In the studio Reed treated his latest work with such an "aw shucks" manner that everyone who was involved with the recording became as laid-back as Jerry was. The entire effort was fun! The playback proved there had been a party going on and that it had been so much fun that maybe the local law enforcement officers should have hauled revelers off. As it turned out, it was the song that would be hauled off, by millions of American record buyers. And its title would become one of the most overused clichés of the day.

Jerry was hoping the very nontraditional "talker" or country rap tune would catch on and give the singer a shot at the top ten again. Little did he guess that "When You're Hot, You're Hot" would top the country charts for five weeks, become a major pop hit, and win the singer a Grammy. Suddenly, after fifteen years of work, he was an overnight success. And it had all been built on a joke. This was great for the bank account, but in the long run may have overshadowed just how inventive and serious a songwriter Reed really is.

But at that moment Jerry wasn't concerned about *how* the world was looking at him, only that it *was*.

In truth, if Jerry's first two novelty hits had led to nothing else but a solid career in country music, the singer/songwriter would have probably been satisfied. But his energetic numbers and his unique way of delivering these musical jokes received enormous play on both coasts, too. In 1974, Burt Reynolds sensed that Jerry's personality would translate well to film and cast him in a movie, *W. W. and the Dixie Dance Kings*. From there Jerry would costar with Burt in the monster hit *Smokey and the Bandit*. Taking a cue from his biggest hit, Reed literally turned his back on Music City and cashed in on being hot by going on to appear in more than a dozen Hollywood entries. But by the late seventies Reed's movie status had dropped and he was back in Nashville living the back half of his only #1 song's title.

As Jerry would soon discover, climbing back to the top is a bit harder than getting there the first time. When you're written off in the entertainment business as one of yesterday's stars, it's awfully hard to get things back together again. Yet even during the days when he no longer was drawing big concert crowds or landing at the top of the charts, Reed's philosophy of having fun and keeping success in focus stayed with him. When he wasn't on tour, Jerry's friends would often find him out in the middle of a lake with a fishing pole in his hand. On slow-biting days he would simply laugh it off by saying "When you're hot you're hot, but when you're not you're not." The glint in his eye seemed to assure everyone that he believed the fish would bite again tomorrow, and that his songs would be hot again one day soon, too. And time would prove him right on both counts. Besides, Jerry had lived his hot period to its fullest. This guitar man hadn't missed a lick. And that made the days of "when he was not" all that much easier to take.

Wild Thing

When the Troggs released "Wild Thing," they probably never thought this song would ever become a major hit, much less one of the most remembered, played, and beloved singles of the hard rock era. It was a demo that the group members had turned down when first reviewing it, believing it to be one of the corniest things they had ever heard. Lead singer Reg Ball thought "Wild Thing" was so bad that simply recording it would doom his band to failure. And in a way, he was right!

The Troglodytes had come out of the English rock scene, having been formed by Ball in Andover. Their shot at fame came as a part of the fallout created by America's love affair with the Beatles. Discovered and signed by Larry Page, who had managed the Kinks, the group flopped when it worked with CBS Records. In an attempt to revive their band's flagging fortunes, the four men shortened their name to the Troggs and earned a second shot at recording, this time with the Fontana label. It was while they were first cutting songs for their new label that they came across Chip Taylor's rather unusual composition.

At about the same time that the four British lads had first previewed "Wild Thing," they also took a listen to

John Sebastian's "Did You Ever Have to Make Up Your Mind?" The Troggs liked Sebastian's song, but their label felt "Wild Thing" was the better of the two tunes. Who knows what would have happened if they had gone for the ballad over the somewhat sleazy rocker. They might have never topped the charts, but their American rock music tenure might have lasted a bit longer.

Released initially only in England, "Wild Thing" quickly became something of a cult classic. The Brits ate it up. The single not only topped the charts, but quickly established itself as one of the standards of almost every English club band; it was kind of a British "Louie Louie." With the success and fame they'd earned in their homeland, the Troggs decided to follow scores of their musical countrymen and try the opposite side of the Atlantic.

Like their English counterparts, teens in the States quickly learned to love the bizarre and unsavory lyrics of "Wild Thing." In truth, the song was about nothing more than a boy who couldn't help falling in lust with a chick (this girl was no lady) who was so wild that she made everything "groovy." It was probably because of the very rebellious nature of the single—in great contrast to the sweet and innocent messages which groups like Herman's Hermits were putting out—that American youth took to it, just as an earlier generation had fallen in love with the image of hoods dressed in leather and riding big motorcycles (thanks in large part to Marlon Brando's *The Wild One*).

Entering the rock charts in the summer of 1966, the Troggs rode their loud and vulgar tome to #1 in early August. The single's quick move to the top seems to indicate that the music which had been spawned by the British invasion did not have much effect on upgrading the taste of the American buying public, as some retro music historians would have us believe. Critics may have shuddered at the huge sales generated by songs about hot rods and surfing in the early sixties, but do they really believe that "Wild Thing," and the song it knocked from atop the *Billboard* list, "Hanky Panky," represented steps forward? Those who argue that these years were the best in pop music history should consider the fact that "Lil' Red Riding Hood" was #2 when the Troggs owned #1.

Initially the American version of "Wild Thing" had been released by both the Fontana and Atco labels. It seemed that each of these two companies believed that it had the exclusive rights to the song. Ultimately it was Atco's version which sold the most copies and was registered as the hit. But as far as collectors are concerned, Fontana's version is worth more now.

"Wild Thing" completely ruined any chances that the Troggs had to challenge the other successful groups of the period. The song pigeonholed their sound, and the hole in which they had been placed had very little to do with displaying the depth and width of their talents. But just because the Troggs faded away into the streets of England didn't mean their biggest hit died with them.

For many years "Wild Thing" remained a favorite with rock bands on both sides of the Atlantic. A decade after the Troggs had been all but forgotten, new groups were fighting the disco craze by playing their own versions of this loud, bombastic cult favorite. Still, as disco faded and fewer and fewer club bands picked the song up, it appeared as though the "Wild" days were finally coming to a close. Then, just when everyone assumed that rap and the soft sounds of folks like Whitney Houston had buried the old song for good, a movie spoof brought it back in a huge way.

Major League was hardly film art. It was a satire of sports movies played out for very broad and cheap laughs. The fact that Bob Uecker had the motion picture's best lines said a lot about the script. Yet what most folks remember from the feature was not the acting, not the realistic baseball scenes, but "Wild Thing." The song played just about every time Charlie Sheen's punkish, ex-convict fastball hurler appeared on the playing field for the hapless Cleveland Indians. And simply because *Major League* made millions, a new generation came to know and love "Wild Thing," not as a rock song, but as a baseball standard. And when the Indians finally made it to the real World Series, the Troggs and their song went with them. Thus, a tune that was an unexpected hit on the charts in the sixties had become a big hit in the nineties on the diamond!

When Chip Taylor wrote "Wild Thing," he never intended for it to become so much a part of the American folk culture that it would be used in scores of product ads and movies and at sporting events. The writer could never have imagined that his "Wild Thing" would be reshaped by orchestra leaders into half-time music for marching bands. Chip, who wrote "Angel of the Morning," "I Can Make It Without You," and "Make Me Belong to You," probably couldn't believe it when one of his least inspired and worst writing efforts was even recorded, let alone when it became #1! But in the long run Taylor came to love his "Wild Thing" all the way to the bank, and it loved him right back! It would seem that whoever said that wild women always cost you money, then break your heart, didn't know what he was talking about.

Winchester Cathedral

Most novelty songs are labeled as such because of their unique themes and lyrics. "Does Your Chewing Gum Lose Its Flavor on the Bedpost Overnight?" had to have been written as a joke. So too were hits like "The Purple People Eater" and "Witch Doctor." Yet there were a few songs whose lyrics were straightforward in every way but which through the use of an offbeat arrangement or production technique crossed over into the bounds of the unusual or even the downright weird.

In the forties Spike Jones and His City Slickers took a host of straight compositions and performed them in a style which was meant just for laughs. The most remembered of these has to be "Cocktails for Two." The Marcels' version of "Blue Moon" also placed a different spin on what had once been considered a classic love song. In country music this approach was employed by entertainers such as Grandpa Jones on several occasions. Yet nowhere is there a better example of the use of a particular performing style's altering the public perception of a song than songwriter/singer Geoff Stephens and his "Winchester Cathedral."

When Stephens composed the song which would give him his lone shot in the spotlight, he was a staff songwriter for a music publishing company in London. Geoff would have had an impact on rock music even if he had never glanced up at a photo of Winchester Cathedral and been moved to write his ode to a love gone bad, for it was he who penned "There's a Kind of Hush," "Smile a Little Smile for Me," "Daughter of Darkness," and a long list of other singles which charted in both England and America. But without "Winchester Cathedral" Geoff would probably have never gotten the chance to gain fame as a performer.

Even though Rudy Vallee and His Connecticut Yankees' greatest days had come before Geoff Stephens was born in 1934, the songwriter was a big fan of the performing style employed by Vallee's and other Tin Pan Alley groups. The nasal tones and the unique sound created through the use of a megaphone had intrigued the young man since his youth. So, while it was unusual, it shouldn't have been surprising to those at Fontana Records when Geoff explained that he "heard" his new composition as if Rudy Vallee himself were scheduled to cut it. In spite of questioning the wisdom of spending money on a musical style which no one alive remembered how to promote, the label booked Stephens some studio time.

Much as Gary Paxton had done with "Alley-Oop," Stephens cut his "Winchester Cathedral" with studio players. Producing the recording himself, the songwriter insisted on re-creating the sound of the Tin Pan Alley days in great detail, using as many of the instruments and as much of the recording equipment of that era as he could find. Geoff even sang the song's lead vocal through a megaphone. It was as if British music had taken a huge step backwards—but it would prove to be a step worth taking.

Without the unique arrangement and sound it is doubtful that anyone would have cared much about the story of an old English landmark and a lost love, but with the "Vallee-boy" effects, people tuned in. At first the song may have won repeat listeners through simple shock effect; certainly there were a host of kids who wanted to know "What in the heck is that thing?" Yet "Winchester Cathedral" seemed to quickly earn the same kind of reputation in the music world that the VW Beetle had earned in automotive circles, and after a few weeks the record was considered so bizarre it was deemed cool.

As the song began to climb the charts in the United States in the fall of 1966, many megaphones were employed at high school and college football games, not for leading cheers, but as a way to imitate the sound of the New Vaudeville Band (the name Stephens had given to his imaginary group) and the country's hottest song. Like mood rings and lava rocks, the Vaudeville sound had become a fad.

With "Winchester Cathedral" charging up both the English and the American playlists, booking agents from around the world were calling Fontana Records in an attempt to find out how to obtain the services of the New Vaudeville Band. Suddenly Geoff Stephens had a problem—as he had never planned on the single's becoming a major hit, he didn't have a band.

With the help of his publisher and label, the songwriter quickly set up auditions and found five men who could play in the style of the record. Working up a host of songs from bygone days, Geoff and the New Vaudeville Band caught a plane to the United States. They landed just in time to sing their now #1 hit on *The Ed Sullivan Show*. There, dressed in the style of the Flapper Era, the sextet reawakened a host of memories for millions of senior citizens, provoked teens' curiosity about the past, and opened the door for Rudy Vallee to come out of retirement and play college campuses for the first time in two generations.

As with most revivals of bygone styles, the Tin Pan Alley sound resurrected by Geoff Stephens with "Winchester Cathedral" and performed by the New Vaudeville Band didn't last long. After playing a few successful gigs in Las Vegas and across the Atlantic in London's better clubs, the band broke up and Geoff went back to writing hits for other acts. Yet for a few moments "Winchester Cathedral" had become a bridge between generations which had been separated by three wars, countless social changes, and a vast number of industrial advances. And though this dialogue was a novelty that didn't last for very long, it did confirm that grandparents and their grandchildren had a lot more in common than either cared to admit. In that way, "Winchester Cathedral" didn't let anyone down.

 **Witch Doctor**

In 1958 a down-and-out songwriter/record producer/ part-time actor, Ross Bagdasarian, was about to lose everything he owned. Behind on his bills, faced with a dismal run of records and songs, and with creditors banging on his door and collection agencies calling him on the phone, Bagdasarian needed a miracle just to make it through the year. What he had to find, many thought, was either a new profession or a magic potion. As it turned out, Bagdasarian opted for the latter.

Bagdasarian had known brief moments of success. He had earned gold and hard cash when he'd penned Rosemary Clooney's monster hit, "Come On-a My House." He had also scored with a few other songs that had charted, and had even made a few appearances in some good films. Yet by 1958, the money was gone. So, it seemed, was his inspiration, and nobody wanted him for movie or television acting jobs. With no one seemingly out there to help him, he knew that his only chance was to make some magic of his own.

For weeks Ross worked feverishly to save his family and his career. One day he happened to glance at his wall of bookshelves and noted a book entitled *Duel with the Witch Doctor*. Most people would have shrugged off all thoughts of turning their fortunes around on the strength of anything in this title, but not Ross. This was a man whose creative juices often flowed backwards and who marched to a band that no one else could hear. In a sudden Faust-like semitrance, Bagdasarian began to jot down lyrics for a song about a young man who gets advice in the art of love from a witch doctor who seemed to have come straight out of a Tarzan movie. The writer made the witch doctor's dialogue easy to write and rhyme by simply throwing together a bunch of gibberish and making it sound something like a curse used by natives in the Bob Hope–Bing Crosby movie *The Road to Zanzibar*.

No one in his right mind would have produced a demo of Ross's "Witch Doctor," but that didn't deter the songwriter from "selling" it to his own publishing company. He then went into his makeshift studio (an old tape recorder in his office) and spent a couple of months trying to make the recording into something that he could market to his friends in the industry. But after he'd played around with the concept for eight weeks, the song was still trapped in a jungle of boredom. It didn't move, it didn't bounce, and not even his own family thought it was any good. Then fate stepped in.

Some have claimed that Ross made an error and recorded the song at the wrong speed on his tape machine. More likely, when he played it back, he jumped the speed up to double that at which it had been recorded. The bizarre high-pitched vocals that echoed from the tape deck sounded like something out of a *Wizard of Oz* Munchkin's mouth. Most people would have rectified their mistake, but Ross liked it and thought it would be perfect for the witch doctor's voice. This, of course, was breaking dramatically with the Hollywood tradition of having jungle healers speak in a deep, booming manner, but that fact bothered Bagdasarian little—his life had been a constant attempt to do things his own way.

The song's key lyrics—"Ooo-eee, ooo-ah-ah, ting-tang," etc.—didn't have much going for them upon first glance. Written out, they looked really strange and made "be-bop-a-lula" seem almost intellectual. But it was the weird nonsensical lyrics, and not the song's pat story line of a young boy who is unable to win a girl on his own, that captured the attention of Liberty Records. The label had all kinds of financial problems, it couldn't attract flies, and it was so desperate that it was willing to take a chance on almost anything. It needed something that might get the IRS off its back for a few months. Few inside Liberty would have guessed that a simple "walla-walla bing-bang" would do just that.

Even after the record was pressed and being readied for shipment, most of those treading water at the label seemed to believe that "Witch Doctor" had about as much chance of generating play time as a magic potion did of fixing the company's financial woes, but Liberty released it anyway. There was only one change that the executives insisted on—instead of Ross Bagdasarian, the performer/songwriter would take on the handle David Seville. It probably brought Ross a secure feeling to know that by his not using his real name, disc jockeys would have a harder time tracking down and blacklisting the performer who had dumped this thing in their laps.

"Witch Doctor" debuted the first week in April of 1958. As it seemed the single was an April Fools' joke, this was probably wonderful timing. Almost, it seemed, to make fun of it, DJs played it. Then, as if the teenage brains of the nation had been put into a trance, the song began to sell. By tax time (a date which the label had been dreading) the single was moving so fast that Liberty couldn't keep up. Two weeks later "Witch Doctor" had saved Liberty Records, allowed David Seville to feed his family and make his car payments, and knocked the Platters and "Twilight Time" out of #1. Though few noted it at the time, this successful single seemed to fulfill the prophesy of many conservative preachers of the day who had proclaimed that rock and roll was nothing but jungle music designed by those who wanted to evoke satanic power over America's youth. Yet in reality, this million-selling song had just the opposite effect. It gave Ross Bagdasarian an almost divine inspiration to create a wholesome children's group that would remain popular three decades later. But why crowd the good doctor with the story of a trio of rodents. We've already shared that story with you.

# Wooly Bully

If you had known nothing about Sam the Sham and the Pharaohs and had just wandered into a club where they were playing in the late fifties and early sixties, you would have quickly realized that here was a group that performed its music more for yuks than meditation. The Pharaohs didn't care if you thought about what they did or what you thought about how they looked—they just wanted you to have a good time.

Dressed in outfits that resembled a cross between the wardrobes from the movie *Cleopatra* and the cult-classic television show *Batman*, this Dallas-based ensemble would have been good for a laugh even if all it had done was stand still and glare. As it was, the group seemed to enjoy making fun of itself in full-range motion and expression. The Pharaohs howled, they kicked, they screamed . . . and they also played real good music. And during a time when most American groups stood very still, dressed in conservative suits, had lost their ducktails, and had begun wearing their fathers' haircuts, the Pharaohs, with their turbans and beards, were a refreshing change. There was nothing else like them anywhere!

The heart and soul of the group was a talented Hispanic

Texan named Domingo Samudio. Growing up in Dallas in the days after World War II, the boy was influenced by everything that was happening in the region's music. From the traditional sounds of Tex-Mex, to Bob Wills, to R&B, and even to classical, Sam, as his friends called him, not only listened, but took the music to heart.

By the time he graduated from high school rock and roll had evolved and Sam was picking up on the sound as he served a tour of duty in the navy. Upon his release the young man used the G.I. Bill and studied music for a couple of years before joining a band and going out in search of fame and fortune.

By the early sixties Sam had taken his nickname, added "Sham" to it (because he "shammed"—danced and moved when he played guitar—as part of his act), and formed his own band. The boys, Ray Stinnet, David Martin, Jerry Patterson, and Butch Gibson, took the name "Pharaohs" from a movie they had watched about ancient Egypt. The handle gave this rather eccentric collection of performers a chance to dress up and set themselves apart from every other band in the Lone Star State. Soon their sound would do that too.

By the time the Beatles had led the British invasion, Sam the Sham and the Pharaohs had carved out a record deal with MGM. By continuing to dress in their unique style and by making their own fashion statement about facial hair and hairstyles, Sam's group went radically against the grain and refused to give in to the follow-the-leader mentality of most American rock bands of the day. There was no way that Sam was going to be a Beatles clone; he was his own man, and his band was its own band, too. Theirs was a rougher, more blues-type music than most and hit on elemental roots of R&B as well as early rock and roll.

In the MGM studio in 1965 the group brought out one of its most beloved Dallas club songs. It was a nonsensical number based on the Hully Gully dance craze. Upon the advice of its legal department, the label turned thumbs down on Sam's "Hully Gully." Unbothered, Domingo suggested that he could rewrite the chorus—after all, it was simply the words "Hully Gully" over and over again—in the matter of a few seconds. Wouldn't any words really work as well? he asked.

Satisfied, MGM rolled the tape. Even as Sam was hitting the song's initial lyrics, most of those watching and listening were also wondering just what he was going to do with the chorus line.

Domingo's mind, which operated in a pattern all its own, had decided that if he couldn't honor a dance he was fond of, then he would honor his cat. The feline's name? Wooly Bully!

Incredibly, singing "Wooly Bully" over and over again made as much if not more sense than the song's three verses, which spoke of animals with two horns, pulling wool, and not being an "L 7" (slang for a square). Yet when teens would say on *American Bandstand,* "It has a good beat and you can dance to it; I'd give it an 89," MGM would soon realize, they were voicing the buying mentality of the American public. The same kids who bought up songs with heavy lyrical messages like "She loves you, yeah, yeah, yeah" probably found great meaning in "Wooly Bully."

For some reason word was passed around that the phrase "Wooly Bully" was slang for something overt and sexual. Hence, many stations decided to ban the song from their playlist. In a way this answered MGM's prayers, as the publicity generated by this ban suddenly made the song a teenage taboo. And as with all things forbidden, everyone had to have it. Hundreds of thousands of kids, and who knows how many of their parents, suddenly rushed out to purchase "Wooly Bully," then rushed home to attempt to decipher the song's hidden message. Many thought they had, and when they shared what they thought the song meant with their innocent friends, many more blushed.

It was amazing how quickly what should have been a simple take-it-or-leave-it dance song that had been renamed after a pet had suddenly became the hit of the year. In rocketlike fashion Sam the Sham and the Pharaohs' initial release shot up the charts and hit #2 on June 5, 1965. It would hold that spot for two weeks and spend almost four months spinning its "dirty" message to American teens before departing to the oldies rack. *Billboard* even named "Wooly Bully" the song of the year! And Sam wasn't finished yet; he was no one-hit wonder.

A year later Sam the Sham and the Pharaohs again scored with a top ten chart-busting novelty smash. That song, "Lil' Red Riding Hood," was written and performed in the same "serious" vein as had been "Wooly Bully." It didn't hurt that Sam, with his goatee and turban, resembled the big bad wolf either. And this wolf was interested in more than lunch!

Having made two trips to the higher reaches of the charts with two classic novelty songs makes Sam the Sham and the Pharaohs one of rock's more interesting groups. Yet in reality, with his eccentric stage shows, deep, scratchy vocals, howling style, and wicked grin, not to mention his rich talents and varied musical taste, all blended into a style of his own, Domingo Samudio would have stood out anyway. As it turned out, Sam was no Sham and the Pharaohs belong in the court with novelty's royalty.

Yakety Yak

*T*he circus had Emmet Kelly, television had Milton
Berle, the movies had the Marx Brothers, and rock
and roll had the Coasters. They were the clowns of their
trade, the good-humor men of youth music, the doo-wop
group who went for chuckles more than blend. Yet beyond everything else, even when the material was not very
good, the Coasters were always real good. And if they ever
begin a Novelty Music Hall of Fame, these guys should
join David Seville, Roger Miller, and Ray Stevens as char-
ter members.

There would have been no Coasters if there hadn't been
a Jerry Leiber and a Mike Stoller. Possibly the most creative minds to ever write pop and rock material, these two
Los Angeles products began composing songs as high
school students and continue to this day to turn out some
of the best-crafted lyrics and melody lines ever. Without
this team scores of acts, including the great Elvis Presley,
would have seen a lot less gold. Rodgers and Hart and
Cole Porter had nothing on Leiber and Stoller, but Mike
and Jerry did a lot of things that other composers never
did—they found their own talent, produced their own material, and even owned their own label.

Jerry and Mike came along at the perfect time. Raised

in Jewish homes where humor helped their families get through not
only the good times, but the bad as well, the boys spent a great deal
of their spare time running with African-American friends. In the
black culture the impressionable duo learned about music, dance, and
spontaneous fun. They essentially caught the R&B fever, and that,
combined with their own cultural experience, gave them a unique
perspective and helped to ready them for the rock and roll explosion
that was just about to happen. So in 1954 when R&B combined with
a bit of country and gospel to start the world a-rockin', the boy wonder songwriters already had suitcases full of material and hundreds
of additional ideas for such needy labels as Atlantic. It was there that
Leiber and Stoller would meet Carl Gardner, Billy Guy, Leon Hughes,
and Bobby Nunn.

Gardner and Nunn had become known to Leiber and Stoller
through a group called the Robins; Hughes had wandered into the
studios during his days with the Lamplighters; Guy had done some
group singing in the L.A. area and had come to Atlantic seeking a
chance to record either as a solo act or with a new group. The songwriting team deemed that these four men could be rolled into one
special sound. They tested this theory in the rehearsal hall and found
that not only did the men have a solid blend, but that they possessed
an energy which consumed the room. Even though they had never
cut a record together, these guys had a chemistry that was different
from that of any other group act Jerry and Mike had ever seen.

Though Leiber and Stoller were rolling in the chips thanks to compositions such as "Hound Dog," there was a side of the boys' writing
that was often overlooked. This involved taking frantic pacing and
close harmonies, blending these elements with solid but simple music,
and adding a punch line. In a sense they were looking for a group
that could tell a three-minute joke and do it so well that folks would
want to hear it over and over again. As they listened to the new
quartet, they sensed that they had found just such a group.

Gardner, Nunn, Guy, and Hughes became the Coasters in 1956.
Less than twelve months later they hit the charts with "Searchin'."
For a year the Coasters achieved some moderate success, but the great
moments didn't begin until Nunn and Hughes quit. Leiber and

Stoller then brought in Cornell Gunter, a former member of the Platters, and Will Jones. It was this mix that took that initial dose of special chemistry and blended it into a really potent brew. These were the Coasters that first fully understood their musical magic and captured the humor that was to take them to the Rock and Roll Hall of Fame.

On March 17, 1958, the new, improved Coasters gathered in the studio and in one session completely debunked the television portrayal of American family life. No more would father always know best; no longer were things all right just because a parent said so. "Yakety Yak" painted life like most teens really viewed it. And this was dramatically different from what they were seeing on *Ozzie and Harriet* and *Donna Reed*.

Like every session that Leiber and Stoller conducted, this one was planned as carefully as the invasion of Normandy. Everyone was tutored on their roles, the music was rehearsed to the point of being automatic, and each of the four singers knew exactly when to deliver his every note and take his every breath. Most important, Carl Gardner was shown how to hit just the right bass roar to emphasize the authority that parents had over their children. Once the songwriters/ producers were satisfied that everyone was on the same page, they struck up the band and set about business. And as the Coasters picked their way joyously through a song that began, "Take out the papers and the trash," everyone in the studio quickly realized that the youth of the nation finally had a voice that brought light to the real relationship most kids had with their parents. In the teen mind it was always, "Do this! Do that! Don't forget this! Don't do that! And whatever you do, don't talk back!" "Yakety Yak" said it all, and a bit more too.

With some novelty songs it seems like it has taken a bizarre act of God for the song to land on the charts. With the Coasters' "Yakety Yak," it was obvious from the first play that nothing was going to keep this single from becoming a hit. This song may have been a two-minute extended musical joke, but it was one that had a great deal to say and that said it in a very humorous way. It also combined two wonderful commodities that most serious songs fail to mix—genius on both the writing and performing sides. While "Yakety Yak" might not have been as dynamic as the Platters' "Twilight Time," it was every bit as good.

"Yakety Yak" hit the charts in the early summer of 1958. It would go to #1 in July. Because the melody was simple and set in a key in which almost everyone could sing, and because the words hit so close to home for so many kids, the single was the top play on jukeboxes and radios throughout the summer. It was a monster that went beyond its initial silly feel and lingered on the playlists for almost four months. It is far superior to all but a handful of novelty-type numbers and on an equal footing with most of the great rock and roll hits of its time.

Leiber and Stoller, who often wrote as many as a dozen songs a day, didn't rest on this moment of success. They got the group back into the studio and penned several more numbers in the Coasters' energetic, yet laid-back style. And as would become the rule rather than the exception, these next releases were also of the novelty variety.

"Charlie Brown," "Along Came Jones," and "Poison Ivy" were all major hit songs of the rock and roll era. And like "Yakety Yak," they were so masterfully written, produced, and performed that the oddball humor which drove the lyrics was almost lost in the genius of the total package.

But as good as the Coasters were, they wouldn't stay on top for long. By the late fifties groups were being phased out as teen idols began to control the rock charts. Nonetheless, even though their hits didn't come as often or as fast, because of their humor and energy the Coasters remained strong concert draws. They had earned the title of the Clown Princes of Rock and Roll, and this would carry them through a time when all the other doo-wop groups folded. Even today the living original Coasters are still touring and making people laugh, giggle, sing along, and view life with a little humor. And in today's world of rap and alternative music, that *is* a real novelty!

# Y.M.C.A.

*I*n the late seventies record producer Jacques Morali
noted two growing phenomena in New York. One was
the huge success of disco music. The other was the growing acceptance of homosexual couples and groups and
their being able to come together in public. As a matter
of fact, some years before, many entertainers, Bette Midler
and Barry Manilow among them, began their musical careers by performing in front of those who frequented
Manhattan clubs which appealed primarily to gay audiences. And now these clubs were becoming trendy! With
both disco and the acceptance of homosexuality as a lifestyle becoming more mainstream, Morali began to assess
how he could put the two together in order to make some
money.

One of the things which the native Frenchman had
noted was that in many gay clubs the patrons dressed up
as policemen, cowboys, construction workers, and other
versions of the supposed "macho" men who represented
the ultimate American image of the straight man. Using
that theme, Morali conceived of a new disco group and
set about making that group a supposed reality. First he
wrote a core of songs for his "Village People"; the name
implied that the nonexistent group was from Greenwich

Village. Jacques then used studio musicians to record a disco album that included his original songs. The album's sole intent was to appeal to the audiences who frequented gay dance clubs. These songs—"Macho Man" was one of them—were then packaged by Casablanca Records into an album which featured a photograph of models dressed as a policeman, a soldier, a Native American, a cowboy, a biker, and a construction worker. These models were supposedly the Village People. Of course, in reality there were no Village People. It was all just a rather cheap marketing concept.

Morali had planned on the record's making a bit of money in the disco market; neither he nor the record label had considered the ramifications if the Village People's product moved out of the gay disco scene and over to pop music. And of course, that is exactly what happened. In the summer of 1978 "Macho Man," the ultimate gay parody song, actually penetrated the mainstream charts. The single would peak at #25. Suddenly, Morali needed a group—a real one—to promote his product and idea.

Auditioning actor/singers who looked a great deal like the original publicity photos of the fictional Village People, Jacques formed a sextet that consisted of Victor Willis, Randy Jones, Alex Briley, Felipe Rose, David Hodo, and Glenn Hughes. In the studio this new group began to perfect its own sound while working on an album. Everyone at Casablanca Records agreed that things were going very well. Whatever vocal weaknesses the six guys had revealed could be covered in production, so all they really needed was a strong single for radio and dance club play. On promotional tours they could lip-sync. It seemed that simple.

Jacques was almost finished producing the new song when, while walking to work, the foreigner noted a sign which confused him. "What is the Y.M.C.A.?" he asked. Within a half hour of finding out what the initials stood for, and finding out as well that it was a place a lot of young gay men stayed when they first arrived in town, he had penned the song which would make the Village People an international rage.

None of those who now made up the Village People considered

"Y.M.C.A." anything special when they cut it. Few thought it would be released as a single. But Casablanca Records, seemingly caught up in the symbolism and irony of a group that appealed to gays singing about a conservative Christian organization, pushed the song as the group's follow-up to "Macho Man." As it turned out Casablanca was right on target—the public quickly embraced the single. But one thing the label hadn't considered, and something which almost derailed the song's hit potential before it had steamed too far up the track, was that the real Y.M.C.A. wasn't ready to allow the label to freely use its name. A suit was threatened even as the song headed up the charts. However, peace was made when the Young Men's Christian Association realized that the single was giving it the best publicity it had experienced in years. Even though it was lost on most of the public, this fact made the song an irony of the highest standing. But it wasn't irony that made "Y.M.C.A." a major hit. "America's Oldest Living Teenager" can claim most of the credit for that!

The move that probably made the Village People's single "the song which would never go away" was the brainstorm of Dick Clark. When the group appeared on *American Bandstand*, Clark had his audience spell out "Y.M.C.A." with their arms as the Village People sang the chorus. Within weeks this innocent move, first spotlighted on national television, had created a fad that was repeated at dances and basketball and football games, and soon, by the New York Yankees' grounds crew. There can be little doubt that Clark, whose simple concept of using hand motions had moved the single from hit to fad status, had a great deal to do with the fact that "Y.M.C.A." outlasted not only most of the other pop songs of the era, but the whole disco movement!

The Village People would hit the charts only one more time and would never again score like they had with "Y.M.C.A." Yet because of this manufactured musical concept, which was originally intended to score big numbers only within the gay and disco communities, the group's greatest hit had evolved into one of the best sing-along party songs of the seventies. For that reason the Village People were still touring almost two decades later. And why not, since the group's trademark song, "Y.M.C.A.," represented the very thing that was at the heart of the music of the gay community of that time—fun! Sadly, the Frenchman who'd dreamed it all up, Jacques Morali, didn't get to enjoy the fun that he had created for very long: in 1984 he died of AIDS.

You Never Even Call Me by My Name

"*I was drunk the day my mom got out of prison*" is just one of the scores of wonderful lines taken from country music's greatest parody song. Hatched from the creative mind of one of Music City's finest songwriters and shaped into a hit by one of the genre's greatest characters, of all the novelty songs in this book "You Never Even Call Me by My Name" is perhaps the finest example of good satire combined with great songwriting. So many of the songs we spotlight in these pages are so bad they're good, but "You Never Even Call Me by My Name" is so good that it's great!

By the time he hit his teens Chicago-born Steve Goodman had decided that he was going to be an entertainer. The influences which shaped his formative years included the likes of Pete Seeger, Woody Guthrie, and Hank Williams. As all of these men not only performed, but wrote, it was only natural that Steve would begin to pen his own thoughts and ideas. Churning out concept after concept, Goodman wrote as if he was living on borrowed time. As it turned out, he was.

By the time Goodman hit his early twenties, the singer/songwriter had found a mentor, in the form of a former teen idol, tunesmith Paul Anka. Anka paid for Steve's initial trip to New York and got the young man an audition with Buddah Records. Paul knew that one listen was all it would take to impress the label. By 1971 Steve had an album and was working clubs in Nashville.

One of the first songs which Goodman wrote and recorded was the magical train epic "The City of New Orleans." Covered by a host of different artists from almost every music field, "City" put Steve on the songwriting map. Soon everyone was listening to *Steve Goodman,* the singer's first album. And a lot of artists were calling and asking if the young man would write something for them too. Goodman was in demand!

It was ironic that so many country music stars were looking for a Goodman song to cut, because one of the more obscure cuts on the songwriter's first LP poked fun at the very heart of country music songwriting. Using the sparest of language, Steve had managed to not only compose one of the most magnificently clever tunes ever written, but had also taken an effective if gentle jab at what made Nashville's cash registers ring. "You Never Even Call Me by Name" attempted to mention every timeworn cliché that had ever been used in a hillbilly song offering, including prison, broken hearts, lost love, trucks, trains, booze, mothers, and pet names. In the process Goodman also managed to drag in some of the day's hottest country music stars (in name only), including Merle Haggard and Charlie Pride. And everyone who heard it, even Merle and Charlie, laughed. Still, no one thought to try it as a single.

Four years after Goodman had laid down the tracks for his original version of "You Never Even Call Me by My Name," another country music songwriter/performer decided to jump-start his career. David Allan Coe had spent most of his life in trouble. Sentenced to reform school at age nine, twenty years later he could honestly state that he had never been out of the state's care for more than six months at a time. He was a hood who seemed doomed to live out his years working on a rock pile.

Finally getting his life under control at the age of thirty, Coe took his thoughts, put them into songwriting and performing, and finally drifted into country music's "Outlaw Movement." Sporting biker-type garb when most acts were clean-cut, David wore earrings and showed off his tattoos at his concerts. He often used abusive language in front of his audience and sometimes showed up drunk. Yet for some reason the more outlandish his behavior became, the more crowds loved him. Sensing that this antihero was a diamond in its most primitive form, Columbia Records signed Coe.

He had been recording for about a year when David uncovered Steve Goodman's "You Never Even Call Me by My Name." In Steve's old cut, Coe and his label knew instantly that they had found the perfect vehicle for Coe's almost belligerent personality. What better way for this man who walked to a very different drummer to make his point and a name for himself than by poking fun at the very core of what made Nashville's greatest songwriters tick? Columbia and Coe figured correctly that DJs would love it and that outlaw fans who lived in places like Austin and L.A. would eat it up too.

When David cut the Goodman song he added a monologue right before the final verse illustrating what it would take to make "You Never Even Call Me by My Name" the perfect hillbilly epic. Coe explained that the songwriter, Steve Goodman, had written a new verse for him that covered everything David thought it took to make the "perfect country and western song." And perfect it was. "You Never Even Call Me" instantly became a well-spun record on radio and jukeboxes across the nation. David Allan not only eventually took the recording into the top ten, but by mentioning Steve within the context of the single also made the songwriter a household name.

Steve Goodman never got to fully capitalize on the fame which had come his way thanks to Coe's salute during the final cut of "You Never Even Call Me by My Name." He spent much of his last few years of life battling cancer, and leukemia finally claimed him in 1984. He was just thirty-six. Yet though he died so young, the thoughtful, insightful, and amusing songwriter's efforts live on today because of their original story lines, their uniqueness, and their flair.

His great work and the tribute to that work by an ex-convict who loved it, make it certain that Steve Goodman's name will never be forgotten. Perhaps more important, whenever people catch David Allan Coe's superb version of "You Never Even Call Me by My Name," they will have to smile when thinking about Goodman. He would have liked that, because the only thing that Steve liked more than smiling was making someone else smile.